Benjamin Franklin

Benjamin Franklin

POLITICIAN

———————

Francis Jennings

W · W · NORTON & COMPANY

NEW YORK · LONDON

FIRST EDITION

The text of this book is composed in Galliard with the display set in Galliard and Snell Roundhand. Composition and manufacturing by The Maple-Vail Book Manufacturing Group. Book design by Marjorie J. Flock.

Library of Congress Cataloging-in-Publication Data

Jennings, Francis, 1918–
    Benjamin Franklin, politician / Francis Jennings.
        p.   cm.
    Includes bibliographical references (p. 225) and index.
    ISBN 0-393-03983-8
    1. Franklin, Benjamin, 1706–1790.   2. Politicians—Pennsylvania-Biography. 3. Statesmen—United States—Biography.   4. Pennsylvania—Politics and government—To 1775.   I. Title.
E302.6.F8J45   1996
973.3'092—dc20
[B]   96-3377
                                                                                                        CIP

W. W. Norton & Company, Inc., 500 Fifth Avenue, New York, N.Y. 10110
http://web.wwnorton.com

W. W. Norton & Company Ltd., 10 Coptic Street, London WC1A 1PU

1 2 3 4 5 6 7 8 9 0

For Richard S. Dunn
and Richard H. Brown

CONTENTS

A PERSONAL PREFACE

THE UNIVERSITY OF PENNSYLVANIA'S Professor Richard S. Dunn became unwitting godfather to this yet unconceived book when I took his graduate seminar in Colonial Pennsylvania, in 1963. He introduced me to the source materials on Benjamin Franklin and bled conscientiously over my awkward exercises with them.

Franklin is everywhere on Penn's campus (he started it) and in Philadelphia, but I was drawn aside to study the Indians of his era, so I put him in a file and made a career in the history of American Indians. Franklin emerged to view once again when I returned to the Newberry Library as a Senior Research Fellow in 1990, after my dear wife's death. Richard H. Brown, an old friend, was Director of Research and Education, and he demanded that I sing for my fellowship supper. We agreed on a book about Franklin.

Hence the reason for this book's dedication.

The delay was beneficial as new materials had been published that I needed to study, and I needed time to think about the very complex person who was my subject. More delay ensued because of distractions like mourning and the Columbus Quincentennial, so I did not seriously start writing until after my second retirement from the Newberry in 1993.

Now, with some patronage from the University of North Carolina at Chapel Hill, I have finally girded my loins, ensconced my *Sitzfleisch,* and done the job. This has been made possible by the kind assistance of Peter Wood and Townsend Ludington.

I would be ungrateful to forget my brother Walter R. Jennings's gift of the first ten volumes of the *Franklin Papers,* and the *Autobiography*. I have added to them, one by one, as published, until their shelf array demanded use. Readers will see that they are cited very frequently herein because they have been edited to include much background material on Franklin as well as careful printing of his writings; and their knowledgeable and conscientious editors often explain detailed processes in a note that simplifies citation and saves printing costs.

I am happy to say that these editors have confirmed my findings of fact although we sometimes diverge in interpretation—for example, in regard to the characters of Thomas Penn and Provost William Smith.

Chapter 1: Introduction will clarify issues posed by the subject matter.

I harbor deep distrust of obvious heroes. I have seen too many raised to pedestals, only to expose their feet of clay. I have not found many statesmen, national leaders, or colleagues who do not have their weak points. That is natural. I expect people to be human, and if they display nothing but virtue my instinct warns me that something must be wrong.

Harrison Salisbury, *Heroes of My Time*

And now I speak of thanking God, I desire with all Humility to acknowledge, that I owe the mention'd Happiness of my past Life to his kind Providence, which led me to the Means I us'd and gave them Success.

Benjamin Franklin, *Autobiography*

Perhaps I shall a good deal gratify my own *Vanity*.

Benjamin Franklin, *Autobiography*

Benjamin Franklin

1 INTRODUCTION

BENJAMIN FRANKLIN WAS A GENIUS clothed in the flesh of a man. This is not always a happy circumstance for a genius. Some have not been able to adapt to the routines and expectations of the mass of common people, and have been frustrated to the point of self-destruction. Franklin escaped that bitter fate by capacity for adjusting to circumstance. He came early to an understanding of his own mental and physical superiority, which he delighted in showing off by constructing mathematical magic squares and performing feats of long-range swimming. Such entertaining displays of vanity threatened no one and made no enemies, and Franklin took good care to hide other manifestations of superiority behind a persona mask of modesty.

This was quite as misleading as he intended. He knew his own preeminence without humility. Even in religion, which much concerned him as a youth, he turned away from the established creeds of churches to create his private, personal system of belief. He adapted to his community by attending Anglican Christ Church for the benefit of which he did more than most of its members, and he was requited by the political loyalty of most of its leaders; but he never joined that church, or any other. By never flaunting his superiority, he permitted other persons to proclaim it. For Franklin, modesty consisted in acknowledging their praise, and thanking them for it.

Events reveal the ego hidden so carefully behind his words. When Franklin discovered that Pennsylvania's Proprietary Thomas Penn, whose cause he had been serving loyally, had spied on him and plotted his political destruction, the furious genius campaigned to extinguish Penn's estate in Pennsylvania. When Quakers worked against his campaign to make the province royal instead of Proprietary, Franklin harbored such deep resentment that he colluded with their disfranchisement a few years later. When officials of the crown of England humiliated him before a fashionable audience, he joined and led the Revolution of colonial secession. Certainly, there were other reasons besides wounded vanity, but more than intellectual analysis was involved in Franklin's conduct. The towering ego of the man swept aside the rationalism of the genius.

To understand Franklin and his roles in great events, one must realize the omnipresence of that ego. But one must also recognize how he mirrored the feelings of other colonial Pennsylvanians. He rose to leadership because he conceived events as they did; indeed, he did not achieve commanding mastery in politics *until* he began to reflect the resentments against exploitation of ordinary people.

In that light, the long life of Benjamin Franklin requires some reassessment of standard thought about the beginnings of the American Revolution. That did not start because some noisy radicals in Boston held a tea party nor because Paul Revere took a ride. Long before those entertaining events, Bostonians and other colonials had chafed under regulation from England. In a curious book, Stephen Saunders Webb traces origins all the way back to 1676.[1] The "salutary neglect" of Britain's Whig administrations was tolerable overseas, but when George III took the throne his Tories tightened the reins and added whips. Like other colonials, Franklin rebelled.

Long before George III, Pennsylvania's Proprietary Penn family made serious efforts to rule by the prerogatives spelled out in their charter, which were only partially offset by liberties itemized in William Penn's subsidiary charter "of liberties," chief of which were religious toleration and the right to representation in an elected Assembly. For Pennsylvanians, it was bad enough to have to buy land at exorbitant prices from the Penns. When lord Thomas Penn schemed to nullify their liberties by plotting to control their Assembly (as George III would later take control of the House of Commons), the colonists resisted, and when Franklin put himself at the head of the resistance, he became the people's idol.

Genius though he was, a decade passed before Franklin realized that his struggle against Penn was also resistance to George. Then he became more than a Pennsylvanian—he became the first American.

His striving against feudal lordship, though it made him

master of the Pennsylvania Assembly, has passed almost unnoticed by historians. Three reasons seem to account for this. One was the elaborate legal case with which Thomas Penn defended his chicanery. Historians have not noticed that Penn's documents were fabricated after original sources were destroyed, but Franklin's supporters understood Penn's "honour."

Franklin was constitutionally unable to admit error or failure, so his defeats by Thomas Penn are omitted from his *Autobiography*. A stronger reason has been the domination of American history, and especially the American Revolution, by New England's historians, for whom feudal lordship was an irrelevant issue. Fascinated by the "patriots" of Boston, these writers have concluded that Philadelphians were a laggard folk who had to be dragged into the Revolution by Sam Adams and Paul Revere. That the Continental Congress met in response to a suggestion by Franklin fails to register.

We must comprehend what Franklin became and why; and when we do, we shall know more about how ordinary Pennsylvanians felt long before they took up arms against their king and his oppressive ministers, and why. I think Franklin reveals motives also for Maryland and Delaware rebels. Those "middle colonies" had all been under feudal regimes.

Historical apologists have tried to portray British rule as not so bad really, so that if only both sides in the Revolution had tried harder to understand each other, it need never have occurred. It seems to me that none of these clever hindsighters has ever been as shrewd as Benjamin Franklin, and certainly none has lived through his experience. He knew very well what he was rebelling against, and why he had to.

To discover the man behind "Poor Richard's" moralizing, one must plunge into the morass of eighteenth-century Pennsylvania's struggles over power, and must watch how Franklin first aligned himself with the feudal Proprietaries until he discovered in the midst of war how basely they sacrificed the people to their greed, and how they betrayed him personally. The older Franklin preferred not to remind *Autobiography* readers of his early association with those feudal Penns. He turned against them and became their most bitter enemy. Doing so, he became the people's tribune, the one man who could lead the multitude of squabbling sects and parties against feudal oppression. Yet this heroic struggle is totally missing from his *Autobiography* and the lives written upon its pattern.

Reasons will become apparent further on in this narrative, but the first requirement is to tell what was omitted. This book is limited to the materials I have found in research about colonial Pennsylvania. It must stop short of the giant of Revolutionary diplomacy and the icon of leadership following 1774. Instead, we see the establishment and enrichment of a clever, preachy tradesman, his retirement from business to enter provincial politics, his shocked discovery of the Proprietaries' ruthlessness in grasping for power, and his outrage which led to the extremity of his campaign to take the province away from them and make it directly royal. Then came his disillusionment and rejection by the British crown, and his conversion to become the oldest rebel.

Students have long known his imperialistic vision. We need only add that his adopted province was always at its heart. When the Penns abandoned their western regions to the scourge of Indian war under French direction, Franklin turned against his lords. When the crown sent an occupying army to impose rule by prerogative, Franklin turned against his king. Again, this turn came after he was assailed personally by royal agents.

His turns and reversals have baffled students needlessly. Franklin the public man was shaped and took direction during the years of imperial war: King George's War, 1744–48, and the Seven Years War, 1754–63. With brief glimpses before and after, these years are where our attention must be focused. In that era we find the making of the hero. As with all heroes, this was sometimes a little messy as well as instructive.

To begin with, Franklin's *Autobiography* is about as valid as a campaign speech. It sounds good. Everything he wrote sounds good. Franklin's public life was devoted to public relations, of which he became preeminent master. The *Autobiography* teaches the lessons that any caring father would want his son to learn. Indeed, Franklin's admonitory lessons were carefully edited to highlight the facts supposedly reported, and they suppress more than they reveal. The book belongs on the same shelf with *Pinocchio* and *Swiss Family Robinson*.[2]

This is not really news. Many writers have commented on the discrepancies between that charming fairy tale and the political rough-and-tumble of that charmed life. What needs to be added is that biographers have shown the man's struggles through rosy hazes of their own devising—under his guidance. Source materials are available today to penetrate the hazes, but first we must realize their existence and origination.

When Franklin left his childhood home in Boston to seek his fortune in Philadelphia, he arrived in a feudal Proprietary, the fief of the Penn family. Founder William Penn had rejected nobility and membership in the English Parliament's House of Peers because his Quaker faith abjured vain show and empty titles, but he had a title, nevertheless, that was far from vain or empty. He was True and Absolute Proprietary of the province of Pennsylvania, chartered owner of all its unpatented lands, and master of many powers that will emerge in this account—more, in fact, than were possessed by any of England's dukes.[3] He had original title to more territory than the island of Ireland, including Northern Ireland (Pennsylvania: 45,000 square miles; Ireland: 38,000 square miles).

However, it is not quite correct to call his ownership "original title," because the land was already occupied, and owned according to Indian custom, by the Lenni Lenape or Delaware Indians and others farther west. To exploit his royal grant, Penn needed to sell land to English purchasers, and to do that he needed to guarantee clear title by lifting the Indian "incumbrance." This would cost money that he did not have, so he and his heirs became involved in some devious devices. More of that later. We shall have to notice how Franklin became entangled in the wake of one of those devices called the Walking Purchase.

William Penn not only had chartered right to the "soil" of Pennsylvania; he also owned the separate right to govern the province. That right entailed more complications because Penn's Quaker religion forbade him to take a required oath of office, so that he was obliged to hire members of the Church of England as deputy governors even while he was personally on the scene in his province. Finding someone qualified and sympathetic proved to be difficult because men in colonial authority aimed at personal enrichment rather than benefits for William, and they were not attractive to potential Quaker purchasers of land. Penn could not dictate to the market.

To attract purchasers and colonizers, William Penn granted a "charter of liberties" subordinate to his own charter from King Charles II, but this did not satisfy his people. He tried again, and again met hostility from the colonists who must approve if his grand project were to succeed. (And it was indeed grand; the fleets of immigrants were greater than any others since the founding of Massachusetts Bay.)

On Penn's third try, a charter was accepted which remained in force until the American Revolution, and which still echoes in part of Pennsylvania's present-day constitution.[4] This charter was the jurisdictional foundation for all of colonial Pennsylvania's politics, and Benjamin Franklin had to cope with the conditions created by it. What made it overridingly important to Penn's brethren in the Religious Society of Friends (Quakers) was its guarantee of religious freedom—something they held as sacred for others as for themselves. Franklin formally agreed with the principle, but he despised the Quakers' pacifism protected under the charter, so his devotion to toleration vacillated in practice.

His conflict of motives produced a temporary alliance with Quakers in politics, then a permanent split from them, and finally a mean revenge upon their leaders. All of this, by the way, is missing from his *Autobiography*. He very carefully omitted even to name those Quaker leaders, and incidentally inflated his own role in events when Quaker activity had been essential. In that respect, his book is pollution in the wells of history, requiring a serious task of purification to save readers from the ethnic and political malaise.

We may postpone further description of Pennsylvania's political system until the time comes to consider Franklin's involvement in it. Let me anticipate a reader's question as to where the information comes from to flesh out Franklin's life as is proposed here. Taken together, accumulations of original documents constitute masses of effectively new evidence. The Penn family papers were donated by Granville Penn to the Historical Society of Pennsylvania in mid-nineteenth century; they require to be dovetailed with other sources. Supplementing them, the privately held papers of Thomas Penn's henchman, Provost William Smith, were deposited on loan at the Historical Society library, and copies were made before their ultimate removal. Many collections of papers written by Quakers have been preserved in various repositories and have been so slightly consulted that, in effect, they are new evidence. A magnificent publication project by the American Philosophical Society and Yale University Press has printed the most complete compilation yet of Franklin's papers with excellent editorial notes. My debt to it is gratefully acknowledged.[5] Besides these, the Commonwealth of Pennsylvania has published official records of colonial government and has preserved the private records seized by the provincial Assembly from the Penns' Land Office in 1757.[6]

As part of my research for earlier books, I analyzed the texts (and exposed their falsity) of fabrications by Proprietary lawyers and "covert" operator William Smith that had misled scholars for centuries.

It is now possible, with all this material at hand, to show how Thomas and John Penn fraudulently dispossessed Delaware Indians and thereby created enmity for which rural people paid with their lives when the Delawares took revenge in the Seven Years War. Scholars have become aware that Thomas Penn "declared war" on the provincial representative Assembly and tried to engross all political power into his own hands.[7] Most important for present purposes, evidence now permits us to see Franklin's successive roles in these events, and what they led to.

His vanity apparently caused shamefaced suppression of the way he had been duped when young, but to me he seems more interesting than ever in the way he turned about to become the people's champion—a *human* champion, let us remember. We need not wallow in gush. Genius, he most certainly was. Superman, he was not.

Four Pennsylvanians (and several Indians) are critical to the account. The Pennsylvanians were Proprietary Thomas Penn; Provost William Smith of the College of Philadelphia; "King of the Quakers" Israel Pemberton, Jr.; and B. Franklin. (The Indians, peripheral to the provincial infighting, will be noticed in their turns.)

One other background factor requires notice, namely, the presence of German immigrants in Pennsylvania, whose negative influence shaped Franklin's thought and career—and were swept under his *Autobiography* rug. Rhineland Swiss and Germans began entering Pennsylvania in 1710, in response to William Penn's invitation and his promise of religious toleration. More came in 1717, and after them a deluge as dynastic and religious warfare along the Rhine impelled inhabitants to seek Penn's peace and liberty. So great did the tide become that by midcentury, Germans made up at least a third of the province's European population; some estimators pushed their proportion up to one half.

This surge coincided with Franklin's business career, and he did not like it. He had contempt for the Germans as persons, and he fretted as they became naturalized and voted solidly to support Quakers in the Assembly. As will be shown, Franklin made repeated efforts to reduce the German "menace," and was defeated by them in ways impossible to disguise. He never forgave, and he carefully erased the record.*

To avoid a hopeless jumble, we must pull out threads of Franklin's life until they can be woven together. We start with the young man.

A PERSONAL NOTE

Some findings of this book have gone against my bias. Since youth, I have admired Franklin intensely and without reservation. As an undergraduate student, I bought the Van Doren biography[8] which, though a cheap reprint, cost me the price of two restaurant dinners, and in those days I had to budget food carefully. I have kept the Van Doren through all removals for half a century. Until I began serious research for the present book, I swallowed it whole.

To the critic, therefore, I request: please do not accuse me of writing with a desire to cry down Benjamin Franklin. 'Twas not so. What is reported herein is the product of evidence that surprised me and taught me that Franklin was a real man rather than the chaste idol of an adolescent. My admiration has not been lessened by its object's assumption of recognizable humanity.

The evidence is cited.

*The German response to Franklin's appeal to provide wagons for General Braddock's army is proudly included in the *Autobiography,* but that was an example of his cleverness. See below, chapter 11, Changing Sides.

Addendum

After this book had been copy-edited, and while type was being set, Robert Middlekauff published *Benjamin Franklin and His Enemies* (1996)* dealing with some of the same matters. I had previously described Franklin's struggles with Thomas Penn and William Smith in 1964 and 1988,† and I am ticked off by Professor Middlekauff's omission of any reference to my name or work. Unprofessional discourtesy should have limits.

As to substance, Mr. Middlekauff shows no awareness of Franklin's early cooperation with Penn's Proprietary party before 1755, especially in regard to the Germans who made up more than 40 percent of Pennsylvania's population. The Walking Purchase swindle of Delaware Indians, and the Quaker involvement in Indian affairs are skimmed over, and Franklin's equivocal relationships with Quakers are not to be seen. A selection of Franklin's individual friends appear, but not the mass of popular supporters who enabled him to control the falsely named "Quaker Assembly," nor the policies by which he won such support. His hatred of what we now call feudalism, which drove him to rebel against first Thomas Penn and then George III, is missing, and thus there is no explanation of Franklin's Revolutionary leadership of Presbyterians whom he had opposed regularly in provincial politics.

Middlekauff's book, though gracefully written, seems to me to be deficient in research and unreliable in interpretation. Comparisons are invited.

---

* Robert Middlekauff, *Benjamin Franklin and His Enemies* (Berkeley: University of California Press, 1996).
† Francis Jennings, "Thomas Penn's Loyalty Oath," *American Journal of Legal History* 8 (1964), 303–313; *Empire of Fortune: Crowns, Colonies, and Tribes in the Seven Years War in America* (New York: W. W. Norton, 1988).

2 BOSTON

Born 17 January 1706 (6 January, Old Style), Benjamin Franklin's mind was formed in boyhood in small-town, bigoted Boston, whose repressiveness in religion and government he came to dislike. Our modern filiopietists who profess to find the spirit of freedom rampant in the town (or demand that we adopt the views of its most offensive characters) get no support in Benjamin's life and works.

Boston was a port city of about seven thousand persons. (In our tilted semantics, an Indian community of the same size is invariably called a village.) It was a respectable size in the British Empire of the early eighteenth century; England's Chester, with about the same numbers, was the largest city in northwest England.

Boston had been founded by Calvinists almost as stiff as those in Geneva and Scotland. Its history included the legal murder of Quakers and the banishment under threat of death of even Roger Williams, Puritan himself and friend of John Milton. By Franklin's time the town's magistrates had been forced by crown power, and under heavy protest, to permit services of the Established Church of England which, most definitely, was not established in Boston. The reigning Mather ministers were half crazed by belief in witchcraft, and Cotton Mather had been prominent in stirring up the hysteria that brought on the infamous witch trials and executions at nearby Salem, only fourteen years before Benjamin's birth.[1] Franklin would have no patience with delusions of witchcraft, but he picked up the Calvinist approbation of militarism, and kept it lifelong.

There were, indeed, men in Boston of more independent thought, as there had always been and as had always been persecuted. They had to be discreet. Two of them, John Checkley and William Douglass, encouraged Benjamin's older brother James to publish the *New England Courant* as a vehicle for ideas unacceptable to Boston's other two weekly papers.

At the age of twelve, Benjamin was indentured as apprentice to James to learn the trade of printer and do whatever needed to be done. The *Courant* became his university where he mastered skills, read omnivorously, and became contemptuous of the inferior education of Harvard and its graduates. It is doubtful that any American high school today could produce a student whose reading and writing has the quality of Benjamin's—nor many universities. Boston had one outstanding advantage for this apprentice lad: it was a seaport town that received news and books from abroad. With their aid, Benjamin's avid intelligence leaped out of the town's stultifying atmosphere, and in his brother's paper he gained practice *and publication* of his earliest writings, the Silence Dogood papers. True, they were anonymous at first, but how many fifteen-year-old boys can feast eyes upon their own print standing side by side with the serious reflections of the town's leading thinkers? And Benjamin could not resist "discovering" himself as he heard the praises of his fictional Mrs. Dogood.

Appetite grew by what it fed on, and Benjamin became a creature of the written word. He had had only two years of formal education, one at what became Boston Latin School, at the age of eight, the second year at a less durable school for writing and arithmetic. "Writing" for Benjamin meant, among other things, production of an elegant, highly legible script that was to serve him well in later years. His father and an uncle took some pains with what was obviously a very bright boy, and the *Courant* provided the learning-by-doing that has become holy writ in modern educational theory.

The paper taught more than techniques. Experience there acquainted Benjamin with two priceless lessons: the danger of offending powerful authority, and the humiliation of being wrong when the enemy was right. Prudence was taught by the arrest of brother James for contempt of the authorities after he had printed a fictitious letter. Benjamin was grilled also, but as a mere apprentice lad he was let go while James served a month in jail and was forbidden to publish the *Courant* evermore. This lesson had a bright side for Benjamin. By a ruse to circumvent the court's sentence, James named Benjamin as publisher, and the boy became rather cocky about it, especially after he leaked the authorship of the Silence Dogood papers. But real relationships had not changed. Brother James frowned on the upstart and beat him too, which was another way of training apprentices.

(A humbling came when Benjamin learned belatedly in Philadelphia that Cotton Mather had been right about inoculation for smallpox, while his free-thinking opponents writing in the *Courant* had been wrong. Many years later, Benjamin added a preface to a pamphlet advocating inoculation, and distributed fifteen hundred copies free.)[2]

In his *Autobiography,* Benjamin claimed to have been a leader among the town boys. When could that have been? He had little time for the casual pursuits of boys. Work at the *Courant* consumed much of his day, and reading before and after work used up most of the rest. (He must have had abundant energy to plow through his heavy tomes after a tiring long day's work.) He exercised by swimming, at which he became adept. The picture emerging from scanty records is of a precocious boy who conversed more with adults than with other boys, and there are no girls in this picture—rather oddly, considering later manifestations of lusty sexuality. Perhaps he simply preferred to omit adolescent dalliance from his memories, but once again we must consider the driving ambition and insatiable curiosity that led him into so many hours of heavy reading after so many hours of heavy work. He may, literally, have had no time for girls.

This boy grew fast—too fast for brother James. Benjamin seems to have considered himself superior in intellect to his nine-years-older brother, and to have let his attitude show. If James accepted that judgment, he certainly felt no happier because of it, and he let his displeasure show. The relationship of master to apprentice could not last, despite the two years remaining in their contract.

In the *Autobiography,* Benjamin remarked that James's "harsh and tyrannical treatment of me might be a means of impressing me with that Aversion to arbitrary Power that has stuck to me thro' my whole Life." On reflection, Benjamin in old age thought, "Perhaps I was too saucy and provoking."[3] Perhaps so, but rebellious young Benjamin was not so even-minded.

His friend John Collins concocted an alibi that enabled him to board a sloop for New York whence he ferried to Perth

Amboy and walked to Burlington, west New Jersey. From Burlington he helped row a skiff downstream to Philadelphia. As may easily be imagined, this seventeen-year-old was not an image of sartorial perfection when he walked up Market Street on Sunday morning munching "a great puffy roll" for breakfast and carrying another under each arm. His humorous account of that saunter has become folklore for the ages.

He entered a Quaker meetinghouse to rest, and the decorous silence of Quaker meditation combined with fatigue from his journey to put him to sleep. Perhaps it was an omen of sorts. Kind Friends woke him after Meeting (they may have had previous experience of the sort) and another guided him to a proper inn.

3 PHILADELPHIA

———————

BENJAMIN FRANKLIN came to Philadelphia because he had heard that a printer's assistant was needed there. Very quickly, he showed his superior qualifications and went to work. For the next few months, his life was that of a skilled tradesman in a small town where, like Boston, everyone knew everyone else. Philadelphia temporarily was smaller than Boston, though that situation was on the way to reversal because of Pennsylvania's welcoming policy of religious toleration.

Despite Philadelphia's growing prosperity and great prospects, the place was a political snake pit when Franklin arrived in 1723.

Writers are apt to mention Pennsylvania rather casually as a "proprietary" colony. It must be stressed that "proprietary" implied feudal qualities which would have been greater if William Penn's desires had been satisfied fully, but officials of the court of King Charles II thought that prudence required restrictions on this overreaching courtier. They therefore created the conditions for the province's future politics by dividing powers between its lord and an assembly representing its "freemen" property holders.

Economics strengthened the restrictions. Penn's lordship could not become real until he had lured enough prosperous investors to buy landed properties from him, and their demands forced him to grant successive "frames" of government with increasing concessions of power. Most of these early investors were English Quakers, with some fraternal German and Welsh pietists. The political origins of Pennsylvania must therefore be attributed as much to Quakers who bought real estate on terms of quitrent as to Penn and his heirs who held feudal rights by royal grant. To William's credit, he negotiated changes instead of imposing his will by authority or force.

At the top, however, William Penn was "True and Absolute Proprietary." If his powers were not quite as absolute as his title proclaimed, they were real enough to create constant conflict between the lord on the one hand and the freemen on the other. For example, no law could be passed without the consent of the lord or his deputy.[1] At the time of the Seven Years War, Benjamin Franklin was to be caught up in these struggles. After some indecision, he emerged as the great champion of opposition to feudal privilege. But we must not load that burden yet on a newcoming immigrant boy.

Founder William Penn died in 1718, throwing the government of this Proprietary colony into confusion. No one doubted that his sons should inherit the government and the vastness of undistributed land. The legal question arose: *which* sons? William had married a second time after the death of his first wife, and had sired sons by both wives. When he died, the two sets of sons went to court. The elders—William, Jr., and Springett—claimed Pennsylvania by right of priority. The juniors—John, Thomas, and Richard—claimed it by right of bequest in Penn's will. Britain's Chancery Court mulled the question at leisure for a number of years. Meantime, until final decree, who was to govern?[2]

The crown agreed that someone must. Pending Chancery's decision, the crown accepted Sir William Keith, the current deputy governor, and told him to continue in office, responsible to no Penns but directly to the crown. It was almost carte blanche. Not quite, because of complications left over from William Penn's rule, chief of which was the founder's steward and general factotum, James Logan. Keith and Logan immediately became bitter enemies as Keith used his new power to hack at Logan's former privileges, and incidentally to enrich Keith.

Among other sources of enmity, Logan was a Quaker grandee, and Keith belonged ostentatiously to the Church of England. Logan drew his authority from service to the Penn family, but Keith flaunted his own service to the crown. Mutual avarice partially blunted their hostility. Keith happily loosened the crown's reins in return for whopping annual retainers from the Quaker-dominated Assembly; and Logan's secretive private business of trade with Indians needed Keith's forbearance in several matters, especially when two of Logan's traders murdered an Indian of the powerful Seneca tribe, which did not regard such incidents lightly.[3]

We must not diverge into the political infighting. What is relevant here is that Benjamin Franklin came to the attention sequentially of both Keith and Logan; Keith first. By pure happenstance, Keith was in company with Franklin's brother-in-law, Captain Robert Holmes, when a letter from Benjamin reached the captain. He showed it to Governor Sir William Keith, who was much impressed by its maturity and command of language. So much so that he paid a visit, with a companion, to the printshop of Franklin's employer; and to the bug-eyed astonishment of that worthy, Keith bore Franklin away for dinner.

Keith had grand schemes (*grandiose* says it better). From the immense authority of his office—the top post in the province—he persuaded the young printer to seek capital from relatives in Boston to set up his own printshop in Philadelphia. Keith would secure its future by giving it the official printing to do. Starry-eyed Benjamin hurried to Boston where he encountered father and brothers of a more realistic view and tighter purses. He came back to Philadelphia without the desired capital.

Still, Keith's grandeur so impressed the young man with dreams of greatness that this "poor ignorant Boy" (so characterized by himself) took Keith's advice to go to London on promises that Keith would send letters of credit to buy the equipment needed for a new printshop—about £100 in Franklin's calculations. In London, Benjamin learned the hard lesson that grand manners may be sham. Certainly, Keith's were. He had maintained his great show by spending money even faster than he got it.

On the passage to London, Benjamin had made friends with Quaker merchant Thomas Denham, who understood Keith's character very well. "No one who knew him had the smallest Dependance on him," said Denham, "and he laught at the Notion of the Governor's giving me a Letter of Credit, having, as he said, no Credit to give." Ruefully, Benjamin confirmed that truth, but he salvaged friendship with Denham from the wreck of his dreams, and it proved to have more substance than Keith's patronage.[4]

We know almost nothing about those first eighteen months in London. The *Autobiography* gives sage advice from old age about how young men should avoid vice and save money, but

Benjamin would have had to be angelic to miss out on the opportunities for easy sex available to a hot-blooded youth. Angelic, he clearly was not, neither then nor thereafter, despite his virtuous maxims.

For whatever reasons, despite his regular employment as a printer again, and his supposed saving, he needed a ten-pound loan when the time came for passage back to Philadelphia; he was even more broke on his second entrance to that town than on the first. Franklin claimed that his roommate James Ralph "had kept me poor. He owed me about 27 pounds."[5] Perhaps so. It seems a bit farfetched that so sober a youth as Benjamin presented himself would let himself be drained of his last penny. In any case, Ralph repudiated the debt when Benjamin made advances to Ralph's mistress and was virtuously repulsed.

Credulity is strained further by what happened soon afterward. Franklin's Quaker friend Thomas Denham advanced the £10 passage money for the voyage home with the understanding that Franklin would clerk in his Philadelphia shop. This arrangement continued for six months, until Denham sickened and died, forgiving Franklin's debt in his oral will. It seems highly pertinent that Benjamin owed more at the end of *that* paying employment in the staid Quaker city than when he had arrived home from London.[6] Young Benjamin had a way to go before adopting the persona of Poor Richard, but he never lacked grave maxims. The boy left Boston, but if Boston did not ever completely leave the boy, neither did London.

4 DOMESTIC

—————————

BEFORE LEAVING FOR LONDON, Franklin had boarded with the family of John Read and had grown fond of daughter Deborah—the same girl who had laughed at him parading with rolls on his first entrance to the town. They proposed marriage, but Mrs. Read objected when she heard of Benjamin's intended voyage to London. Absence, she knew, did not always make the heart grow fonder. So it transpired. For Franklin's probable amours in London we have his own account, though imprecise.[1] Debbie married another man.

This was not a happy choice. Only his surname, Rogers, has come down to us. Deborah parted from him when she learned of his other wife in England, and Rogers ran away to the West Indies to escape debts in Philadelphia. Reports that he had died were unconfirmed, so poor Deborah was left neither maid, wife, nor widow. "Our mutual affection was revived," writes Franklin. He pitied her "unfortunate situation," and remedied it in his practical way by marrying her, 1 September 1730, by the common law; that is, by living together and announcing their union publicly.

Common law marriage obviated the difficulties sure to be met with from clergy of any denomination, and it had a long tradition of legality in England as it still has in some American states, Pennsylvania among them. It was especially practical for Franklin because he had an "unfortunate situation" of his own. He had begotten a child, William, on another woman (she remains anonymous); and it seems, much to his credit, that he wished to acknowledge and rear the infant. Complaisant Debbie accepted the boy, and the couple thus solved easily and practically some problems that law and religion could just as easily have turned into prolonged misery.

They begot two children, but this was obviously a marriage of convenience, never passionate, yet notably affectionate. Debbie's reputation was saved at a time and place where it was a woman's most important asset. She was a good housewife, as Franklin gratefully acknowledged; she kept a clean and orderly household and a tight rein on its expenses. *And* she raised his illegitimate son without a murmur. It appears also that she turned a blind eye to Benjamin's tomcatting, and she made no recorded protest when he left her behind in later years while he traveled abroad for years at a time. As his share in this arrangement of convenience, Franklin worked hard to be what came to be called "a good provider," succeeding so well that Debbie's tasks in later life were lightened by servants. One need not endorse a double standard of sexual morality to comprehend that they coped with admirable practicality. Debbie, it seems, was as practical as her famous husband. From all reports, Benjamin and Deborah lived happily, if often separately, ever after, pillars of the community.[2]

In our era of "female liberation" it is worth a pause to consider this partnership. For Benjamin, its benefits are obvious. It gave him a comfortable base, a helpmeet who neither nagged nor pried, the social standing of a family patriarch, and the freedom allowed to males by the contemporary double standard of sexual morality. He took full advantage of them all. In return, he fulfilled his part in their partnership.

For Debbie, one must understand that many of today's assumptions are irrelevant. Her instant benefit from this marriage, common law though it was, came from the preservation of her *name* as a good woman. In that era, the term "liberated" had not been coined for sexually flexible women; if lucky enough to have powerful protectors, they were "courtesans." Others were merely members of "the oldest profession."

Debbie was not invited to the gentry's homes. However, especially after Benjamin bought their pew in Christ Church, Debbie became the social equal while seated there of the grandest ladies of the city.[3] When Benjamin sent her fine silks from London or Paris, her attire excited envy.

Perhaps more mundanely, but far from negligibly, her husband provided servants in an era when house maintenance involved more, and more unpleasant, labor than today. The servants emptied and scrubbed chamberpots daily and kept the privy clean. They laundered when "Monday was wash day, Tuesday ironing day," and so on. They cooked over open fires, and served at table. They split kindling and brought it in to tend the multiple fires. They scrubbed floors and everything else scrubbable. They stripped the beds and aired the bedding every day and remade the beds in the evening. Periodically they leached wood ashes to make lye and boiled it with fats to make soap, not without stench. Servants were among the greatest benefits a woman could enjoy, but she became one herself if she did not have a husband-partner.

Debbie loved and ruled her children. She was mistress of her domain, completely so during Benjamin's long absences, only slightly less so while he was at home. Her freedom within that realm does not accord with some modern values, but it was genuine.

Finally, it is apparent that she basked in her husband's glory, which was far beyond her own comprehension except for the admiration paid to him with consequent deference to her. As to what he did privately beyond her realm, she simply accepted that he was like other men—young William's presence proved that—and inquired no further.

Debbie was not a misanthrope. From today's standpoint, Benjamin Franklin was far from an ideal husband, but he was utterly reliable in the things that mattered to Debbie, and she was glad to have him. By the time of his marriage Benjamin Franklin was in a fair way to prosperity. His superior skills as a printing craftsman enabled him to stop working for others. He took a partner with capital, ordered equipment from London, and opened his own business.

As Thomas Denham's store clerk, Benjamin had acquired the skills of accounting and selling. He had learned printing in Boston and typefounding in London. In 1727, he gathered together twelve intellectually curious young men to found the Junto—a discussion club with serious aims—and his friends in the club functioned like Rotarians to help each other along. (One of them brought Franklin the first customer for his new business.) In 1731, he became a Mason. His competitor Samuel Keimer succumbed to being not fully competent as either tradesman or businessman; Keimer ran into debt, sold out, and left town. Franklin bought Keimer's weekly paper and reissued it in 1729 as *The Pennsylvania Gazette*. And, as Carl Van Doren tersely remarks, Franklin "was the best writer in America."[4]

There were special problems of reporting news in Philadelphia, some of which were quite different from what Franklin had known in Boston. Boston's Puritans demanded conformity to a narrow creed and obedience to established authority. Philadelphia's Quakers were hardly less narrow as regarded their own members, but they had no "priests" (as they scornfully called Boston's ministers), and they preserved complete toleration for non-Quakers, even pariah Roman Catholics. When Maryland's Lord Baltimore hounded presumptuous Jesuits out of his province, some of them fled to refuge in Pennsylvania, and Philadelphia's St. Joseph's Chapel became the only place in the British Empire where Roman Catholic mass was openly celebrated. Catholics were a tiny minority of the people of Philadelphia and Pennsylvania, and they generally kept a low profile in fear of the persecution they met everywhere else under British rule, but their worship in Pennsylvania was free.[5]

Such a situation was unheard of in Boston, and it made difficulties for Franklin as an editor of local news even in Philadelphia. In 1733, a Presbyterian mob advanced with axes on newly erected St. Joseph's Chapel, but Quakers intervened and saved the building. In 1734, Thomas Penn, who was then in Philadelphia, demanded that St. Joseph's be outlawed, but his provincial council withstood his demand. The tradition of religious liberty established by William Penn continued vital and strong, and it seems that members of other faiths agreed with the Quakers to keep it so. But Franklin's *Pennsylvania Gazette* kept silence about both of these episodes.

Franklin's personal religious beliefs were aroused by infighting among the Presbyterians who corresponded in Philadelphia to Boston's familiar Congregationalists. He attended the Presbyterian church for a while, and when a minister was charged with heresy in standard Presbyterian style, Franklin rallied to his support with a contentious pamphlet. Did he believe that religious freedom was right for Presbyterians, but not for Catholics? His man lost in this case, and angry Franklin took the rejection personally. He refused to attend that church again.[6]

When he filled his newspaper with his own writing, it immediately became lively and interesting, as Van Doren has observed. By modern standards, it seems to have evaded as much of the news as it reported, but with a very light, gossipy touch. Very plainly, Franklin remembered what had happened to his brother in Boston when the brother criticized men of power. Perhaps Benjamin felt wary about exposing his *new* newspaper to hostility; in later years he was to take on journalistic crusades. By way of compensation for oversights, he took pains to make his paper technically superior to others, and in 1730 the members of the Pennsylvania Assembly were so favorably impressed that they made Franklin their official printer.

Thus, by the age of twenty-five, this ambitious, energetic, and capable man had become one of Philadelphia's leading commercial citizens with the means to exert considerable influence in public affairs. Such a man could not escape notice by the province's most important persons. Franklin drew attention as his kite one day would draw lightning.

Though Franklin took quick advantage of opportunities to gain prominence, he did not rely on chance to enhance his reputation. "In order to secure my credit and character," he wrote and described conduct so virtuous as to seem a mite prissy, concluding with the rather stagey device that, "to show I was not above my business, I sometimes brought home the paper I purchased at the stores through the streets on a wheelbarrow."[7] Virtue so cunningly advertised lacks innocence. The incident warns of his *Autobiography* purposes.

Publicized virtue seems to have achieved the desired effect. Busy, busy Benjamin included among the virtues an intention to serve the public good. With this in mind, he agitated his Junto friends in 1731 and persuaded fifty bookish men to start the Library Company of Philadelphia with founding fees of 40 shillings each and dues of 10 shillings annually. This Library Company proved its value by enduring to the present day to the great joy of bibliophiles.[8]

It was not exclusively altruistic. To paraphrase John Donne, nothing done by Franklin was ever an island; he had a knack for benefiting himself by the most impeccably laudable public projects. From the Library Company he gained two especially useful long friendships with men well placed to help him. Peter Collinson was one of these—a Quaker merchant in London through whom Franklin bought the Library's books. Collinson was a gentleman scientist and member of the Royal Society who became one of Franklin's principal sponsors among London's intelligentsia.[9]

Pennsylvania's James Logan also became friendly with Franklin through the Library. Logan had been the Penn family's chief provincial steward for thirty years. Governors came and went, but Logan was the Poohbah lord-everything-else who seemed to go on forever. He was also an amateur scholar and scientist with a lovingly collected large, private library. Logan happily agreed to help select the titles for the new Library Company's collection, in return for which service he was granted the privilege of using the Library without paying fees.[10] Easily and naturally, Logan was drawn into conversations and association with the Library Company's leading spirit, was impressed by him, and became his advocate to the ever suspicious Proprietary Thomas Penn.

5 PROTÉGÉ

FRANKLIN DID NOT SLANT HIS *Autobiography* by actual lying. Rather, he contrived strategic omissions and suggestions to guide a reader to self-delusion. However, one passage in the book comes close to outright falsehood and is worth special notice.

He wrote of being summoned in 1756 to a private conference with Governor William Denny, then newly arrived in Philadelphia to represent Proprietary interests. Denny remarked that if Franklin would cease opposing the Penns—which he had begun to do in 1755—Franklin "might depend on adequate Acknowledgements and Recompences, &c., &c."

As Franklin reported the incident, he repulsed the offered bribe in virtuous indignation. "My Answers were to this purpose, that my Circumstances, Thanks to God, were such as to make Proprietary Favours unnecessary to me; and that being a Member of the Assembly I could not possibly accept of any."[1]

This would read more candidly if Franklin had noted that he *no longer* needed Proprietary favor such as he had enjoyed in ample measure in the past. He had not turned hostile to the Penns until the advent of the Seven Years War. To the impressive list of civic projects initiated and nurtured by him, one must add the honors and offices conferred upon him by patronage of the placemen appointed by and dependent upon the Penns. "The Governor put me into the Commission of the Peace [i.e., made him justice of the peace]; the Corporation of the City chose me of the Common Council, and soon after an Alderman."[2]

So early as 1737, Franklin was appointed deputy postmaster at Philadelphia (by favor of Virginia's Governor Alexander Spotswood rather than Thomas Penn), and Franklin learned how the post could be made advantageous to his newspaper. "It came to afford me a very considerable Income."[3] Therefore, when larger vistas opened after the death of the Deputy Post-

master General for all the British colonies, Franklin applied for
the post, and, in 1753 was appointed by the crown jointly with
William Hunter, a printer in Williamsburg.[4] Relevant here is
the strenuous effort made in his behalf by William Allen, provincial chief justice and political boss for Thomas Penn. It appears
that Allen's intervention had not been needed—Franklin had
used other connections—but it is beyond doubt that Franklin
knew of Allen's patronage, which is invisible in the *Autobiography*.[5]

Besides this royal post's obvious potential for profit and
prestige, Franklin used it for patronage by himself by appointing his relatives to the local offices in Philadelphia and Boston.[6]

One of the most beneficent influences upon Franklin's early
career came from his friendship with James Logan, the Poohbah
who had guarded Penn family interests since being brought to
the province as William Penn's secretary in 1701. Logan was a
"birthright" Quaker, but not a pacifist. Franklin delighted to
tell how Logan had taken up arms against the threat of attack
while William retired below their ship's deck. Further, when
Franklin organized a military Association to defend Philadelphia in 1747, Logan contributed heavily. Franklin never had
any patience with pacifism. He heartily deplored "these Embar-
assments that the Quakers suffer'd from having establish'd and
published it as one of their Principles, that no kind of War
was lawful."[7] But Franklin respected James Logan's variety of
"defense" Quakerism.

A stronger bond was their shared deep affection for books.
Logan had carefully assembled what is usually called the best
library in British America, and he kept his linguistic skills alive
by annotating the margins of his books in their own languages:
Greek, Latin, Hebrew, Arabic, French, and Italian. (They can
still be seen in the Library Company of Philadelphia.) It was
natural for Logan to take interest in the young tradesman who,
without benefit of schooling, read books of serious scholarship
and taught himself languages. Just as naturally, Franklin gravi-
tated to the learned elder and the two relished conversations
about matters far over the heads of most Philadelphians. For
the young man it was a heady experience to be accepted as an
intellect worthy of respect by the learned and powerful official.

There were more practical bonds also. It was remembered

in Logan's family that Franklin "acknowledged obligations to him in the beginning of Franklin's career and valued himself on his friendship."[8]

When Franklin conceived a project for the first subscription library in America, he asked Logan to choose the basic stock, to be rewarded by free membership. Carl Van Doren lists the books: "On this or the second list were Pufendorf on jurisprudence, Hayes on fluxions, Keill on astronomy, Sidney on government, L'Hospital on conic sections, Gravesande on natural philosophy; Palladio, Evelyn, Addison, Xenophon's *Memorabilia,* Defoe's *Compleat English Tradesman, Gulliver's Travels,* the *Spectator, Tatler, Guardian,* Homer's *Iliad* and *Odyssey,* Dryden's *Virgil,* Bayle's *Critical Dictionary* . . . and Newton's *Principia.*" It is not hard to infer that Franklin's young companions were a serious lot.[9]

But I digress. Franklin's library directors, we are told by the editors of the *Franklin Papers,* "had learned that the Proprietor [Thomas Penn] would welcome an address praying his 'Countenance and Protection.' " (They probably learned that from James Logan.) Figuratively tugging their forelocks, the directors sent Franklin to invoke benediction on the Penns: "May every kind of humane Felicity attend the Proprietary House thro' all Ages to the latest Posterity." Thomas Penn took the address "very kindly."[10]

That was in 1733. Thomas was in Philadelphia with a mission to tidy up provincial administration and to get his family out of their quagmire of debt by selling lands. He still subscribed publicly to his father's Quaker faith, he needed support from Quakers on both sides of the Atlantic, and he was eager to acquire public goodwill from his constituents. We shall have to follow the winding paths by which all this was transformed into opposites. At this point, however, it is enough to notice that he was gracious to susceptible young Benjamin Franklin and even patronized Franklin's stationery shop, though without condescending to pay for what he bought.[11]

For the time being, Thomas maintained a generally conciliatory attitude that was necessary because he had only shaky control over even the administrative functions of the government. These had long been dominated by Quaker grandee James Lo-

gan and his friends. Thomas suspected, correctly, that income
for his family was being siphoned off to other quarters, and his
first objective was to pry Logan's cronies loose from their grip
on offices. This determination was the edge of a wedge that
soon would face the Proprietary family in bitter enmity against
the provincial Quaker establishment and their religious allies
in Britain.

One would naturally look for Franklin to take sides with
Logan against the Penns, but their dispute was conducted in
great secrecy. Logan could not afford to precipitate an open
battle because he had been embezzling Penn property,[12] and
Thomas had the evidence in hand.[13] If their contest came to
showdown, Logan faced ruin. On the other hand, Thomas understood how Logan could be uniquely valuable in some under-
handed dealing by Thomas himself in connection with Indian
affairs. As will be shown, Thomas intended to get formal quitclaims from Delaware Indians for their lands along the Delaware River. He needed such releases in order to sell the lands—
no one would buy while Indians claimed ownership—and he
needed to sell those lands in order to keep himself and brothers
out of debtors' prison. Thomas was not concerned about legal
or moral niceties, and James Logan readily cooperated to save
his own skin, quickly abandoning his earlier warnings about
Indian rights.[14] (See chapter 6 below.) Thus Thomas Penn and
James Logan maintained a facade of friendship, and Benjamin
Franklin's admiration for Logan rubbed off into the good
wishes for "every kind of humane Felicity" for the Penns.

During the 1730s, while Franklin built his business, Thomas
Penn created his political machine.

Thomas had much work to do because of the confusion of
provincial offices and powers in the clutches of James Logan
and his Quaker grandee associates. Thomas divided Logan's
post as "Secretary" into council secretary and Land Office secretary, and he put two new men in the new jobs. One of them
kept the council minutes for the governor (I'll drop the "Deputy" part for convenience). The other secretary wrote the Land
Office minutes for no eyes but the Penns' because unpatented
land was entirely their own property to dispose without governmental intervention.[15] The Penns guarded their land business

with great secrecy. Since every Pennsylvanian hungered for land that could be granted or withheld at Penns' pleasure, they were probably as powerful in this respect as in the government itself. Until 1757 no elective Assembly intruded into the Land Office.

Between the government and the Land Office, Thomas established a network of posts and placemen, all entirely dependent on him; and few persons desiring to create estates dared to incur his disfavor. When he returned to England in August 1741, the executive branch of the province had been reduced to tight controls, the Penns' outstanding debts were paid, and the surrounding Indians had been effectively conquered without a shot. Though Thomas Penn was a most unlovely man, one has to admire his executive ability. Only the mature Benjamin Franklin could cope with it. It is worth a moment's reflection that behind Penn was the great power of the sovereign crown. Behind Franklin was only the support of the province's admiring people. Events were to prove that Franklin and Penn were well matched in wits.

Until the threat of King George's War (1744–48), Franklin sought patronage where he could find it, not excluding the Quakers whose pacifism so offended him. So to speak, he played both sides of the street, a feat made possible because Thomas Penn was still negotiating with the Quaker elite rather than trying to crush them.

Thus it was possible for businessman Benjamin to win favor with Quaker businessmen already in 1729 by printing a pamphlet endorsing paper money.[16] (Franklin was a strongly political editor as well as a printer.) The Penns opposed paper money despite the strangling of business by inadequate amounts of specie constantly being drained off to England. The Penns feared inflation with consequent loss to themselves when paid in depreciated currency. Losses to the inhabitants concerned them not at all.

This was an early occasion when the Assembly defied the Proprietaries. £30,000 of interest-bearing notes were printed and circulated before the law could be disallowed by the crown, and another £40,000 soon followed.[17] On that issue, Franklin saw eye to eye with the dominant Quakers. To stimulate business was to profit *his* business.

(One of the factors in eighteenth-century colonial politics
was the length of time required to send a law to the crown and
receive a response. A royal veto took so long in arriving that the
game could be won by that time.)

Quakers joined Franklin's Library and fire company, and
the assemblymen approved his neatly legible handwriting by
appointing him their clerk in 1736. As he observed, "the Place
gave me a better Opportunity of keeping up an Interest among
the Members, which secur'd to me the Business of Printing the
Votes [decisions], Laws, Paper Money, and other occasional
Jobbs for the Public, that on the whole were very profitable."[18]
At this stage of his career, Quaker patronage was very desirable,
perhaps essential. If Franklin was a self-made man, he had lots
of help.

Franklin's friend James Logan declined in health and influence and died in 1751. Unlike him, the rising "King of the
Quakers," Israel Pemberton, Jr., held strictly to the pacifism that
Franklin scorned and detested. As provincial issues gradually
hardened into enmity between Thomas Penn and the Assembly,
relations between Pemberton and Franklin became decisive.

And mysterious. Israel was a third-generation, rich Quaker
merchant, fervent in the faith, dedicated to good works, and
absent from Franklin's *Autobiography*. That gap must be filled.

Israel Senior had been born to Phineas Pemberton, who
sailed to Philadelphia in 1682 to become one of the colony's
founders. Phineas bought land in the Quaker stronghold of
Bucks County, and built the house called "Bolton" which remained family headquarters throughout the lives of the Senior
and Junior Israels.[19]

These were "weighty Friends" whose quick success in the
rapidly growing colony gave them wealth, and the wealth (as
well as their intense dedication) put them high among the oligarchy controlling Quaker Meeting. To the present day,
Friends' doctrine requires the Meeting to decide by consensus
rather than a mere majority, and it is customary for losing dissidents to fall silent or absent themselves. As Theodore Thayer
remarks, the eighteenth-century Meetings listened to leaders'
decisions and "the rank and file were quite certain to fall in
line."[20] Discipline was strong.

It had to be if Quakers were to preserve political leadership where, after the founding generation, they quickly became a minority. Philadelphia's Germantown preserves the memory of Mennonite Germans who immigrated in William Penn's day to his colony, which guaranteed religious liberty. About 1710, Swiss pietists, along with Germans from the Palatinate and Rhineland, began coming in substantial numbers to settle in a broad arc just beyond the Quakers of Bucks and Chester counties. In the twenties, Scotch-Irish refugees from poverty and absentee landlords started to trickle in, and they soon became a tide. Englishmen of the Established Church arrived in a steady stream. Who was to govern? How could such diversity be reconciled and kept from violence? In a much quoted remark, Assembly Speaker Isaac Norris, Jr., explained concisely (in 1756) why the small minority of his fellow Quakers were constantly supported and elected by more numerous constituents.

The Church of England are well Apprized that their Interest is not sufficient Alone, and upon search they have found it Difficult to find men among Themselves, with whom they Could Confide Their Liberties. They dread the Presbyterians, and the Germans more, so that in the Nature of things upon a Political System only, the Church of England know, they must keep in with the Quakers to keep the others out. . . . And the Dutch [Germans] Joyn them in dread of an arbitrary Government.—So that it seems Absolutely Necessary to keep the Quakers as a Ballance here.[21]

The Pembertons carried as much weight among the "political" Quakers as in their religious Meeting, and Israel Junior was as active as Benjamin Franklin in Philadelphia's civic affairs outside the Assembly. It appears that the competition rankled Franklin, who could be generous to the Quakers who were deferential to himself.

Besides administering Friends' Annual Meeting, Pemberton acted for thirty-six years as Clerk of the Quaker schools—Penn Charter School is still functioning—and he was active in Franklin's Library Company from 1738. Like Franklin, he became prominent in the fire company, where his support may have been essential for its success. Certainly Pemberton was one of the most important Philadelphians, and for much the same reasons as Franklin himself, but he is a nonperson in the *Autobiography*. Was it mere spite that caused Franklin to consign him to oblivion? Perhaps a sense of guilt was involved also. It should have been.

In his own way, Pemberton was as hard-driving as Franklin, and at least as sure of himself. Theodore Thayer's dry observation foreshadows the crunch that was to come when Pemberton, Franklin, and Thomas Penn locked horns in struggle: "Israel was not the person to question his opinion regarding the proper means of promoting the happiness of others."[22]

Meanwhile, Thomas Penn was not idle. While Pemberton emerged to leadership among the Quakers, and Franklin built his business, Penn created a political machine. He had to circumvent the same obstacle that had given so much trouble to father William Penn; to wit, that he could not assume the post of governor himself because he was still a Quaker and no Quaker could swear the oath of fealty to the crown required of all colonial governors. (The oath requirement will recur importantly in this narrative.) William Penn had had the peculiar and highly awkward task of finding a non-Quaker deputy governor who was formally the chief executive in the government even while William, who owned the government as a property, was in the province.

The same difficulty descended to William's sons. As noted above, Sir William Keith made a good thing of it after William Penn's death until the younger Penns could replace him with a sufficiently compliant Patrick Gordon in 1726. They got a secret kickback of £200 per year from Gordon.[23] While subservient, Gordon understood that though his appointment came from the Penns, his salary came from the Assembly, so that he had to be compliant in that direction also. (To the annoyance of the Penns, Gordon passed the Assembly's paper money bills.)

Assemblymen were not handicapped by oaths, and Pennsylvania's Assembly followed the examples of other colonies by constantly seizing opportunities to encroach upon the executive. The stinginess of British royalty offered invitations. The empire had been acquired at little more cost to the crown than the price of charters, and even that had to be paid by the charter recipients. Still striving to rule on the cheap, the crown required colonists to pay for their own governance by crown appointees. So doing, however, royalty forgot the adage that he who pays the piper calls the tune. The colonists remembered.

The same process occurred from South Carolina to Massachusetts: alert assemblies demanded concessions before granting governors' salaries, and governors everywhere balanced their instructions from England against the need to repair the typically broken fortunes which were their reasons for wanting to be governors.

Thomas Penn observed the process in his own propriety, and determined to retrieve the powers that the Quaker-dominated Assembly had acquired. In 1736, Thomas and his brothers hired a new deputy governor, George Thomas, for a minimum of four years, and gave him highly detailed instructions as to the laws he was permitted to sign. This pattern of secret contract with governors was to continue throughout Thomas Penn's life and to occasion much friction with the Assembly. No matter the stringencies and hazard of events, through war and peace, Thomas enforced his instructions as rigidly as British law permitted.

When George Thomas solicited the post in 1736, he promised to give security "for the performance of whatever shall be demanded by you."[24] Thomas Penn was in Philadelphia at the time, so his older brother John dealt with the new applicant. "He has agreed to pay to Me in London," wrote John, "£500 Sterling per Annum . . . I shall Injoyn him by his Instructions to dispose of no place, nor pass no Law without your Approbation, and on His following all instructions sent with him or that He shall from time to time receive . . . no person whatever may Know the above Terms which are upon Honour to be Kept Secret."[25] It may be seen from this how the Penns conceived honor.

Having acquired that puppet, Thomas Penn gained control of the entire law enforcement and judicial machinery in the province. All judges were the governor's appointees, and when elections were held for county sheriff the governor chose the one he liked from the top-running three, even if that one had come in third. The governor also nominated members of the provincial council, who were usually ratified automatically by the crown. In short, Thomas Penn not only *owned* the government along with his brothers; he *ran* it—except for the elected

Assembly. He still had the problem of the family debt to solve, which will require a separate chapter.

In the eighteenth century, it was customary for enterprising, ambitious men to make themselves useful to others with patronage to dispense. (English novels are full of episodes in which clergymen scrounge "livings" out of prosperous squires.) Businessman Benjamin Franklin could see quite clearly where patronage was to be had in Philadelphia, and he took pains to make himself available for it. Such conduct was considered laudable rather than shameful.

Substantial patronage in Pennsylvania required an applicant to solicit from two separate sources. Besides the Assembly controlled by Quakers, there was the Proprietary Penn family and its entourage of placemen and hangers-on. So long as these two groups maintained uneasy cooperation, it was possible for Franklin to cultivate friends among both, though he was always contemptuous of orthodox pacifist Quakers—"stiffrumps," as he called them. Until 1747, he was discreet about expressing the contempt.

Franklin's earliest substantial help came from Quakers. Well before the "very profitable" Assembly connection, we have seen how merchant Denham brought him back from the fiasco of his first trip to London, and how Denham gave him a fresh start. Regretfully, it must be said that Franklin never showed much gratitude toward the Quakers. Indeed, when Thomas Penn turned Anglican and "declared war" on the Quakers, Franklin rather hypocritically served Penn.

Was it only because Penn's patronage was so much more potentially valuable in material terms? That inference is possible, but other factors seem likely also. Franklin feared the Germans whose electoral support kept the Quakers in control of the Assembly. There is no denying his strong feelings of ethnocentrism. He was also more at ease with the Proprietary's men than with the Quakers (always excepting James Logan, who was both). As we would say nowadays, the Proprietary men were more "cultured"; they had read more widely than the orthodox Quakers, who seemed narrowly limited by religious strictures and scruples.

Nor can one forget that Franklin was a militarist with dreams of empire that could not be reconciled with the creed of the Society of Friends. This much of his outlook was quite independent of considerations of patronage.

Being Franklin, he worked his way out of the dilemma of dual dependency, first by establishing thriving businesses, then by creating his own political machine. The process took some time.

6 THE WALKING
PURCHASE

THOMAS PENN WAS TO EXTRACT his family out of deep debt and to create one of Britain's greater fortunes. While in his province, he was handicapped by father William's careless ways with money and careful scrupulosity about business dealings. Thomas himself suffered from neither handicap, with the consequence that the means he used for success have been buried under documents altered and fabricated by his squad of legal retainers, whose prosperity depended on his.[1]

I have done much homework on Thomas's devices, the details of which need not be repeated here, but enough must be given to show how Benjamin Franklin became involved variously as Thomas's dupe, his ally, and ultimately as his bitter enemy.

The foundation of Thomas's success came from cheating Indians out of the value of their lands, which he then sold to English colonials at full value with annual quitrent. William Penn had recognized Indians' rights to land and had taken pains to distinguish different tenure customs of different tribes. His agents scrupulously bought a series of tracts along the Delaware River, carefully identifying the family chiefs whose rights were acknowledged by their neighbors, and just as carefully specifying the boundaries of each purchase. He got bargain prices, and he sold at profitable markups, but William's way with money was loose.

Unlike our image of Quakers as prudent and thrifty, William was extravagant and reckless. He had big mansions in England, Ireland, and Pennsylvania, fully staffed with servants (including some Black slaves in Pennsylvania who scandalized his pietist neighbors), and he lived high.[2] When the time soon came to buy more Delaware Indian land, he lacked the wherewithal. As several customers presented themselves, he sold anyway, knowing that they did not intend to emigrate to the colony in the near future, and he meant to pay off the Indians later.

His royal charter granted the "soil" outright to William, saying nothing about Indian tenure, so he was clear under English law; but he was not so clear in the market. Purchasers wanted lands patented with guarantees that Indian "incumbrances" had been lifted. To get more buyers, William had to get more Indian quitclaims, and to get more of those he had to lay out more money that he did not have. The situation worsened as the Indians learned they could charge much higher prices than at earlier times. It was a nasty bind, and it raises great respect to see how William nevertheless maintained his principles for dealing fairly with the "poor Indians."[3]

A particular negotiation could not be consummated during his lifetime. This was for a tract belonging to Chief Nutimus north of the Delaware River's Tohickon Creek. William had bought the land north *to* Tohickon Creek from a chief called Mechkilikishi, but Nutimus insisted that the land across the creek had not been sold and still belonged to him. William was recalled to England to meet a political crisis. (He really was a great lord, regardless of title.) He left Nutimus with an understanding that he would return to finish the land transaction, which called for bounding the purchase by a walk of one and a half days along a line. William had thought that the walk was to follow north across Tohickon Creek along the Delaware. Nutimus said no, Mechkilikishi had no right to sell north of Tohickon; in Nutimus's understanding, William was to walk a day and a half west *along Tohickon's southern bank.*[4]

William was never able to complete the purchase, but he left a draft document concerning it among his papers. The draft had strategic gaps about the walk, so that it was obviously worthless in a court of law, but Thomas Penn brought it to Pennsylvania in 1733, and it became the key to the skulduggery of John and Thomas Penn.[5]

William Penn had died in 1718, but his extravagance had run to such an extreme that he briefly served time in debtors' prison until a group of rich Quakers ended that scandal by paying his debt and taking a mortgage on the province, naturally with interest. The rental income and purchase instalments from lands already sold were supposed to clear the mortgage.

James Logan was commissioned to supervise the lands, sold and to be sold, and he thus became immensely powerful.[6] William's heirs constantly begged Logan, who was also executor of William's will, to divert money to them from the mortgage payments; and he obliged enough to keep them subservient.

One characteristic that did descend to them from William was extravagance. Quite apart from their mortgage debt, they ran up big bills of their own. John was to defend Thomas against charges of being spendthrift by saying that his brother lived "in as frugall a Manner as was Possible for any Person that Must appear as the first Man in the Place he resides in."[7] This was a tolerable standard of austerity for Thomas, but it was not cheap, not even considering Thomas's quaint way of living on unpaid credit.

In 1729, a stroke of luck enabled the brothers to pay off the mortgage, upon which they sent Thomas to shake Logan's controls loose and accelerate their income. Thomas was unable to work fast enough. John Penn chased after him in 1734 with the gasped information that debtors' prison doors yawned open for them for £8,000 owing.[8]

At that point the lands of Delaware Chief Nutimus became essential to saving their hides or their "honour." They chose without difficulty. Hides came first. Honor could be salvaged by sufficient attention to certain arrangements.

Their proceedings became highly interesting to Benjamin Franklin twenty years later when he would be commissioned to protest them to the crown, but for the time being they were secret. It is unlikely that his friend and patron, James Logan, who became intimately involved, disclosed to Franklin any of the clandestine goings-on. Possibly because of Logan's involvement, Franklin omitted the whole affair from his *Autobiography* though he had had to cope with its fatal consequences. And none of its doings got into his *Gazette*.

The brothers Penn understood very well what they were about. James Logan had stressed to them that Nutimus's lands had never been purchased; indeed, Logan had a highly personal interest in getting those lands legitimized under provincial law because Logan was part owner of an iron mine at Durham, high on the Delaware River, within their bounds. He had paid Nutimus £60 to let him go ahead with the isolated mine, but he could not establish legal title until the Penns purchased by treaty. The law was very plain: No purchase from Indians was legal except purchase by the Proprietaries, no matter how the Indians might regard it. The land had to be ceded by treaty before provincial property in it could be patented by law.[9]

Logan prepared the way to overpower resistance by Pennsylvania's Indians by contriving an alliance with the remoter Iroquois Six Nations from New-York. What he had in mind was to hire them as backwoods police to suppress unrest among the tribes fringing the province's settlements. The Iroquois balked at first. While they debated the matter at home, the Penn brothers summoned Nutimus to confer at Logan's Durham in October 1734. Logan had been crippled by a fall on ice, so he sent his son William, who remained notably close-mouthed about it ever afterward, and won much Penn patronage.

Many Indians attended this conference, but this fact must be inferred from sources other than the document presented by Penn lawyers as minutes. It is clear that they had fabricated this crude forgery after someone had destroyed the original, too-informative record. What is especially pertinent now is that Logan had advised the Penns (again) that a purchase was in order, that the Indians' claims were valid. On the whole, he thought, a good price would be £2 per thousand acres, "but you have the sharpest fellows to deal with that I have known amongst the Indians . . . but I think you should purchase."[10]

Nutimus and his associates refused to sell at Logan's fire-sale price. They had been offered ten times as much by some interlopers from New-York, and they wanted fair compensation. At Durham, Nutimus was annoyed. "When We Were With [Thomas] Penn to treat as usual with his Father. He keep begging and plagueing us to Give him some Land and never gives us leave to treat upon any thing till he Wearies us Out of Our Lives."[11] The conference ended with its only agreement being to meet again at the Penns' manor of "Pennsbury" (on the Delaware River near Bristol) in May 1735.

John and Thomas knew that they could not possibly satisfy Nutimus's terms, so they decided instantly to steal his lands— with a show of legality for honor's sake. They would treat their draft of a deed that had been left unfinished by William Penn in 1686 as though it were a genuine deed. With a little hocus-pocus they could fool illiterate Indians with it, and they could keep it away from serious examination in a court. After all, Pennsylvania's chief justice James Logan was complicit in the scheme.

First, the plotters tested the document's vague, ambiguous terms for maximum results. They hired a party of men to walk for a day and a half (the only specific words in the document) and sent them across Tohickon Creek well into and through Nutimus's lands.[12] Satisfied with what they learned from that rehearsal of a walk, they went on to other arrangements.

When the treaty conferees met at Pennsbury, John and Thomas knew that their secret walkers had blazed a trail that could be made to encompass not only the lands of troublesome old Nutimus but also the entire "Forks of Delaware" where the Lehigh River pours in, and the upstream "Minisink" beyond. The Penns moved confidently now.

They presented their 1686 draft of a deed and called it a contract. James Logan, who had privately and repeatedly told them it was no such thing, now told Nutimus that "Purchase had been fairly made for a large Consideration made by the said old Proprietor [William Penn] to the Ancestors of the said Indians." A young Delaware named Teedyuscung added what does not appear in the minutes once again fabricated. Teedyuscung observed that Logan *threatened* Nutimus and flaunted provincial power: "He did not value Newtymas, but look'd upon Him as the little Finger of his left Hand, but that he himself [symbolizing the province] was a great big man; at the same time stretching out his Arms."[13]

The Indians still politely disagreed, but the Penns shrugged them off and immediately went ahead with more pressing business—selling the land that the Indians refused to cede. They surveyed large tracts of it high along the Delaware River (37,000 acres are still on record, but the record was then kept secret in the Penns' Land Office).[14]

They organized a land lottery for 500-acre tracts (at £2 a chance) which would have provided a bonanza of about £15,000, enough to pay all their debts with a tidy sum left over. But—woe!—the lottery not only contravened Quaker morality but violated provincial law enacted by the Quaker-dominated Assembly. One of the Penns' staunch supporters reported that the lottery was "discouraged" even by persons who had obligations to the Proprietaries. It failed to sell out, and the money was to be returned.[15]

The lottery was advertised in the newspaper of Franklin's competitor, Andrew Bradford's *American Weekly Mercury,* nos. 814, 816, 817, 831, 833, and 834. It is not possible that Franklin was unaware of it, but it did not get into the pages of his *Pennsylvania Gazette*. Why?

Despairing John Penn tried to sell the province in England—he had an offer of £60,000[16]—but Thomas would not agree because Thomas wanted to become governor, despite the handicap of an oath of loyalty to the crown. He was frustrated in this desire by Quaker opposition. Brother John had actually signed a commission for Thomas, "but our Friends were exceedingly Concerned at the thought of your taking the Oath . . . they also told me how very ready they had been in our absence to support our Interest and should still be ready to do anything in their power to assist us, but that if you took the Government Wee must never Expect to have any assistance from them againe as a Body, nay some went so far as to talk of Publickly disowning you." Thomas protested, but John hired another man.[17]

From subsequent events it is clear that Thomas never forgave the Quakers. For the time being he solved the immediate problem of debt by peddling real estate secretly to raise more than £10,000 in a hurry. He sold twenty-one tracts of five hundred acres each to close friends for £500 each. These knowledgeable purchasers understood perfectly well that the Indian "incumbrance" had not been lifted, but they trusted Thomas to handle the Indians, and intended to cooperate in that process. The greatest among them, to the tune of £3,000, was William Allen, the province's richest man and a good friend and patron of Benjamin Franklin.[18]

I have seen no direct evidence that Franklin knew what was going on, but he certainly must have seen the advertisements for the failed lottery that ran in competitor Andrew Bradford's *Weekly Mercury,* and it is hard to believe that so shrewd a man remained ignorant, considering his friendships with Logan and Allen, not to speak of his association in his Junto with Nicholas Scull, the surveyor who laid out the tracts ultimately purchased in the secret "little" lottery. Perhaps Franklin realized that some game was afoot and preferred not to inquire too closely. The

participants were all his patrons. Investigatory journalism had
not yet been invented.

The illegality of these sales of Indians' lands was carefully
concealed in nebulous dateless phrases in the deeds: "by
agreement some time since made." (And not long after James
Logan died, William Allen became chief justice.) No patents
were issued until 1737, though warrants were given and surveys
were made in 1736, all of which were recorded secretly in the
Land Office. As the purchasers bought purely for speculation,
they soon began reselling to intending settlers on terms with
staggering markups, and settlers moved in.[19]

Nutimus and his men were consternated, but James Logan
contrived a way to keep them under control by neatly combin-
ing carrot and club. The carrot was for old Delaware Chief
Sassoonan, whose lands along Tulpehocken Creek (which
poured into the *Schuylkill* River) had been sold off years earlier.
Landless Sassoonan was not a party to Nutimus's claims, but
Logan considered him influential among the Delawares and
worth buttering up. Presents and soothing words were given
to Sassoonan.[20]

Rougher treatment was in store for Nutimus. He was put
off until Logan could wrap up the treaty with the Iroquois.
When the chiefs of four of their nations arrived in Philadelphia
in 1736 (the Mohawks absent), Logan sounded them about
Indian ownership of the lands claimed by Nutimus and his associates. The Iroquois acknowledged Delaware ownership. But
when they stopped off for a party at their town of Shamokin
(Sunbury, Pa.), Conrad Weiser dealt with them. Weiser was the
provincial interpreter, deeply involved in the schemes of Logan
and Penns.

Logan wrote Weiser to convert the Iroquois *refusal* to claim
Nutimus's lands into a *release* of claim. "It may be proper for
them, under their hands, to Declare that they release to the
Proprietors of Pennsylvania . . . all their Claim and Pretensions
whatsoever to all the Lands between Delaware and Sasquehan-
nah." Admittedly, "They do not grant us any Land on Delaware
. . . they only release and quit all their Claims there and as they
make none it is in reality nothing."

The Iroquois were not fooled, and they resisted. "It went
very hart," Weiser responded to Logan. "They war afaired they

shoud doe any thing a mis to their cousins, the delawars." Logan
raised his price. "They Charges will be some what larger than
you most Expect," wrote Weiser, and he hired ten horses to
carry the goods of the material bribe.

But Logan dangled a more seductive lure. "We are not willing to enter upon Treaties" with the Delawares "as with our
Brethren of the five Nations for whom we keep our fire and
therefore *would treat with them only in behalf of all or any of the
others.*" In short, he offered a bloodless conquest which the
Iroquois could not resist. As Paul A. W. Wallace has remarked,
the Iroquois undertook to police Pennsylvania's woods "in return for Pennsylvania's recognition of their sole right to do
so."[21]

The agreement was made secretly in Shamokin after being
rejected in Philadelphia. With it in hand, Logan and Thomas
Penn held a new meeting at Pennsbury to prepare for the day-
and-a-half walk which they now insisted on organizing. Governor George Thomas played a carnival, pea-under-the-walnut
trick on the Delawares by showing them a purported sketch of
the streams along the Delaware River. They could not read, and
he simply lied about the names on the creeks to make his case.
When they signed the release he presented to them, they
thought they were signing the bounds of land that all agreed
had been sold long ago to William Penn. What they actually
signed, as labeled, was something else again, as they soon
found out.

The Walk was walked—sixty-four miles in the day and a
half, with lines drawn strategically at the end to dispossess all
Delawares. Thomas Penn "reduced" the minutes of the treaty
to an "exact" manner that took in "as Much Ground as any
Person here ever expected." When the Delawares protested,
Logan summoned the Iroquois to discipline them. Onondaga
Chief Canasatego invented an ancient conquest to mask the real
one taking place at the moment, and historians and ethnologists
were led astray for centuries.[22]

But not the Delawares who were evicted from their homeland, and not the European colonials who settled there. Quakers
in the region kept alive the tradition that fraud had been committed. Moravians, who came later, listened to the Delawares
and became fearful, but dared not protest publicly though they

offered compensation to the ousted Indians. Scotch-Irish immigrants who swarmed in were accustomed to seizing lands from
natives in Ireland. They cared nothing about fraud or fairness,
were interested only in getting rid of Indian occupants, and they
harassed the Delawares who resisted eviction.

Emigrant Delawares waited for the opportunity of the
Seven Years War when they took bloody vengeance, and incidentally aroused the curiosity of the provincial Assembly and its
leader who, by that time, was Benjamin Franklin; and by that
time, too, Franklin had become Thomas Penn's bitterest enemy.

The people who suffered from that revenge were the home-
steaders who had paid very high prices to the Penns' land speculators for the right to settle and make a living on the land. Logan
and Penn were beyond Delaware revenge. Logan died in his
bed in 1751. Thomas Penn returned triumphantly to England
in 1741 where, incidentally, he immediately rejected the Quakers who had frustrated his schemes. Penn talked to the Archbishop of Canterbury, who was very glad to welcome into the
Church of England fold this great lord and landowner. In 1741,
Franklin was still working hand-in-glove with Penn's placemen
who were so strategically placed to be advantageous to Franklin,
and he continued on that team until 1755.

Let me explain why this seemingly extraneous chapter became necessary in writing about Benjamin Franklin, who was
not strictly part of it. Standard histories have assumed the validity of the Penns' version of the Walking Purchase and, in consequence, have poured out viciously racist and bigoted
denunciations of the Quakers who eventually exposed the fraud
and tried to reconcile the Delawares. (At much cost, financially
and politically, to themselves.) In histories of colonial Pennsylvania, the Quakers are commonly presented as "Indian lovers"
comparable to the diatribes leveled elsewhere at "nigger lovers."
It should not be necessary to expound further on that score.

Franklin, though he was the little man who was not there
during the Walking Purchase, contributed to this false image by
omitting the Walk from his *Autobiography,* having learned full
well in later life what had happened.

The effect on history has been to trivialize the struggle by
Pennsylvanians against their feudal lord by permitting Thomas

Penn's carefully fabricated self-image to stand without challenge. Given an assumption that he was really honorable and just, then his Quaker and Franklinite assailants appear as libelers with malignant motives squabbling over petty issues of privilege and patronage.

When, instead, it is realized that Pennsylvanians came to understand how lord Penn exploited them and exposed them heedlessly to the wrath of even more exploited Indians, Franklin's subsequent great campaigns to overthrow lordship in Pennsylvania make sense. Then arise historical issues that have been neglected and misrepresented far too long.

The self-consciously wise Franklin of the *Autobiography* could not admit how he had been duped by Penn and, worse, had actually worked hard to support Penn's political machine. We turn to that process now.

7 CLIMBING

For CLARITY, chapters 7 and 8 cover the same time period with distinct though related themes. Chapter 7 (this one) continues Franklin's success in business and his rise to civic prominence. It shows how he walked a tightrope between the Assembly Quakers and the Proprietary placemen, carefully avoiding the creation of enmities and equally carefully drawing personal profit from both sides while he initiated and organized new civic institutions.

Strive though he did to give an appearance of impartiality, this was illusory because the Proprietary side was "more equal" for Franklin. This will become more evident in chapter 8, which shows his efforts to erode German support for the Quakers. When Thomas Penn sponsored an elaborate political machine to divide the Germans, and thus to reduce their electoral support for Quakers in the Assembly, Franklin joined the machine. Further comment can be put off until the next chapter.

As soon as Thomas Penn returned to England, he began plotting to control his province's Assembly. His conversion to the Church of England has already been noticed. It guaranteed many strong friends at court, and he would use their support in future, not only independently of Quakers, but in active hostility to them, often in secrecy.

So far as the Assembly was concerned, he needed support on the western side of the Atlantic. The brute fact that he and his lawyers could not evade was provision for Assembly elections in the royal charter of Charles II, which was the foundation of all his power and property. Penn's adherents had never won an Assembly election (and never would). They tried violently to break their losing streak in the election of 1742.

At that time, citizens had to come in from surrounding counties to vote in a Philadelphia polling place. They had to mount a flight of stairs to the building's upper story. Proprietary partisans complained that their supporters were crowded out of access to the poll by gangs of Quaker partisans who controlled the stairs. (I cannot confirm or deny this; elections in Pennsylvania have always been rough.) William Allen, who was political boss for the Penns, resorted to direct methods. He hired sailors from ships in port to advance on the polls with clubs, much to the outrage of the Quaker partisans. However, pacifists though they were, their German adherents included men who responded to the sailors with clubs of their own, and they were more numerous. The sailors retreated to shipboard sanctuary, the elections continued; and, as usual, the Quakers won.[1]

Franklin's *Gazette* report named no names and carefully avoided categories, noting that "some of the Magistrates, and other Persons of Note" expostulated with the sailors, but the latter knocked down "Magistrates, Constables, and all others who oppos'd 'em." In the *Gazette,* the restorers of order were undistinguished "Inhabitants" who pursued the rioters to their ships and dragged them out "one by one" to commit "near 50 of them" to prison.[2]

As the chief magistrates included the men who had hired the sailors, it does not seem likely that the culprits remained in prison very long. On that point the *Gazette* is silent. However, the persons at the polling place apparently caught on to what was happening, helped by the contrasting experiences of William Allen and Israel Pemberton, Sr., Allen surveyed the scene unscathed; Pemberton was knocked about.[3] Voter opinion showed in their ballots. Franklin demurely reported that, except in Bucks County, "the Majority in favour of the old Assembly was extraordinary."[4] (In Bucks it was normal.) In short, this Proprietary approach to gaining Assembly control backfired, and Penn's men had to devise new strategy. Equally clearly, Franklin straddled. Though he could not have been ignorant of the facts, his reporting in effect absolved the Proprietary side of guilt.

Perhaps he really was ignorant of the eviction of Nutimus's Delawares that occurred in the same year, 1742. That affair had been conducted in some secrecy at distant Easton,[5] and Franklin had no correspondents among the Indians. If he had known, it is unlikely that he would have protested. Despite some romantic propaganda of recent days, Franklin's interest in Indians was limited to their fighting abilities and their lands, and in 1742 he had no personal involvement in their affairs nor any opportunities to acquire their lands. These came later.

In 1742 Franklin was a community booster. To be pleasant, one may say he believed in accentuating the positive. More harshly, he deserved the word "opportunist."

Tradesman Franklin, acquiring property and status, had some of the same attitudes as aristocrat Penn acquiring property and power. Franklin was no bleeding heart. "To relieve the misfortunes of our fellow creatures is concurring with the Deity, 'tis Godlike," he wrote, "but if we provide encouragement for Laziness, and supports for Folly, may it not be found fighting against the order of God and Nature, which perhaps has appointed Want and Misery as the proper Punishments for, and Cautions against as well as necessary consequences of Idleness and Extravagancy."[6]

In the circumstances, that was not entirely as callous as it sounds; in Franklin's fast-growing Pennsylvania, except for the handicapped, unemployment was voluntary and opportunity was seemingly boundless. Yet, regardless of reasons or mitigations, it was an upper-class attitude (that can still be heard today in certain quarters), and it fixed Franklin's sympathies in the same patterns as those of Penn and his entourage. Young Franklin's pursuit of Virtue (still maintained as a facade) was largely displaced by the mature man's achievement of Success, and he had small patience for persons of smaller achievements.

This man's genius was not to be contained in the account books of a printshop, no matter how carefully he kept them. However much he realized the need to acquire wealth in order to achieve independence, his intellectual needs transcended matters of business. In May 1743 he published *A Proposal for Promoting Useful Knowledge among the British Plantations in America*. Botanist John Bartram had been discussing with him a project for founding a learned society to correspond with England's Royal Society, and for Franklin to get an idea was the same thing as to print it.

He named nine members, and held "several Meetings," but the project failed to excite a following. Even learned James Logan refused to get involved. As the editors of the *Franklin Papers* observe, "The Society was already moribund by the time Bartram began receiving inquiries about it from his European friends."[7] But Franklin had his teeth in the project and did not let go. In 1755 he revised it as *Proposals for an American Philosophical Society,* which he transmitted to London.[8] His society made no waves until 1769, when it merged with another group, elected Franklin president, and began to achieve the renown it enjoys today. In later years, Thomas Jefferson became its president while in office as President of the United States. It seems safe to say that no other printer-businessman who had set type with his own hands can be respected for such prowess in the learned world.

Franklin was not only a projector and organizer. Within an astonishingly few years he became the world's foremost scientist in the field of electricity. In 1743, while visiting Boston, he observed some experiments with static electricity performed not very expertly by Archibald Spencer, an itinerant lecturer from Scotland. These aroused curiosity, and when Spencer passed through Philadelphia, Franklin bought his equipment, which was supplemented by a present to the Library Company from Peter Collinson, Franklin's friend and correspondent in London's Royal Society. Collinson included "some Account of the Use of it in making such Experiments."

Excited Franklin "eagerly seized the Opportunity of repeating what I had seen at Boston, and by much Practice acquir'd great Readiness in performing those also which we had an Account of from England, adding a Number of new Ones."[9]

Franklin was not merely a technician. His "new" experiments led to new conceptualization that has enriched our language by the terms he invented or adapted: *currents, conductors, positive* and *negative charges*. He perceived and explained that lightning was "Electrical Fire . . . taken from the whole Cloud, and in leaving it, flashes brightly and cracks loudly." Not content with identification, he explored processes as, for instance, "When a great Number of Clouds from the Sea, meet a Number of Clouds raised from the Land, the Electrical Flashes appear to Strike in different Parts, and as the Clouds are jostled and mixed by the Winds, or brought near by the Electrical Attraction, they continue to give and receive Flash after Flash, till the Electrical Fire is equally diffused."[10] The entire document from which these quotations are taken is strong evidence that Franklin deserves credit for the science of meteorology as well as electricity.

More was to come. As Franklin carried his experiments forward, he wrote about them to his Quaker friend Collinson in London. In 1751, Collinson, as a fellow of the Royal Society, compiled five letters in a pamphlet, *Experiments and Observations on Electricity, made at Philadelphia in America, by Mr. Benjamin Franklin*. This was widely read in England and translated into French by Thomas-François Dalibard, whose assistant performed "the Philadelphia experiment" of drawing electricity from a thundercloud. Another Frenchman, named Delor, repeated the experiment in Paris, and it was repeated again in England and Germany.[11] One must make a special effort of imagination to conceive the tremendous excitement over the opening of a whole new world of science.

It was "Mr. Franklin's hypothesis" that they tested in 1752. Franklin tested it independently with his famous kite and key experiment, the greatest wonder of which is that he was not electrocuted on the spot. He drew lightning with his kite, according to Joseph Priestley, "in June 1752, a month after the electricians in France had verified the same theory, but before he [Franklin] heard of any thing they had done."[12]

On 30 November 1753, the Royal Society awarded its Copley Gold Medal to Franklin. The president, Earl Macclesfield, seemed in his presentation speech to be a little bemused that the medal should have been deserved by a remote man who was "not a Fellow of this Society nor an Inhabitant of this Island." Happily, however, Franklin was "a Subject of the Crown of Great Britain, and must be acknowledged to have deserved well of the Philosophical World, and of this learned Body in particular."[13]

Franklin received the medal in May 1754, delivered by the Reverend William Smith, who was to figure very prominently in his life thereafter.[14] The Copley Medal was for contributions to science of world importance. It added immensely to Franklin's prestige at home and in Europe (where he had formerly been an unknown inhabitant of the barbarous colonies); but he had been gaining in prominence at home because of other activities as well.

We must backtrack a little. When King George's War between Britain and France broke out in 1744, it spread as usual to the empires' colonies; and, as always, it posed a harsh dilemma for the Quaker and pietist pacifists of Pennsylvania. Doctrine required them to avoid participation or any sort of support for military measures. Common sense warned them that enemy ships could sail up the Delaware to attack Philadelphia. And hobgoblins in the woods howled portents of raids by French-allied Indians.

The Quakers then controlling the Assembly accepted some risks and resorted to casuistry. They calculated that the Delaware River had too many navigational hazards for an enemy to get by without a local pilot. They counted on Pennsylvania's alliance with the Iroquois to secure approaches overland. When authorities demanded money for defense, the Assembly evaded responsibility for its purpose by granting £4,000 "to the King's Use" and specified purchase of "Bread, Beef, Port, Flour, Wheat or other Grain."[15] Governor Thomas interpreted "other Grain" as gunpowder, bought it, and Franklin remembered that "they never objected to it."[16]

But the assemblymen dug in their heels against creation of a militia, and a disgusted Franklin abandoned his stance of even-handedness between the Quaker and Proprietary parties. In 1747, he wrote and published *Plain Truth: or, Serious Considerations On the Present State of the City of Philadelphia, and Province of Pennsylvania.*[17] This passionate outburst flailed away at the "Dissensions of our Leaders [who] thro' *mistaken Principles of Religion,* joined with a Love of Worldly Power, on the one Hand; thro' *Pride, Envy* and *implacable Resentment* on the other" continually exposed families and fortunes to destruction. "It seems as if our greatest Men . . . had *sworn the Ruin of the Country.* . . . Where then shall we seek for Succour and Protection? The Government we are immediately under denies it to us."[18]

The strong language professed balance, but its specific target very plainly was the Quaker-dominated Assembly, so Franklin's bold words risked losing his lucrative place as Assembly Clerk. Nevertheless, as he boasted later, he was continued in that post by unanimous vote. His gratitude was far from fervent. The *Autobiography* takes a backhanded slap at his employers. "Indeed I had some Cause to believe, that the Defence of the Country was not disagreeable to any of them, provided they were not requir'd to assist in it." Though opposed to offensive war, many Quakers "were clearly for the defensive."[19]

As for the opposite party, its leaders simply ignored implications of fault. (We shall see their reason in a moment.) When Franklin followed up his outcry by recruiting an Association for a voluntary private militia, response was instantaneous and strong. Volunteers signed a compact, companies were formed and drilled, and substantial donations of money were made for buying arms, including cannon. Governor George Thomas invited Franklin to meet with the provincial council when Association affairs were before it. The whole affair rocketed Franklin to prominence throughout the province even as his experiments with electricity were drawing attention abroad.

But this Association, like so many of Franklin's remembered experiences, was not quite what he made it seem. On its face it was purely spontaneous, but that picture is shaded by the report sent to the Proprietaries by Secretary Richard Peters, their most trusted confidant. Peters wrote that Franklin had concocted the Association scheme by consulting with three important members of the Proprietary party "to fall foul of the Quakers and their opposers equally . . . and by this Artifice to animate all the middling Persons to undertake their own Defence in opposition to the Quakers and the Gentlemen." Peters carefully noted that Proprietary boss William Allen had been aware of the scheme "before it was reduc'd to any settled form or Plan." Allen and Franklin "and the other Persons concern'd" wanted Peters to induce the Penns "to believe the Associators were heartily in their Interest."[20]

Their assurances failed to persuade Thomas Penn, who took a very dim view of popular movements and was darkly suspicious of Benjamin Franklin. Penn was alarmed by the very fact that the Association rocketed Franklin to prominence as the people's defender. This was "Contempt to Government," fumed Penn, by which he meant independence from himself and his appointees, certainly not the Quaker Assembly. (Penn's semantics must always be watched closely.) The Association was "a Military Common Wealth" leading to "Anarchy and Confusion" in a manner "little less than Treason."[21] Thomas held very different views from those of his own supporters, who were keenly aware of being within reach of French power. At his greater distance across the Atlantic, Thomas had his own concerns. He worried that that "dangerous Man" Franklin had seduced even the Proprietary's friends, so Thomas felt he must bide his time. Since Franklin had become "a Sort of Tribune of the People," he had to be "treated with regard," but at the very moment when Franklin gained highest esteem from Penn's friends, Thomas himself began to wish this "Tribune" in "any other Country." A few years remained, however, before he felt it expedient to attack such a tribune openly. Ironically, when that moment came, the attack was launched simultaneously against Franklin and the Quakers whom Franklin himself had attacked.

War ended in 1748 and Franklin's Association disbanded. For the time being he interrupted his function as "Tribune," and resumed the gratifying process of increasing his personal wealth. As we have seen, he neatly fitted into his printing business his roles as Assembly Clerk and Philadelphia postmaster. One hand washed the other. His innovative imagination reached out to organize a precedent for today's franchising schemes, which he did by forming partnerships with printers in other cities. Franklin supplied the equipment, his partners managed the businesses, and they split the profits.[22]

We have seen also how Franklin became actively involved in electricity research in ways that were to win international celebrity. Yet all these activities and the Association failed to consume completely the time on the hands of this busy, busy man. (His Debbie probably saw very little of him.) He sensed a need for higher education beyond the limits of the Quaker school already teaching rudiments. Like other pietists, Quakers feared the "worldly" influences of higher learning. (They have changed, as their colleges now testify.)

In his *Autobiography,* Franklin remembered that he had proposed to start an Academy in 1743, but was distracted in other directions.[23] He kept the project in mind until he could free more time for his avocations by retiring from business. This he did in 1748 by taking assistant David Hall as partner to handle physical and financial matters while Franklin continued as editor and writer of what we would now call special features.[24] Unhampered by details of daily routine, Franklin used the printing press more than ever as a powerful means for setting public policy.

With time free, money available, and connections well established, he revived his project for an Academy of higher education. In 1749, he printed a pamphlet, *Proposals Relating to the Education of Youth in Pensilvania,* which ignored the existing Quaker school.[25] One might justifiably ascribe that gap to oversight, but it soon takes on a different coloration as the lists of subscribers and trustees are examined. No pacifist Quakers were on either list though several token "defense" Quakers appear, two of whom, William Coleman and Robert Strettell, had been "disowned" (excommunicated) by Friends Meeting.[26] The trustees named within a month after publication of the pamphlet were all Proprietary supporters, James Logan and William Allen prominent among them.[27] Annual financial pledges were contributed for a total of £2,000, and an idle building was immediately bought. Rarely has an institution of learning started so apparently spontaneously.

However, appearances were illusory. The editors of the *Franklin Papers* note that the "Constitution of the Academy of Philadelphia" was drawn up jointly by Franklin and Attorney General Tench Francis,[28] who had earlier strategized with Franklin on launching the military Association. After careful deliberation, the Proprietary Penns patronized the Academy, chartered it, and actually donated "as an earnest of their Benevolence Five Hundred Pounds Sterling."[29] Franklin, who made that remark, was no stranger to the Penns' tightfistedness. It seems warranted to comment that the Academy trustees formed up as the executive committee of the Proprietary party.

Again, the *Autobiography* is uncandid and misleading. It remarks that Pennsylvania had no provision "for a complete Education of Youth."[30] The word "complete" sends a reader on the wrong track while preserving an appearance of legitimate qualification. In fact, as Theodore Thayer has noted, "a school was established by the Quakers and chartered by William Penn soon after Philadelphia was settled." Indeed, Penn Charter School still functions, with an excellent reputation.

How "complete" was its offering? Thayer tells that Franklin's Academy "had a somewhat fuller course of studies than the Quakers offered, but until the Revolution one was essentially as much a college as the other."[31]

In short, the Academy was founded as competition for the Quaker school, and it was soon to give clear signals that Quakers were unwelcome in it. This became unmistakable when its administration was taken over by Provost William Smith.

William Smith came to New York in 1751, apparently to seek fortune, equipped with little more than a letter of recommendation from the Archbishop of Canterbury and an overwhelming urge to spill ink on paper—anonymously. Smith was passionately imperialist. He was also passionate about "regular" religion, by which he meant the Church of England. Immediately on arrival in New York, Smith became involved in a Presbyterian-Anglican controversy over a proposed new college for New York. He strongly favored an Anglican establishment. "As to the Political Uses of national Establishments [of Religion], he must indeed be a very shallow Politician who does not see them. . . . The Statesman has always found it necessary for the Purposes of Government, to raise some one Denomination of religions above the Rest to a certain Degree." The government "is thus enabled to turn the Balance and keep all in Subjection . . . [if] all Sects and Persuasions be equally favor'd . . . how shall they be influenc'd or how rul'd?"[32]

This concept at the opposite pole from the principled toleration of Quakers seems also to contradict the easygoing attitudes often expressed by Benjamin Franklin, yet Smith and Franklin came to terms of intimacy with each other for three years during which they worked in close cooperation. I have to wonder about the means used by the younger man to charm, even to entrance, the older.

They met after Smith wrote a tract embodying his ideas for an ideal college which he sent to Franklin, who thereupon invited him to Philadelphia. Franklin quickly warmed to Smith, who just as quickly calculated how he could use Franklin for advancement. Together they traveled to Connecticut to visit the leading Anglican churchman in America, Dr. Samuel Johnson.[33] The custom then was for men to share a bed in inns, and we may presume that "pillow talk," if nothing else, contributed to intimacy. Certain it is that Franklin became positively fatuous about young William Smith in a letter to "my Pupil."[34]

Smith got what he wanted. When he soon returned to England for ordination in his Church, he was fortified with impressive credentials, the purpose of which was to bring influence on Proprietary Thomas Penn to patronize Franklin's fledgling Academy of Philadelphia *and* to establish Smith at its head. He approached the Archbishop of Canterbury again, this time with a letter from Samuel Johnson. From Archbishop Herring he went on to Thomas Penn (with an assist from Franklin via Peter Collinson who was friendly with both Franklin and Penn).[35]

Pennsylvania's problems were discussed and considered at length in 1753 by the trio of Smith, Penn, and Archbishop Herring. These three discovered among themselves an identity of interests, and Smith emerged from their conferences as the trusted agent of the two men of power.[36]

One of their prime concerns was Franklin's Academy. As Smith reported to Franklin, the Academy interfered with a plan of Penn's own. "But," continued Smith, "when I was able to shew the worthy Gentleman the necessity of such a seminary in a political light, he generously agreed to ingraft his Scheme upon yours in the two Foundations proposed, provided I would undertake to be the person to execute them." As we have seen, Franklin had founded the Academy as a Proprietary party project, so there was no conflict on that point. Nor could Franklin take exception to the second "Foundation" mentioned in Smith's report. (For clarity, it must be deferred to the next chapter.)

Franklin ought properly to have become thoughtful at Smith's happy boast of obtaining "an uncommon share" of Thomas Penn's confidence "such as no indifferent person ever before enjoy'd." That Smith reciprocated Penn's goodwill, while aware that the Proprietary was unpopular in his province, was underlined by the remark to Franklin, "I hope whatever opinions some on your Side of the water entertain of him, they will now be convinced that he is not the *nominal* but the *real* father of his Country."[37]

What Smith did not confess to Franklin, either in this correspondence or later, was his acceptance of the function of undercover agent and spy for Thomas Penn, with Franklin as one of the primary objects of his spying.

Yet again, it is necessary to look beyond the *Autobiography* in which Smith is nonexistent. To mention him would have required Franklin to confess that Smith had used and made a fool of him, had outsmarted him, and such a confession would be intolerable.

The beginning of delusion came as Smith and Thomas Penn altered the Academy from Franklin's original plan. Before Smith had journeyed to London for ordination, the trustees petitioned for a charter, and Thomas Penn acceded to their desire. This first charter, which was signed by Governor James Hamilton on 13 July 1753, empowered the trustees "to erect, set up, maintain and Support an Academy or any other kind of Seminary of Learning in any place within the said Province of Pennsylvania."[38] The broadness of this language is noteworthy because Smith's biographers have contended that this charter narrowly precluded the founding of a college. Not so.

Smith convinced Penn of "the necessity of such a seminary in a political light."[39] These two schemers contrived a new enterprise rather different from the Academy that Franklin thought was to be his own. To restructure it, they needed a new charter countermanding the old one, but some delay was required to prepare the nice legalities.

Smith returned to Philadelphia in May 1754.[40] He was hired by the Academy trustees "on trial" to teach "Logick, Rhetorick, Ethicks, and Natural Philosophy" (i.e., science).[41] Such lowly status did not last long. Within a year, Smith drafted the new charter (January 1755) with provision for appointment of a *Provost,* and Smith was promptly made executive head of the new *College.*[42] His salary was set at £200, a solid sum for the time. It was made even more solid by the secret fee of £50 from Thomas Penn for Smith's covert operations.[43]

The new charter sharply restricted the broad terms of the first one. Significantly, this new charter required qualifying oaths for trustees, officers, and faculty. They had to swear in blood-curdling terms to uphold King George II against all rebels, and also to deny under oath the Roman Catholic doctrine of transubstantiation.[44] A loophole for Quakers permitted affirmation instead of swearing, but they were shy of any institution requiring oaths (as intended) and they soon turned hostile to Smith and his very political College.[45] Presbyterian Charles Thomson, who was to become Secretary of Congress during the American Revolution, immediately resigned from the faculty (and was picked up by the Quakers for their school). Thomson could sign the oath without qualms, but he was not going to work under Smith.[46]

If Franklin had qualms, they did not appear; he was elected to the showy and toothless post of president, which he held under sufferance of good political behavior.

Within the scope of this book, only a selection of Franklin's multifarious schemes and projects can be noticed; but, besides those already described, one more demands notice. This was the Pennsylvania Hospital, first suggested to Franklin by his friend Dr. Thomas Bond. In contrast to the Association and the Academy, the Hospital shows no signs of political motivation. Indeed, it could not have started without an act of the Assembly to grant £2,000 if private philanthropists would raise that much in matching funds.

That was Franklin's scheme, but the year was 1751 when the Assembly was wholly dominated by an absolute majority of Quakers and included Israel Pemberton, Jr., "the King of the Quakers," so there can be no doubt of orthodox Quaker approval for the Hospital. Non-Quaker physicians Thomas and Phineas Bond, who had supported Franklin's military Association, offered to serve the Hospital without fee. In complete contrast with the Academy-College, the Hospital was a nonpolitical project. When the conditions were met, the money raised, and the Hospital began operations, Pemberton as well as Franklin took an active role on the board of managers. In fact, Pemberton became more active and stayed on the board for the rest of his life. By contrast, Franklin kept this nonpolitical post at the Hospital for only five years, though he remained a lifelong trustee of the College.[47]

Regardless of his multitude of interests, Franklin was, above all, a political animal.

$\mathcal{8}$ GERMANS

No one in a responsible position could have escaped concern about the tide of immigrant Germans. By midcentury their numbers rose to half the population as estimated by three very different gentlemen. Franklin's eventual enemy William Smith placed them at half. Franklin's ally Joseph Galloway made them 50 to 55 percent. The Reformed missionary Michael Schlatter, who had counted houses in his tours around the settlements, put Germans at 90,000 persons among a total of 190,000 European colonials.[1]

At first Franklin was ambivalent about these newcomers, whose numbers did not begin to swell until after his own arrival in Philadelphia. In his usual astute fashion he saw them as possible sources of profit. In May 1732 he started publication of the *Philadelphische Zeitung* in the German language, taking advantage of his newly arrived *Gazette* employee Louis Timothée, who became his *Sprachmeister*. But the paper failed to attract subscribers and died after a second issue.[2]

In 1747, Franklin still counted on "the brave and steady Germans" to join his military Association. But they stayed away. Franklin never accepted rejection with indifference, and the circumstances of the German rebuff angered him. Where his newspaper had failed to attract the three hundred subscribers necessary for continuance, Christopher Saur, a tough Anabaptist in Germantown, not only succeeded famously with a new *Pensylvanische Berichte* and a German-language almanac that competed successfully with Franklin's English-language *Poor Richard;* but Saur dared to attack Franklin's military Association and was a major influence persuading the Germans to avoid it.[3] Franklin's ambivalence turned to hostility against Saur and all the Germans supporting him.

By 1751, Franklin had formed a strongly adverse opinion about those stubborn "Dutch" whose "Disagreeableness of disonant Manners" was causing English settlers to move away from them. "How good Subjects they may make, and how faithful to the British Interest, is a Question worth considering." Their numbers in Pennsylvania were "too great." Unless measures were taken to stem the immigration, "This will in a few Years become a German Colony: Instead of their Learning our Language, we must learn their's, or live as in a foreign Country."[4]

Franklin's growing hostility coincided with the feelings of the Proprietary placemen whose favor he had been courting. They had gradually whittled away at Quaker power in the 1720s and 1730s until John Kinsey, Quaker Speaker of the Assembly, outsmarted them with special attention to German interests. Kinsey's strategy became all the more effective after the Proprietary men overreached themselves with the violence of the 1742 election (see pp. 59–60 above). After that, though the Germans kept a low public profile in their own right, they piled up the vote for Quaker candidates.

Their voting habits were skewed even further toward Quaker support by the similarity of religious assumptions of their more aggressive constituencies. The Germans actually spread across a wide range of faiths, from a few Roman Catholics and a much larger number of "High Church" Lutheran and Reformed Protestants, through the Moravians, to the pietist radicals of the time—the Amish, Mennonites, Dunkards, and Schwenkfelders. The pietists were anti-authoritarian pacifists. From long experience with suppression and exploitation in Europe, they suspected all noblemen of base motives, and they were rightly sure that the Penns were noblemen. High Church Germans did not hold this attitude uniformly, but for a long time they avoided politics while the pietists warmly supported Quakers as the best security for their liberties. The result was a dependable phalanx of Quakers in the Assembly, at constant conflict with the Anglicans and Presbyterians among the Penns' placemen.

As Dietmar Rothermund has observed, "The unity and strength of the Quaker-German coalition was a source of deep frustration to the men of the Proprietary party. . . . The rapid increase of German immigration in the 1740s and early 1750s seemed to turn this nuisance into a menace."[5] Franklin's fears, quoted above, were exactly in line with the placemen's attitudes.

Church authorities in Germany and Holland were also concerned about what seemed like irreparable loss of souls as well as bodies in the migration. The 1740 settlement of Moravians at Nazareth and Bethlehem in Pennsylvania excited horror among Lutherans who were indifferent to the souls of heathen Indians. The Moravians were followers of martyred Jan Hus, who had almost been exterminated in Europe by Lutheran persecution. They had kept a "remnant" alive in Saxony under the protection of sympathetic Count von Zinzendorf, but these fled to the New World when pressures became too intense. Lutheran authorities would not let them slip away to spread their abominable heresies unhampered. In 1742, only two years after Moravian arrival, the Lutherans' Reverend Heinrich Melchior Mühlenberg pursued them. Though Pennsylvania's laws and policies of toleration prevented any thought of renewed persecution, Mühlenberg feared losing his own church's "sheep" to the Moravians' extremely active missionaries. Dietmar Rothermund notes that from 1742 to 1745, more than forty Moravian missionaries "preached almost daily in many German settlements of the Middle Atlantic region. The regular ministers of the Lutheran and Reformed churches were few and could not match these efforts."[6]

In 1746, the German Reformed synods of Amsterdam sent the Reverend Michael Schlatter to look after their flocks. Schlatter lacked Mühlenberg's tact within his own denomination. His dogmatism alienated Reformed religionists, including their pastors, already in Pennsylvania. He seems to have been a rather stupid man whose chief talent was raving. Though the mass of Pennsylvania's Germans were honest, industrious farmers whose superior agriculture and devotion to the land was the very foundation of Pennsylvania's prosperous export trade in premium wheat, these hardworking families were to Schlatter a mass of "pagan blindness and fearful ruin."[7] Back in Amsterdam, where he returned in 1750, he solicited support to save the "tender children, who, without [orthodox] instruction or care, grow up as for hell, and become a prey of Satan and his seducing apostles."[8]

The clergy of Amsterdam did their bit to rescue those tender children from Satan, hell, and Moravians. They collected donations from churches throughout the Rhine Valley and in Scotland, and raised £12,000. A canny lot, they did not turn it over to Schlatter; instead, they put it in charge of trustees, who invested it and sent income directly to Pennsylvania's Reformed churches.

At their behest, Schlatter went off to London to solicit help from Proprietary Thomas Penn. Approaching Penn, Schlatter warned that the Germans in Pennsylvania were "in danger of growing savage" in a manner that historically had "often made Sovereigns tremble on their thrones." Schlatter proposed to fund the introduction of an orderly discipline and ministry "to prevent the fatal effects of ignorance and vice," thus to make good subjects of those "who at present can scarcely be called men." Remarkably, this phrasing about his own countrymen echoes Christian denunciations of heathen Indians.[9]

Reforming religious ministries was not the sort of crusade to fascinate Thomas Penn, but Schlatter did arouse his attention with a promise that "regular" ministers would make "good subjects" of those German voters. At that point, Penn recognized the possibility for enlarging his patronage machine at minimum cost to himself while most desirably driving a wedge between Germans and Quakers.

Benjamin Franklin became part of the process through a letter about the Germans that his friend Peter Collinson passed about to, among others, the king's chief minister and the president of the Board of Trade.[10] As this was to become one of the most important writings of Franklin's life, both in its immediate effects and in its ultimate boomerang against him, it will repay extensive quotation.

"Why should the Palatine Boors be suffered to swarm into our Settlements, and by herding together establish their Language and Manners to the Exclusion of ours? Why should Pennsylvania, founded by the English, become a colony of *Aliens,* who will shortly be so numerous as to Germanize us instead of our Anglifying them and will never adopt our Language or Customs, any more than they can acquire our Complexion?"[11]

In a later letter passed about by Collinson, Franklin was specific:

I remember when they modestly declined intermeddling in our Elections, but now they come in droves, and carry all before them, except in one or two Counties. . . . They begin of late to make all their

Bonds and other legal Writings in their own Language, which (though I think it ought not to be) are allowed good in our Courts, where the German business so encreases that there is continual need of Interpreters; and I suppose in a few years they will also be necessary in the Assembly, to tell one half of our Legislators what the other half say; In short, unless the stream of their importation could be turned from this to other Colonies, as you [Peter Collinson] very judiciously propose, they will soon so out number us, that all the advantages we have will not (in My Opinion) be able to preserve our language, and even our Government will become precarious.[12]

Several currents of thought and action came together after Michael Schlatter made his heartrending appeal to Thomas Penn. Penn hustled about among royalty and courtiers and at least one important Dissenter-Presbyterian cleric, the Reverend Samuel Chandler. With their support, Penn founded the London Society for the Support of Schools among the German Protestants in Pennsylvania. King George II gave £1,000, the dowager Princess of Wales gave £800, four noblemen contributed substantial sums, and Penn engaged personally to give a typically nonspecific "considerable sum yearly," this for promoting "the most essential part," also not specified.[13]

This, in short, was the second "Foundation" that Thomas Penn combined with the Academy-College, as reported by William Smith to Franklin (see chapter 7, p. 69). Smith and Penn collaborated as closely on this project as on the other.

Two weeks after Smith's arrival in London on 1 December 1753, he prepared an enormous memorandum about the Germans, clearly echoing Franklin's remarks to Collinson, and he scribbled page after page of advice to the gentlemen in Penn's nascent London Society for Schools for the Germans. In the midst of Smith's masses of verbiage, two sentences stand out. "It is obvious," he wrote, that education for the Germans "must be calculated rather to make good subjects than what is called good scholars. The English language, together with writing, something of figures, and a short system of religious and civil truths and duties, in the *Socratic* or *catechetic* way, is all the education necessary to the people."[14]

Two days later, Smith was ordained priest in Fulham Palace.[15] Archbishop Herring thought Smith's scheme for schools for Germans "as great and as necessary to be put into Execution as any that was ever laid before the British Nation." Out of Smith's speech to the Society for the Propagation of the Gospel (SPG) and the archbishop's commendation, somehow an appointment emerged for Smith as a member of a board of trustees empowered and financed to create the German schools. But it was not the SPG that so appointed Smith; it was the "charitable society" of peers and gentlemen for the relief and instruction of poor Germans.[16] More than likely, the appointment was Thomas Penn's, and just as probably, Penn's unspecified annual contribution to the charitable society's purposes was his secret £50 retainer to Smith for covert operations in the province.[17]

All this was not exactly what Michael Schlatter had had in mind when he appealed to Thomas Penn. Schlatter very quickly was reduced to subordination. He returned to Holland, where his explanations of his accomplishment failed to impress the Reformed Synod. They had good reason. As William Smith had commented to Franklin and Richard Peters, Smith's aim "was to have the management of this important Trust devolved upon Men of the first rank of Pennsylvania and not upon Clergy who depend on Dutch Synods." For Smith, Schlatter's fault was "his too great Attachment to foreign Synods and clergy who would counterwork our design. Ecclesiastical power from Holland will not go down in Pennsylvania."[18]

Political associations for religion were well understood by the members of the Dutch Synod, who were no babes-in-the-wood. They saw at once that they not only had no part in the English society's German schools, but were positively excluded, and they dismissed Schlatter. He came back to Thomas Penn, hat in hand. He borrowed £100 from Penn, and was seized upon by Smith to be the actual manager of the schools. Schlatter, the apparent originator of the schools for Germans, became in actuality no more than a hireling, utterly dependent upon and subservient to the Englishmen. He became, in fact, a mere "front."[19]

He was not a very effective front. The Germans quickly realized that the German schools had become English schools for teaching the Germans the English language and possibly English religion; and the Germans never gave up their congregational efforts to establish their own schools. The Dutch Synod directed their own subsidies to Pennsylvanians without intermediaries.[20]

Penn and Smith set up a complex of organizations to establish their schools, and by no great coincidence the general board of trustees was composed of Proprietary wheelhorses. These were the governor, Chief Justice William Allen; Land Secretary Richard Peters; Allen's business partner Joseph Turner; Benjamin Franklin; and the interpreter to the Indians, Conrad Weiser. William Smith became the trustees' secretary and dispenser of funds, and this general board spawned regional boards of "sober and respectable persons denominated *Assistants* or *Deputy Trustees*."[21] These deputies in turn hired schoolmasters and the whole personnel were Proprietary supporters to a man. They constituted political outreach into such solidly German communities as York, Lancaster, Reading, New Hanover, Skippack, and Goshenhoppen (Bucks County's Churchville). The whole machinery cost Thomas Penn very little. This was patronage at its most ideal.

Or it would have been if it had worked; but the Germans were not taken in. They noticed immediately that instruction was to be in English. They rejected the authority of English noblemen to make Michael Schlatter their "Rector" after they had earlier rejected him as the emissary of the Dutch Synod. Worried religious denominations set up their own schools to teach in the German language. Though the Lutheran leader Mühlenberg sought alliance with the Proprietary men, Anabaptist printer Christopher Saur launched bitter attacks against the whole charity school procedure in his widely read and much trusted *Pensylvanische Berichte*.[22] He was so effective that Penn's men determined in 1755 to establish their own German-language newspaper ("at the expense of the society in London," of course). Saur needed no sponsor or patron; his paper paid its own way with a profit that constituted his living.

Franklin lent his name and a contribution to the competing Proprietary journal *Philadelphische Zeitung,* printed by Anthony Armbrüster, but this paper never made headway against Saur; it started in 1755 and expired in 1757. At the same time, Michael Schlatter met with such hostility that he gave up and went off to be a chaplain in the British Army.[23]

But when Smith returned to Pennsylvania in May 1754, he had put together an intricate political machine that showed much promise. It involved diverse groups on both sides of the Atlantic, and Franklin was privy to all Smith's manipulations concerning Germans so far as the records show. First, there was the Proprietor, with his intrinsic, material power of patronage. It cannot be forgotten that all the executive and judicial posts of government in the province were filled at Penn's discretion. Second were the Archbishop of Canterbury and the SPG and the ecclesiastico-political apparatus controlled by them. Third was the "Charitable society," though its importance as a source of power was probably minimal in all respects save one; to wit, that it included the participation of Dissenters (i.e., Presbyterians), and their London general secretary Samuel Chandler was a leading Presbyterian divine who seems to have been on singularly good terms with the Anglican hierarchy. As we shall see, Thomas Penn recruited him later for an effort to exclude Quakers from the Assembly.

In Pennsylvania, Smith had the support of the "Old Light" Presbyterians, led by the veteran Proprietary guardian William Allen and the senior professor in the Academy, Reverend Francis Alison. Besides the Proprietary placemen, there were the Anglicans who looked for leadership to provincial secretary and Anglican minister Richard Peters; and some of the Anglicans accepted Franklin's leadership. There were the trustees and faculty of the Academy—soon to be the College—of Philadelphia. And there were the trustees of the German schools who were to spawn yet more trustees (three English and three German) for each individual German school. Then there were the payrolls for the schools, tightly controlled by Smith, which included fees for German ministers who would be employed as catechists for each school and thus kept "under proper awe." All in all, it was a formidable apparatus for a province whose total population, excluding Indians, was about 220,000 according to Smith's calculation—smaller than the population of Philadelphia's Germantown neighborhood today.

Behind it were the fertile ingenuity of Franklin and the drive and dash of Smith himself. The combination seemed invincible, but it wrecked upon the rock of German solidarity.

As electioneering strategy, the whole affair was a sad flop, one that Franklin preferred to forget and that its sponsors let die with hardly a whimper. True though it was that William Smith had been the key man, Smith rightly claimed that he had based his plans on Franklin's ideas. For once in his life, Franklin had not known what he was talking about. The Germans were not so stupid as he had believed. Generations would pass before they abandoned their native language for English. Nor, despite hostile rumors, were they ready to give up Pennsylvania's peace and toleration for life under French conquerors. Franklin was on better grounds when he noticed the frugality and industriousness of the Germans. Their support for Quaker assemblymen was not merely a product of clever Quaker management; it was a reasoned conclusion about the available alternatives.

9 INDIANS

In 1751, FRANKLIN CAMPAIGNED SUCCESSFULLY for election to the Assembly. In retrospect about this, he adopted a pose of having modestly accepted a call from the people—not an unfamiliar stance among politicians: "My Election to this Trust was repeated every Year for Ten Years, without my ever asking any Elector for his Vote, or signifying either directly or indirectly any Desire of being chosen." Perhaps such easy acceptance may have been possible as his fame mounted in later years, but in 1751, despite the popularity of his former military Association, he needed the usual machinery of electioneering. The editors of his *Autobiography* note dryly that he "may not have solicited votes directly, but he certainly had lieutenants working very hard on his behalf, and was himself fully engaged politically."[1] Franklin *wanted* that post and strove for it. He was not yet celebrated as the master of electricity, and Assembly membership was the most direct road to provincial fame and power for this aggressively ambitious man.

He resigned as Clerk of the Assembly, but assured continuation of special access to its printing by securing the post for son William. Nepotism was generally considered a natural human activity in those days. Franklin's placement of relatives in the post office and the Assembly shows his acceptance of the practice.

During his own tenure as Clerk, he had become familiar with relations between Assembly and Governor which were, in many respects, second-hand relations between Quakers and Proprietaries. But this description needs qualification. Writers generally have dubbed the Assembly as the creature of the Quaker party, and certainly Quaker majorities controlled it until 1756. It is a mistake, however, to assume therefore that only Quakers opposed the Penns, and that Quakers had to ram opposing measures through the body over the resistance of non-

Quaker minority members. The Penns and their self-serving programs were *not* popular.

Franklin had had plenty of opportunity to observe how often the Presbyterian and Anglican assemblymen followed the Quaker lead to make *unanimous* representations against Proprietary demands. Franklin was much too acute to fail to see these struggles, as, for instance, in the matter of issuing paper money.

Indeed, the paper money dispute was very much at the center of Franklin's attention, both as a businessman and as the contracting printer. Opposed as he was to Quaker doctrines, and much as he courted favor with the Proprietary party, he knew that the Quakers led a following greater than their own flock, and that they responded to desires and interests from those others. Franklin certainly knew of the massive Quaker support from the Germans that his own cleverness and industry had failed to dent.

Among the murkier issues facing assemblymen was the matter of provincial expansion westward, which caused great concern to Quakers in several respects. Their lords Proprietary envisioned multiplication of Penn family wealth as new immigrants sought and bought western lands, and the placemen in position to buy up large tracts for profiteering resale shared the excitement. Westward Ho! did not necessarily imply personal removal by the placemen to greener pastures, but it promised gratifying income from out there.

If only the Indians would get out of the way. Other colonies had solved that problem by attacking the obstructors. The mere fact that wars against Indians were inordinately expensive in money and lives did not darken the dreams of expansionists; the money and lives would be sacrificed by other people while the land speculators comfortably cheered them on. By the eighteenth century that tradition had been well established in New England, Virginia, and the Carolinas. But Pennsylvania was different. No matter how much Thomas Penn's henchmen might yearn for quick conquest, financing would have to come from the Assembly, and the Quakers there were having no part of attacks on Indians.

Not all Quakers were alike, and it is possible to think cynically that they simply preferred to buy their way westward rather than fight. On this issue I am not quite so cynical. From William Penn onward, the pattern of treaty *negotiation* with Indians controlled Quaker thinking and practice. Even if one succumbs to cynicism, it seems to me that Indians would rather be bribed to leave their homeland than to be removed by murder. It does not seem like a hard choice.

The consequence of Quaker attitudes was an accelerating expense for the Assembly as it appropriated money for presents to the Indians. One of Franklin's first assignments as a new assemblyman was to serve on a committee to review the cost of purchasing Indian goodwill.

He went into mild shock.

All treaties with Indians, and all cessions of land from Indians, were exclusively the right of the Proprietaries, yet all expenses for such negotiations were paid, without recompense, by the Assembly. Since Assembly funds came from taxes, and the Penns paid none, this arrangement meant that the province's citizens were paying for the acquisition and preservation of the Penns' enormous estate, of which the same citizens then had to purchase individual tracts and pay perpetual quitrent upon them.

More was to come. (Thomas Penn's avarice had no limits.) Events elsewhere impinged upon the province to make a political crisis. Because the Ohio Company of Virginia began in 1750 to expand into territory that Thomas Penn rightly believed to be within his chartered bounds, he tried to inveigle the Pennsylvania Assembly into building a fort for him. It would "in some measure protect the trade and be a mark of possession."[2] The trade with Indians was the bait on his hook. The possession of lands would be his own, not the Assembly's. He gave this project an air of fairness by offering £400 toward the fort's construction and £100 annually toward its maintenance. Cleaning and repairs would have been the smallest component of "maintenance" in the circumstances then prevailing. The fort would require a garrison to fend off Virginians and Frenchmen who claimed the same territory. Penn's less than generous offer could not have been more than a fraction of the sums required for his fort.

The Indians on the scene were also to be considered. Quaker

assemblymen refused to be Penn's catspaws for several reasons. They feared becoming involved in the hostilities clearly shaping up in the Ohio country, and they understood how cheap his supposed magnanimity really was.

Historians following Francis Parkman's detestation of Quakers have seen this affair as yet another example of dogmatic betrayal of the lives and security of western settlers, and some writers indignantly exclaim that even the Indians concerned had requested a fort. As to that, there are forts and other forts. Ohio Indians requested a simple refuge for their women and children while the warriors campaigned; but the Virginia Company intended, and Thomas Penn's "possession" implied, an establishment with a supporting settlement—in short, exactly what all Indians rejected flatly. (Franklin was to learn some of these complications later when he attended a treaty at Carlisle.) The two kinds of forts were conflated confusingly into one in reports by interested trader-politicians from the Ohio region, who made it seem that the Indian request for a small refuge was in fact a request for a major extension of the colony. This has fooled some historians; it did not delude the Assembly.[3]

Franklin approved heartily of building empire westward, but his business instincts rebelled at the cost being loaded onto the Assembly while the benefiting Proprietaries paid nothing. The flap about Penn's fort proposal occurred before Franklin's election to the Assembly, but as soon as he took his seat in 1751 he was appointed to the Indian affairs committee by the perspicacious Speaker, Isaac Norris, Jr. Franklin's colleague on this committee was "stiffrump" Israel Pemberton, Jr., whose general outlook opposed Franklin's nearly 180 degrees. But both were businessmen, and both could count. They found that from 1733 to 1751, the Assembly had laid out £8,366 for Indian expenses, "near £5,000 of which had accrued within the past four years."[4]

Accepting their report, the whole Assembly resolved that "the Proprietaries Interest will be so greatly advanc'd by keeping up a firm Peace and friendly Correspondence with the Indians, that they ought to bear a proportionable Part of the Charges expended upon all such Treaties as tend to those good Purposes." No ultimatum was given. Instead, a request was made "in the most reasonable, and in the most respectful Manner, to agree upon a proportionable part"—with the tart reminder, "as in Justice they ought to do."[5]

If the Assembly eschewed ultimatums, the Penns' rejoinder proclaimed one. "They do not conceive themselves under any Obligation to contribute to Indian *or any other publick Expences*."[6] Naturally the Assembly protested, but it got nowhere. If Quakers were stiffrumps, Thomas Penn was cast in concrete.

Franklin had begun to think of Indians in imperial terms ranging well beyond provincial issues and certainly conflicting with Quaker attitudes. As between scientists, he had corresponded with Cadwallader Colden in New-York, and when Colden's *History of the Five Indian Nations Depending on the Province of New-York in America* was reprinted in 1747 at London, Franklin eagerly ordered copies for his bookshop.[7] Possibly Franklin did not realize that Colden's history was the culmination of a long campaign by Yorkers to acquire domination over all Indians by a one-two assertion: first, that the Iroquois had conquered all the Indians within a vast territory; and secondly, that the tribal empire thus acquired had become Britain's by virtue of Iroquois acknowledgment to be *subjects* of the King of Great Britain.

Through this argument, British diplomats hoped to claim territories beyond the Appalachian Mountains from which they had been excluded by French maneuvers. French officials laughed at the effort. As one of them wrote to New France's Governor General in 1752, "it is certain that the Iroquois have no claim there and that moreover this pretended sovereignty of the English over them is a myth."[8] But English imperialists, who had nothing more substantial to work with, doggedly insisted on the myth of an Iroquois empire that belonged to Britain.

Franklin accepted what the French rejected. War loomed in 1750 as Virginians tried to penetrate the French protectorate in the Ohio country. When Franklin was asked to comment on the manuscript of a book about the importance of Iroquois alliance,[9] he reached for an imperial solution. Most important, he thought, was fair dealing with the Indians. The English would need "to unite the several Governments [of the colonies] so as to form a Strength that the Indians may depend on for Protection, in Case of a Rupture with the French; or apprehend

great Danger from, if they should break with us. . . . A voluntary Union entered into by the Colonies themselves, I think,
would be preferable to one impos'd by Parliament."

He went on to argue, in terms that have been seized upon
nowadays by some Iroquois propagandists who claim Franklin
as an endorser of their traditional tribal League: "It would be a
very strange Thing, if six Nations of ignorant Savages should be
capable of forming a Scheme for such an Union, and be able to
execute it in such a Manner, as that it has subsisted Ages, and
appears indissoluble; and yet that a like Union should be im-
practicable for ten or a Dozen English Colonies, to whom it is
more necessary, and must be more advantageous; and who cannot be supposed to want an equal Understanding of their Interests."[10]

How this contempt for "ignorant Savages" can be twisted
into praise for them is beyond my comprehension, more especially as Franklin meant his union to create "great danger" for
those Indians. But people believe what they want to believe in
the face of logic and evidence.

It remains to note that Franklin suggested that "every Thing
relating to Indian Affairs and the Defence of the Colonies"
could be put under "a general Council form'd by all the Colonies" with "a general Governor appointed by the Crown."[11]
This was certainly not in imitation of Iroquois custom, and it
disappears from the modern propaganda. Imperialist Franklin
warmed to the idea and thought it through in detail. He was to
bring it up again at Albany in 1754, where it became fodder for
a different set of future propagandists who also imposed their
desires on the facts. These were nationalist historians seeking
Franklin as patron saint for their own variety of wish thinking,
as we shall see a few paragraphs further on.

Franklin's imperialism was not the sort of attitude to endear
him to his Quaker colleagues in the Assembly, and (as we shall
see) his independence in regard to Thomas Penn's desires
caused great dissatisfaction in that lord Proprietary. Though
Franklin suffered, as independents always do, from crossfire, he
was nevertheless seen by Proprietary men as working in their
interest. Therefore, when a party of Ohio country Indians came
to Carlisle, Pennsylvania, in 1753 to solicit help against advancing French armies, Governor James Hamilton appointed Frank-

lin as one of three commissioners to meet with them. Franklin was the "swing vote" between the unbending Proprietary man, Secretary Richard Peters, and the Assembly Speaker, "defense" Quaker Isaac Norris. So far as I can make out, the three men worked harmoniously in the negotiations, one reason being that they were all diddled and manipulated by some experts traveling with the Indians.

The Indians were all from the Ohio country, but from different tribal origins in the East. They included Delawares, Shawnees, and "Mingo" Iroquois—a mixture of emigrant Senecas, Cayugas, possibly other New-York Iroquois, and possibly also Conestogas from the Susquehanna Valley. They shared one major goal—to repel French advance into their territories—but otherwise they had objectives as varied as their origins. Leading them, and shakily pretending to supervision over them, was the Oneida "half king" Scarouady (Monacatoocha). He was recognized by English colonials as spokesman and commander over the Ohioans, but the Indians had other notions, as they demonstrated in Winchester where they had earlier treated with Virginia's William Fairfax; again at Carlisle, the Delawares and Shawnees were far from obsequious to Scarouady.

They were all shepherded along by the Irish "king of the traders" George Croghan, and the synethnic Andrew Montour, a much used interpreter between the English and the Iroquois. Both Croghan and Montour regarded the troubled times as preeminently opportunities for personal enrichment. They managed the Carlisle treaty for their own satisfaction, outwitting Indians and commissioners alike.[12]

Franklin learned that the Indians wanted a "strong house" for refuge, but not a settlement.[13] They wanted immediate help in the shape of arms, and the Assembly had provided £800 worth as "presents"—a semantically adjusted compromise of the pacifists. These "presents" had been held up on the road. To prevent further delay, the commissioners bought some more to start negotiations with. When the big present of goods arrived, Croghan and Montour convinced the commissioners that the money would not be safe on the trip back west (where it was needed) but should be left in a sort of escrow in Croghan's hands until ordered for delivery by the governor.

This trick ruined the treaty so far as the Indians were concerned. No record hints that these arms were ever delivered as Pennsylvania's presents, though George Croghan probably reduced some of his outstanding debt by selling arms on his own account.[14]

In short, Franklin's theoretical approach to Indians and empire was no match for the very practical expertise of George Croghan. It was Richard Peters, the Proprietary's man, who came closest to understanding the situation as he explained privately to Thomas Penn that Croghan was not a fit man "nor any Indian trader" to be trusted with presents for Indians.[15]

The Ohioans returned home with empty hands and a sense of betrayal. They soon eliminated Scarouady's facade of supervision by chasing him away; he fled to refuge in Philadelphia where the falsity of his pretensions was not so well understood.

The commissioners also returned home, and Franklin made a little extra profit out of the affair by printing and selling the official minutes in an impressive folio edition that delights the eye. It is too bad that those minutes are not as reliable as they are decorative. Like most official minutes of Indian treaties, they require much correction. It must be conceded, however, that Franklin printed them in good faith. He lacked modesty enough to realize how profound was his ignorance of tribal cultures and the complex politics involved in Indian affairs. So he continued to think of solving all those problems by uniting the colonies under one command to overawe the Indians by sheer strength. That brainstorm had yet to encounter the rock of reality.

The period was rife with Indian disillusion. Matching the Ohioans' realization of the vast gap between Pennsylvania's promises and performance, in 1753 the Mohawks in New-York stormed at that royal province's Governor Clinton that they would stand for no more encroachments on their lands. Chief Hendrick declared, "the Covenant Chain [of alliance] is broken between you and us."[16]

Virginia was challenging New France; the French were marching a great army down the "backs" of the Appalachians; and now the Iroquois backbone of Indian support for the British had broken. In London, the colonies' supervising Board of Trade and Plantations sat up and took notice.

Even from distant London, those experienced gentlemen knew they could not oppose New France without Indian allies.

They ordered a great multicolonial treaty to be held with the Iroquois in the king's name. It was to "redress" Indian complaints and renew alliance. Unfortunately for the Board's intentions, the treaty would have to be held by the same gentlemen who had been causing the complaints.[17]

Once again Pennsylvania was to be represented by Commissioners Franklin, Norris, and Peters, with the addition at Albany of Thomas Penn's nephew, John Penn.[18] At Albany they were to be accompanied also by Conrad Weiser, the province's veteran interpreter and diplomat among the Iroquois. Weiser was not sent just to expedite translations; he had a special mission. He was to find "some fellows greedy for money"[19] and get a deed for a large tract of land in northeastern Pennsylvania, perhaps better stated as within the Penns' chartered bounds. It was also within the sea-to-sea charter of the colony of Connecticut, and by no great coincidence an agent for a Connecticut colonizing company had the same mission as Weiser's to acquire the same land.[20]

Neither Weiser nor Connecticut's John Henry Lydius concerned himself overmuch about ethics in his transactions, nor about validity of the signatures to his deed. Both poured rum like water and lavished bribes. What they were doing, of course, went precisely counter to what the Board of Trade had wanted to accomplish. Instead of redressing Indians' complaints, they were exacerbating them.

The Indians understood what was going on, but joined in what they seem to have conceived as a game. So far as they were concerned, neither Weiser's deed nor Lydius's could have any validity because neither had been transacted with the Iroquois League at its headquarters in Onondaga. So five of the same chiefs signed cessions of some of the same territory to both provinces, and others sold land to which they had no native right. Clearly they thought these deeds would be invalidated by the League, so why not enjoy the rum and bribes? It is fairly clear also that they did not understand how such documents could become effective in English courts regardless of the League's cancelation. Franklin witnessed Weiser's deed, and Speaker Norris too. I have to assume that they lacked knowledge of the legitimate methods for land cessions from the Iroquois.

In Indian metaphor, the deed racketeering was business "in the bushes"—actually in gentlemen's lodgings. William Brewster acerbly qualified it thus: "Two private land grabs, consummated at Albany at the time, were more important in future results than all the doings of the congress."[21] Nevertheless, the Congress did function overtly and formally, and its transactions became part of the mythology of nationalist historians. Their prophet was Frederick Jackson Turner, for whom the frontier of his invention "stretched along the western border like a cord of union. The Indian was a common danger, demanding united action. Most celebrated of these conferences was the Albany congress of 1754. . . . It is evident that the unifying tendencies of the Revolutionary period were facilitated by the previous cooperation of the regulation of the frontier."[22]

Briefly to the contrary, the frontiers were regions of *competition between* colonies rather than a cord of union. There was no such thing as "the Indian"; some Indians were hostile, others were allies. As for united action, Virginia stayed away from the Albany Congress to avoid restraint of Virginia's bold adventurism in territories claimed not only by New France, but also by Pennsylvania. (And Indians.) And *no* cooperation was accomplished by the Albany Congress. Turner mesmerized his own generation of historians and others following, and Benjamin Franklin's fertility of device fed the myth.

Franklin revived the notion he had mulled over since commenting on Archibald Kennedy's *Importance of Gaining and Preserving the Friendship of the Indians to the British Interest, Considered*. In 1750, Franklin had seen great need for union of the colonies. He was all the more convinced of that by 1754, so much so that he had become willing to let Parliament impose union instead of relying on the quarrelsome colonies to unite voluntarily. Outspoken in advocacy, he convinced no Quakers. William Penn's charter to his people guaranteed their liberties. Who could foretell what might happen to them if a new authority were set over the separate provinces?

The Board of Trade's order for a general treaty at Albany aroused mixed feelings in Pennsylvania as in other colonies also. New-York's Governor James De Lancey was to manage the treaty. His proposal to the other colonies was vague about unity except to advocate concerted action for a series of forts in Indian country—a measure dear to imperialists but not calculated to arouse wild enthusiasm among Indians.[23] Nor among Quakers. Franklin was for it, and despite their misgivings the Quaker assemblymen had assented to his being sent as commissioner to Albany, reserving the right to ratify or reject what the commissioners brought back.

They made their own feelings explicit. First they showed obedience to the crown's directive by appropriating £500 as their own present to the Indians. They followed that action with a declaration that "no Propositions for an Union of the Colonies, in Indian Affairs, can effectually answer the good Purposes, or be binding, farther than are confirmed by Laws, enacted under the several Governments, comprized in that Union."[24] In short, conference but no union. Franklin did not sit on the committee that drew up that statement. When he went to Albany, he ignored it. He was beginning to feel his oats as a celebrity, first from the fame of his electricity experiments and recognition by the Royal Society; and on top of that his appointment as a *royal* official as Deputy Postmaster General for all the colonies. Mere provincials were not going to tell him how to think.

(In the English patronage system, an officer was appointed without any expectation that he would do any work. He hired a *deputy* who performed the functions required of the office. Thus, as Deputy Postmaster General for the colonies, Franklin factually was in charge. This confusing nomenclature still is common in Britain.)

Pennsylvania's Governor Hamilton resented his Assembly's tough stance. He suggested to Governor De Lancey that perhaps a way could be found around the Assembly's obstruction. Perhaps "something of a general Utility may be agreed upon" at the congress, or an invocation of higher power: "a candid Representation of our Condition may be made to his Majesty, and his Interposition implored for our Protection."[25] Hamilton seems to have had Franklin in mind; for that newly fledged royal official wanted union in the worst way. On his way to Albany Franklin discussed with several Yorkers a scheme for uniting the northern colonies by act of Parliament. At its head would be "a

Military man" appointed by the king and "to have a Salary from the Crown."[26] Few things could have more horrified the Quakers.

As Governor Hamilton had foreseen, Franklin persuaded the delegates to the Albany Congress to subscribe to a plan of union of his devising. We need not go into its details here. However sincere the delegates may have been, a question arises about the objectives of their sending provinces; for, though the delegates acted *in behalf* of the crown as instructed from London, they did so *by authority* of their provincial governments. That distinction foreshadowed what was to happen to Franklin's plan.[27]

Quite simply, not only Pennsylvania's assemblymen rejected it, but so did all the other colonial assemblies. The crown's ministers rubbed salt in that wound by refusing even to consider the plan. Assemblies rejected the power given by the plan to an overarching governor. The ministers disliked the power reserved for assembly controls on the governor.[28]

Yet some important results emerged from Albany, largely because of attendance there of Thomas Pownall, a sort of unofficial inspector general sent out by the Board of Trade. Pownall's recommendations carried great weight because he was very well connected, especially through his brother John, who was the Board's secretary. Thomas Pownall observed the shenanigans used by Governor De Lancey to manipulate the Indians attending at Albany, and Thomas was not fooled. He compared notes with another unofficial observer, the landlord-merchant William Johnson who lived among the Mohawks, and both observers were disgusted with the obvious chicanery going on. Pownall reported back to the Board of Trade that the crown had better take over Indian affairs with its own servants because the provincials would look after their interests rather than the crown's. He recommended William Johnson as a knowledgeable man who had the Indians' confidence.[29] The upshot of that recommendation was to be the royal appointment in 1755 of William Johnson in charge of relations with the Iroquois.

Pownall was impressed by Benjamin Franklin, and his good opinion did Franklin no harm. At the time, however, Franklin made an even more important contact in Boston, where he journeyed after Albany in his capacity as Deputy Postmaster

General on a tour of inspection. There he met Governor William Shirley (Franklin's royal post opened all doors).[30] He and Shirley were likeminded imperialists who hit it off famously. All unknowing, Franklin was cultivating the man who was to become the colonies' commander in chief within a year. Franklin really had the luck of the devil. Even as his plan of union went down to the most ignominious kind of defeat, he himself benefited politically from the connections he made at Albany and afterward.

By yet another irony of history, the crown decided within the year to unite the colonies by royal prerogative instead of parliamentary action, and the military commanders that Franklin had dreamed of became reality. As he observed their behavior, he lost ardor for that way of solving intercolonial unity. We must not jump ahead of events.

As so much importance has been ascribed to the Albany Congress, a few words of summary seem in order. William Brewster was right in assessing the land transactions outside the official sessions as "more important in future results than all the doings of the congress."[31] And certainly the congress was far from foreshadowing unity of any kind. Instead of beginning something new, the congress was a culmination of multicolonial treaties with the Iroquois that had begun under Governor Edmund Andros, who founded the Covenant Chain system of alliance in 1677. What was new after Albany was the rejection of treaties conducted by provinces and the substitution therefor of treaties conducted directly by royal officials. Albany was the end of a system rather than a beginning.

In one sense, however, the trickery and intrigues of Albany did exemplify a growing colonial attitude of disobedience to royal command. Ordered by the ministry to satisfy Indian grievances, the participants not only turned their attention to business of their own devising, but actually added to the already existing Indian grievances. Back in the provinces, the assemblies unanimously rejected Franklin's and the congress's proposals to erect an intermediate lordship between the colonies and the crown. The ferment working at Albany was indeed something new.

10 ASSEMBLYMAN

FRANKLIN APPARENTLY took the easy way from Albany to Boston, by boat down the Hudson to New York City, then up the coast. Undoubtedly it was more comfortable for a man of middle age than the short way across the Berkshires. In New York City he met an old acquaintance just arrived from England on a new mission. Robert Hunter Morris, Chief Justice of New Jersey, was newly commissioned by Thomas Penn to replace James Hamilton as Governor of Pennsylvania, and Morris's arrival portended trouble.

Former Governor James Hamilton had grown weary of the constant struggle his Proprietary's demands had imposed on him, but Morris was spoiling for the fray. To Franklin's advice to avoid disputes with the Assembly, Morris returned an equivocal answer. He would heed Franklin's counsel "if possible," he said, adding the pleasant observation, "You know I love disputing; it is one of my greatest pleasures."

Morris did not disclose his knowledge that Thomas Penn intended soon to take the governor's post himself. Morris was not restrained, therefore, by hope that a conciliatory approach to the Assembly might win him a long and lucrative tenure. Even before Franklin returned from his business in Boston, Morris was locked in "high contention" with the Assembly; and, as Franklin ruefully observed, "it was a continual battle between them as long as he retain'd the government."[1] It could hardly have been otherwise because Penn meant to bring the Assembly to heel, and Morris was his willing agent for the purpose.

Morris really had no alternative. He was under bond to obey Thomas Penn's instructions as an obligation for appointment as governor, and one of the instructions prescribed that Morris was to insist on being joined with the Assembly—i.e., to require his approval—in the spending of all monies raised by excise taxes and the issuance of paper money.[2]

Modern division of governmental functions into executive, legislative, and judicial had not yet become rigid in the eighteenth century. Today, a legislature would appropriate funds for a governor to expend from the public treasury as prescribed by the appropriating law, and taxes would be paid directly into the executive department's treasury. Colonial Pennsylvania's Assembly had seized some of the functions of the executive. It maintained its distinct treasury and spent the funds as it pleased without consulting the governor, much less requesting his approval. In fact, the Assembly was inching up on sovereignty for itself long before the American Revolution.[3] Thomas Penn's assertions of Proprietary prerogative were a rational response of authoritarianism, also foreshadowing the policies of prerogative in the Revolution.

Benjamin Franklin's resistance to government by prerogative began almost on the first day of his membership in the Assembly. He served on the committees opposing Governor Morris, and wrote many of their responses. Throughout this chapter, what the Assembly articulated was what Franklin wrote.

Showdown with the Assembly came quickly, in December 1754. Young George Washington had surrendered Fort Necessity to the French on 4 July (while Franklin was at Albany), and large hostilities threatened. In response, the Pennsylvania Assembly voted a bill to raise £40,000 by issuing paper money. Half of this was to be turned over to Governor Morris with the familiar euphemism "for the King's use." The remainder would be issued in exchange for worn and torn old bills, and the whole would be retired gradually with income from an excise tax over a period of years ending in 1766. It was trickily devised. Each year more money would be raised than would be required for the sinking fund. Thereby the Assembly would come into possession of a surplus fund that could be spent as it pleased. Governor Morris could happily accept the £20,000 he was handed "for the King's use," but he perceived instantly that the bill would raise extra income about the spending of which he would have nothing to say. This was precisely what Thomas Penn had forbidden.

Morris was in a dilemma. He wanted to say plainly that all spending must be done with his concurrence, but his advisers—

James Hamilton, William Allen, and Richard Peters—knew that there was precedent for the bill. Hamilton had passed such a bill during his term as governor.[4] What to do? Morris and Peters studied the Proprietary instructions closely. Hamilton and Allen, according to Peters, were "very willing to do all in their Power for the regaining just Authority." What would the Assembly permit?

The governor could take a stand openly on the Proprietary instructions, or he could assert, with some show of legal support, that he was bound *by the crown* to let no paper money bill pass without a clause suspending its operation until royal assent had been obtained.

It was agreed that to publicize Penn's instructions would arouse the Assembly's opposition and create a risk of censure in England. While war was was impending, it would not be well received that the Proprietaries were "insisting at this Time on a particular Matter respecting themselves, which they might have done at any Time for these Twenty Years without Inconvenience to the King's Business, and it Might endanger the carrying of their Point against the Assembly." There was the matter of the £20,000 for the king's use being held up if Morris refused to pass the bill. On the other hand, by insisting on *royal* authority, "the Assembly would be gravelled, it was thought, in the most sensible manner, and be put under the Necessity of appropriating whatever they should raise to the King's Use, without leaving any Remainder for their own Disposal." Such an approach would eventually bring the Assembly to terms after its current funds ran out. After that, when the need arose to issue more paper money, Morris could raise the Proprietary instructions with greater likelihood of success.[5]

Morris bowed to this advice and duly prepared his response to the Assembly. "I am forbid," he wrote, "by a Royal Instruction, to pass any Law for creating Money in Paper Bills, without a suspending Clause, that it shall not take Effect till his Majesty's Pleasure be known."[6]

As a trial balloon, this one was made of lead. Assemblymen's suspicions, growing ever since Morris's arrival in the province, were confirmed. They sent for candles and worked into the night, and they knew law. Within twenty-four hours they replied to Morris, discussing each point and precedent raised by him, and putting them back into the contexts he had over-looked. They added a Board of Trade ruling in support of their own position, and they stripped off the placemen's mask. "We entreat the Governor will be pleased to inform us, whether the Royal Instruction is the only Impediment; or whether he has any further Instructions from our Proprietaries."[7]

Frustrated Morris reverted to his first idea; he now pro-posed to object to the Assembly's bill on the plain grounds that it would give him no say in spending the surplus funds. It had occurred to him that if the Assembly agreed to a suspending clause—i.e., that the bill was not to take effect until the crown approved—the Board of Trade ruling made it likely that the crown *would* approve, and then the Proprietary game would be lost.

There was need for a distraction, so Morris acknowledged that he did indeed have Proprietary instructions, "perfectly cal-culated to promote and secure the Prosperity and real Happi-ness of the Inhabitants of this Country." One such instruction was to press upon the Assembly the necessity of putting the inhabitants into a posture of defense—to create a militia and build forts.[8]

This strategy apparently was supposed to put the Quaker assemblymen on the defensive, but it failed to work. Speaker Norris threatened that a petition would be made to the crown, and "those Proprietary Instructions, and the Force and Validity of them," would be the question raised by it.

All of this happened while Franklin still was away on his postal business, and the deadlock was what he faced on his return. He found that the assemblymen understood what Mor-ris was up to, and why; further, that those Quakers understood the law better than Morris did. No less a person than Thomas Penn himself confirmed that point—but privately, of course. It was "very plain," he wrote to Secretary Peters, that governors "are obliged to conform to Instructions from their Proprietors, tho' they are not from the King." In a Proprietary colony the prerogative of its lord was greater than that of the king. And Penn ordered that Morris should let no appropriation bill pass without the explicit clause to join himself with the Assembly in spending the money. As for fears about popular reaction to this ultimatum, Penn "would not give one halfpenny to have the

Instructions conceal'd, to avoid any ill consequences." Why should he? He was 3,000 miles off. His supporters in Philadelphia would have to take the heat, as they very well knew, and they were not so indifferent as Penn to popular feelings.

Penn offered justification for "why they should not have the appropriations to themselves," and listed Philadelphia's proudest civic possessions. "I think their Hospital, Steeple [on Christ Church], Bells [also for Christ Church], unnecessary Library, with several other things are reasons." These objects of Penn's contempt had all been projects by Franklin. It needs to be said very plainly that Thomas Penn had no concern for the growth and glory of his province; for him it was a source of wealth, nothing else.

Further, from his safe perch beyond the ocean, he cared not a whit about the lives and security of *persons*. The threat looming on the western horizon actually gratified him. He ordered Morris to stick to his instructions. "I hope," he added, "the dangerous situation the People were in will force the Assembly to a Bill for appropriating so much of the Money to the King's use, as to make it not worth while to refuse it for the sake of the remainder."⁹ Plainly, this meant that Penn would let the inhabitants suffer murder and rapine until their elected representatives gave in to his demands. I cannot refrain from noticing that bigoted writers have reversed the situation by blaming the Quakers for supposedly failing to protect frontier inhabitants, at the same time painting a noble image of Thomas Penn's concern for them. Judgment cannot be qualified; the histories of such writers are rotten.

While Governor Morris was locked in struggle with the assemblymen, Penn's undercover agent, Reverend William Smith, worked in an extralegal way for Penn's prerogative. Smith's ego was fully as expansive as Franklin's, but Smith had not learned Franklin's saving grace of pretended humility. Smith expounded dogmatically and at large to anyone who would listen. His aggressiveness—he was possessed of demonic energy—won him few friends, as he seems to have complained to Thomas Penn. "I am concerned to hear Philadelphia is shy of strangers," responded Penn. "When I was there it was esteemed a place where Strangers were well received by the people in general."¹⁰

Busy with his chores as provost of the new College, Smith yet found time to put his poison pen to work against Quakers and Germans. He produced an incendiary pamphlet, anonymously as usual, entitled *A Brief State of the Province of Pennsylvania* . . . , which he placed in Governor Morris's hands late in December 1754. Morris was dubious about the work, but Secretary Peters was rapturous. Peters wrote to Penn that Smith was "ungracious" in delivery and accent, "but he speaks the Language of Angels & has the heart of a Saint." Morris found that the pamphlet was "intended for the Press in England, in order to induce the Parliament to take measures for the future security of this Province by excluding the Quakers from the Legislature." Thus it would circumvent Quaker influence in the Assembly by simply keeping them out of it, regardless of the will of the electorate.[11]

As part of his argument, Smith lashed out at the Germans whose votes had supported the Quakers. "They are grown insolent, sullen, and turbulent," wrote this man in charge of charitable schools for their education. He continued the theme to frighten Englishmen into thinking the province harbored a mass of traitors. The French, he wrote, "know our *Germans* are extremely ignorant, and think a large Farm the greatest Blessing in Life," and therefore plan to draw them willingly away from the English. That there was not the slightest evidence for such an assumption did not bother Smith; he fabricated evidence with other writings.[12]

Even Thomas Penn was alarmed. "I fear the harsh manner in which they [the Germans] are treated will disoblige and sower them, and prevent their coming so cordially into the other Scheme"—i.e., the charitable society schools. As to attacks on Quakers, however, Penn's only concern was practicality. Ministers of government were unlikely to be swayed by appeals to the public. Penn suggested that a representation to the king would be more likely to achieve the desired results. In that respect he wished the scheme for Quaker exclusion "all imaginable Success."[13] Smith immediately bustled about to get the desired representation to the king.

Like many such feverishly patriotic and irrational effusions, the *Brief State* aroused a great furore in Britain. Smith had understood his target audience well. In the province, however, where circumstances were more familiar, the reaction to the pamphlet when it arrived in April was quite contrary. It had been written and sent abroad in December 1754, as part of the general campaign to increase Proprietary prerogative, and well before any substantial number of Pennsylvanians felt exposed to immediate danger. Governor Morris knew and informed the Assembly (19 December 1754) that royal forces were on their way; he knew that all the money requested for their support had been offered already by the Quaker Assembly; *only his own signature was wanting.*[14] The "clamours of the People," as Peters made clear to Penn, were directed not against an oppressive oligarchy in the Assembly, but against the Proprietary and his few friends.[15] The effort to disqualify the Quakers was an act of desperation, an effort not to befriend the populace but to behead it.

In England, Penn danced attendance on the Duke of Cumberland, second son of the king and captain general of the forces. When Cumberland appointed Major General Edward Braddock to command a new expeditionary force in America, Penn went to him with "informations and advices . . . for the good of the Cause." It was Penn's own cause rather than the province's.[16]

Braddock arrived in Virginia on 19 February 1755, soaked with Penn's indoctrination. His aide, Sir John St. Clair, preceded him to make preparations for reception of the army. St. Clair asked Governor Morris for help from Pennsylvania, and Morris told him falsely that the Assembly would not give money "upon any Terms but such as were directly contrary to his Majesty's Instructions and inconsistent with their own dependence upon the Crown."

This was an outright lie. On the same date that Morris wrote it, an Assembly committee was ordering 14,000 bushels of wheat to be ground into flour and delivered to Braddock "on the first advice from [Virginia's] Governor Dinwiddie that the British Troops are arriv'd."[17]

Only Morris's lie came to the army's headquarters to be fuel on the fire that Penn had stoked so carefully while Braddock was still in England. Not strangely, Braddock erupted with a denunciation of the "pusillanimous and improper Behaviour in your Assembly." He ranted on about the Assembly's "absolute

Refusal to supply either Men, Money, or Provisions for their own Defence while they furnish the enemy with Provision," and he threatened to "repair by unpleasant Methods," including the quartering of troops, "what for the character and Honour of the Assemblies I should be much happier to see cheerfully supplied."[18]

Morris was delighted with the general's "high stile" that suited his purposes so precisely. He egged Braddock on, provocatively denouncing the Assembly again and exaggerating the wealth and population of the province to make its efforts seem proportionately meaner. Then he recalled the Assembly into session, 17 March 1755, and laid Braddock's fuming letter before it with the complacent expectation that it "would have some influence upon their conduct."[19] But Franklin was back in the Assembly now.

At first, Morris thought Franklin would work against the Quakers, "labouring hard" with them for a £40,000 grant. Morris assumed that Franklin, like himself, was Penn's man; but when the Assembly compromised for £25,000, all to be given in one manner or another to the exigencies of the moment, Franklin was willing to call it a bargain. Morris stuck to Penn's instructions. When he vetoed this measure too, Franklin became unexpectedly independent.

Perhaps he thought a special exertion was needed because a special appeal from his new friend, Massachusetts Governor Shirley, had been joined to the demands for Braddock, and Franklin wanted to make a good impression on Shirley who was so well connected in London. Shirley's representative, Josiah Quincy, had asked for support of a New England expedition against Crown Point on Lake George. When Morris presented the request to the Assembly, its members incorporated a £10,000 gift to Shirley's expedition in its bill. And when Morris vetoed again on the familiar pretext believed by nobody that it would violate his instructions from the crown, the veto meant that Quincy would go home empty-handed.[20]

In desperation, Quincy appealed to Franklin, who devised a new stratagem. Quincy wrote a new letter, to the Assembly directly this time, deprecating the governor's veto, praising the Assembly, and renewing the appeal. This was the first kind word given to the Assembly by an official during the entire crisis.

Perhaps the Quakers had had something of the sort in mind, but no one could have known that better than Israel Pemberton, Jr., who commented that Franklin "perfected the Scheme which some others had projected."[21]

To bypass Governor Morris a little financial sleight of hand was performed. From the provincial Loan Office under its own jurisdiction, the Assembly borrowed £15,000 which the Loan Office did not have, by issuing bills of credit against future payments by debtors to the Loan Office. Strictly speaking, it was not paper money because it was not legal tender, but it served effectively as paper money without going through the formal process legally required for such an issue. By this technicality the requirement for the governor's signature was circumvented, and Quincy returned to Massachusetts with £10,000 that had been passed not only without Governor Morris's approval, but in the face of his determined opposition. While at this pleasant occupation, the Assembly issued enough of those bills of credit to have £5,000 for General Braddock's expenses, and thereby disarmed the threat from that quarter. It was a masterpiece of elegant maneuver, and everyone knew that Franklin was responsible.

Here again is a foreshadowing of the American Revolution, though only hindsight shows its outline. As the Revolutionary assemblies set up committees of correspondence to facilitate defiance of authority, so Franklin's Assembly sent help to Massachusetts in defiance of Governor Morris's assertion of prerogative. Much challenge to authority was brewing in that era which would bubble up irresistibly twenty years later.

Morris was furious, and so was Thomas Penn when he learned of the episode of help to Massachusetts. Morris wrote hotly to the Secretary of State in England, denouncing "such Powers in the Hands of any Assembly, and especially of one annually chosen by a People, a great Part, if not a Majority of whom are Foreigners [the German menace again] unattached to an English Government, either by Birth or Education."[22] But Quincy was grateful, and so was Shirley, neither of whom was much concerned about Thomas Penn's prerogative.

The assemblymen, knowing what they had done for the war effort, and what Governor Morris had refused to do, wondered why General Braddock was so angry with them. They knew nothing of Thomas Penn's indoctrination of Braddock, nor of Morris's falsehoods because Morris's letters were recorded in the secret minutes of his council. It was evident, however, that Braddock had been prejudiced somehow. An opportunity to clarify matters came with Braddock's request for a postal service between his camp and the provincial capitals. Who could better set up such a service than the Deputy Postmaster General? The Assembly promised to underwrite the deficits of the service, and with this little tidbit to appease the general, Franklin went traveling again.[23]

Amusingly, his traveling companions for part of the way included Governor Morris, as well as Governor Shirley of Massachusetts and Governor De Lancey of New-York, all of whom were on their way to an interprovincial strategy conference with Braddock at Alexandria, Virginia. Morris always presented a pleasant face, and Shirley was grateful for what Franklin had done for him. We may imagine some sprightly repartee enlivening the trip for the portly dignitaries.[24] They parted for their distinct destinations, Franklin going on to Braddock's camp at Fredericktown.

What Braddock learned at Alexandria disquieted him, but it put Pennsylvania in intercolonial perspective. He was told flatly that the governors, royal as well as Proprietary, could not dictate to their assemblies. The assemblies would raise money, but they all rejected commands to raise specific amounts for Braddock to spend as he saw fit. Actually, something of the sort had been foreseen in London. Despite all of Braddock's sound and fury about needing money, he had been provided with an ample war chest in specie, as the French found out later when they captured it.[25]

Braddock was not quite so blustery when he rejoined his camp at Fredericktown, where Franklin awaited him. They dined together daily, and Franklin "had full opportunity of removing all his prejudices, by the information of what the Assembly had before his arrival actually done, and were still willing to do, to facilitate his operations."

Shrewd Franklin understood the political importance of opinions below the level of top command. He "commiserated" the poverty of the junior officers, and quietly suggested to the Assembly committee with available funds that a gift of little luxuries would be well received. Typically, he enclosed a list. The Assembly promptly responded with twenty horses well laden with old Madeira wine, Jamaica rum, hams, cheeses, chocolate, tea, coffee, and so on. Each horse, with its welcome burden, was presented to one officer, and there were no more slurs on Pennsylvania's Assembly in the officers' mess.[26]

It has become part of legend that Franklin performed the indispensable task of getting the army on the road. Theretofore, it could not advance until it received horses and wagons that had been promised by the governors of Virginia and Maryland. Now Braddock had a genuine reason for fury because only 10 percent of the promised vehicles appeared. Braddock despaired that there could be no expedition, whereupon Franklin "happen'd to say" that he thought the needed wagons might be obtained in Pennsylvania.

Braddock commissioned him on the spot, and Franklin rushed off to Wright's Ferry (now Columbia), Pennsylvania, where he consulted with Quaker assemblyman James Wright and his sister Susanna. Franklin seized on Miss Wright's suggestion of calling the population together, and he passed it on to Chief Justice William Allen (a Presbyterian) who was then at nearby Lancaster, riding circuit. For once, partisanship was forgotten. Though other Proprietary men looked on defense measures primarily as a political football, Allen differed sharply. He presented a strong appeal from the bench and ordered the constables to call in the people.

Franklin publicized the proceeding with a broadside that nicely combined appeals to cupidity, fear, and patriotism, and the wagons rolled in. Motives of the Germans may have been mixed; Franklin warned them of how the army might confiscate their wagons if cooperation was rejected; but whatever the reasons, the heavy Conestoga wagons (the kind that later were to become "prairie schooners") came to Franklin's receiving station. The refugees from the warred-over Rhineland had no faith in generals; they wanted security from someone known. Franklin was obliged to give his own bond to indemnify farmers whose horses or wagons should be lost.[27]

Sir John St. Clair gave tribute to "the People in Pennsylvania ... by their Assistance we are in motion."[28] Thomas Penn, however, was less happy about the outcome. Franklin, who was

supposed to be one of Penn's minions and had been favored
with Penn's patronage, had suddenly seemed to turn about and
foil Penn's scheme for power at just the moment of apparent
success. Penn wished (to William Smith) that his charitable
society's German press "could have been under any direction
but that of Mr. Franklin." Warming up, "I am astonished at Mr.
Franklin's telling you he was my Friend." The subject preyed on
Penn's mind to the very end of a long letter to Smith. "His
professions of not desiring to hurt our estate I cannot account
for."[29]

The difference of viewpoint was fundamental. Franklin believed that he had served his king and his province. That he
had also helped some Quaker politicians in the process was
irrelevant to his goals; events were to show that he had not
adopted a new attitude toward the Quakers. Penn, however,
saw Franklin's actions as betrayal of himself and his party. The
two held to such distinct courses of thought and action that
they were bound to come into direct collision, and did.

In this chapter I have drawn attention to popular challenges
to assertions of prerogative that have been overlooked (it seems
to me) by historians searching elsewhere for seeds and origins
of the American Revolution. In part, this oversight was caused
by pacifist Quakers holding to neutrality in the Revolution.
Another cause may have been the greater drama of violence in
the streets of Boston and New York. A third, perhaps controlling, cause has been the domination of historiography by professionals trained in New England whose pride in that region's
Revolutionary spirit is clearly apparent and to a degree for-
givable.

Nevertheless, we must not forget popular unrest elsewhere,
including the Pennsylvania Assembly, where Presbyterians and
Anglicans accepted Quaker leadership to defy prerogative rule
as imposed by a Proprietary lord in a fashion soon to become
crown policy. Resistance to the lord evolved into resistance
to the king, nowhere more clearly evident than in the life of
Benjamin Franklin.

11 CHANGING SIDES

PRECISELY WHILE Franklin was engaged in making Braddock's army mobile, the ship *Carolina* arrived in Philadelphia with its passenger the Reverend Thomas Barton. This newly ordained Anglican priest was a protégé of William Smith, who had recommended him so strenuously to the Society for the Propagation of the Gospel as to arouse some touchiness about being ordered about. Nevertheless, the SPG did accept Barton as a missionary for the Carlisle-York region. (A missionary to the European settlers there, not to the Indians.)

Barton brought copies of Smith's *Brief State* pamphlet, already in circulation in England, attacking the Assembly, the Quakers, and the Germans.[1] It made such a "prodigious Noise," and was so far-reaching in its intended and unintended effects, that it deserves examination in some detail. Its title page describes its author as "a Gentleman who has resided many Years in Pennsylvania." This set the keynote for the pamphlet's deceptions; Smith, at the time of writing it, had visited Philadelphia for several weeks in 1753, and had resided there less than eight months in 1754.

The pamphlet opens with a brief review of population statistics on the generous side, and lays down maxims of government. Popular government is all right for infant settlements, it says, but as communities grow their government should become less popular and more "mixt." Pennsylvania has become more of "*a pure Republic*" than at its founding. A "speedy Remedy" is needed. The province has too much toleration; "extraordinary Indulgence and Privileges" are granted to papists.[2] (They were allowed to celebrate mass openly.) The Quakers conduct "political Intrigues, under the Mask of Religion." (As all the organized religions did, in England as well as America.)[3] For their own ends, the Quakers have taken "into their pay" a German printer named Saur, "who was once one of the *French* Prophets in Germany, and is shrewdly suspected to be a *Popish* emissary."

(Saur was an Anabaptist, fiercely independent.) The "worst Consequence" of the Quakers' "insidious practices" with the Germans is that the latter "are grown insolent, sullen, and turbulent." They give out "that they are a Majority, and strong enough to make the Country their own," and indeed they would be able, "by joining with the *French,* to eject all the *English* inhabitants . . . the French have turned their Hopes upon this great Body of Germans . . . by sending their *Jesuitical* Emissaries among them . . . they will draw them from the English . . . or perhaps lead them in a Body against us."[4] The Quakers oppose every effort to remedy this evil state of affairs, attacking all "regular Clergymen as Spies and Tools of State." Thus the Quakers hinder ministers from "having Influence enough to set them right at the annual Elections." The greatest German sect is the Mennonists—people like the Quakers. A quarter of the Germans are "supposed" to be Roman Catholics. (Even Thomas Penn understood that there were only about two thousand Catholics in the province. But he did not make that knowledge public.)[5]

In Smith's dark, gothic imagination, even the Moravians, whose break with the Vatican long antedated that of Smith's own church, became a "dangerous People" who held "some Tenets and Customs . . . very much a-kin to those of the Roman Catholics." From beginning to end, his work is a violent propaganda harangue without scruple or nicety. It comes to a climax with a demand for Parliament to enact a law. The law should provide a test oath for members of the Assembly and should disfranchise all the Germans for "about twenty Years." It is absurd to indulge "such ignorant, proud, stubborn Clowns" with "the Privilege of Returning almost every Member of Assembly." Without such a law, there is "nothing to prevent this Province from falling into the Hands of the French."

Ministers paid little attention to this demand, perhaps because English Quakers were attached to the governing Whig cause; the great merchant John Hanbury, for example, looked after the Duke of Newcastle's interest in Bristol. In response to the *Brief State,* Thomas Penn suggested that a "representation from People of the Country" should be sent to the crown. Then "some answer could be given to it."[6] He meant that some answer would have to be given to it. In due course the Proprietary

men produced the suggested representation. Though Smith
wrote it, he carefully avoided signing it.

If Thomas Penn was somewhat ambivalent about the pamphlet, the Quakers were not. They held frequent consultations
within a week of its arrival in Philadelphia, and they began to
try to pin down the author. Speaker Isaac Norris warned the
province's agent in London to beware of "These Inferior Officers of our Academy, which I fear is dwindling into a narrow
System of Politicks & Priestcraft."[7]

The pamphlet contained a giveaway in its support of the
governor's position on tax bills. Only a very few people in the
entire province took that position, and they were all in the
Proprietary clique. The "sober" Quakers saw handwriting on
the wall.

The Quarterly Meeting of Pennsylvania Friends sent a formal Epistle to the London Meeting for Sufferings (an organization for relief of persecution). Help was needed. Pennsylvania's
Proprietaries, the Philadelphians said, seemed "essentially
changed" from the truly honorable William Penn. "Most un-
wearied Endeavours" were being made "to wrest from us our
most valuable Priviledges." Their government was loading
them with heavy "charges" in order to make them seem unwor-
thy of the liberties earned so dearly by their forefathers.

They would stand faithful. In spite of difficulties, they believed that the fundamental interests of the Proprietaries were
identical with those of the people. So, would the London
Friends "confer" with the Proprietaries to clarify misunder-
standings? In itself this Epistle hinted at division among the
Quakers foreshadowing more to come. The Epistle was signed
by eight of the weightiest Quakers, none of whom sat in the
Assembly. It was but one of several actions taken by the Quarterly Meeting to found a Meeting for Sufferings.[8]

Its avowal of identity of interests between the Penns and
the people expressed assumptions of the most deeply orthodox
Friends; such feelings were not shared by more political Friends
who were involved daily, by necessity, in anti-Penn activity.
Some of these would soon become "defense" Quakers, supporting military activity against attacks on the province. They had
precedent in the example of Quaker grandee James Logan
whom Franklin had so much admired.

Logan had maintained membership in Friends Meeting until he died, but the new atmosphere proclaimed by Smith's *Brief State* worried more devout Quakers into closing ranks and insisting on unqualified adherence to fundamental doctrines, especially pacifism. This would soon lead to rebellious defense Quakers following Franklin's lead instead of Israel Pemberton's, and such deviation led to the Meeting's "disownment" or excommunication of the heretics.

The schism thus opened resulted ultimately in a transformation of the Religious Society of Friends in America as it withdrew completely from electoral politics. Quaker solidarity would be tested as never before in the flaming up of Indian attacks, but the worst harshness of the crisis was averted while General Braddock marched toward the French Fort Duquesne. Yet it began with the evil fabrications of Provost William Smith's *Brief State*.

It was into this wholly unanticipated turmoil that Franklin stepped as he returned from his triumphant mission to and for Braddock. While he was absent, the *Brief State* had opened a horrifying vista to Quakers, Germans, assemblymen, and people of all persuasions, of the lengths to which the Proprietary partisans were willing to go. "All ranks of People" were alarmed, as Israel Pemberton, Jr., saw it.[9]

The Assembly voted unanimous thanks to Franklin when it reconvened on 12 May 1755. He was asked to write the Assembly's reply to Governor Morris's latest assault, and he finally burned all his bridges to the Proprietary shore: he called the governor the foe of his own people. "While we find the Governor transforming our best Actions into Crimes; and endeavouring to render the Inhabitants of Pennsylvania odious to our Gracious Sovereign and his Ministers, to the British Nation, to all the neighbouring Colonies, and to the Army that is come to protect us; we cannot look upon him as a Friend to this Country."[10]

The political Quakers who had so long opposed Franklin, because of his militarism, now looked to him as their champion. Pemberton hoped he would "act Steadily and Zealously in our Defence." Speaker Norris was confident. He wrote to the agent in England, "We have now very much Thrown our Disputes from being a Quaker Cause to a Cause of Liberty."[11]

Norris was only partly right. As has often been remarked, the events of 1756 marked a reorientation of Quakers in public affairs, a withdrawal from politics into the shell of religion. The process began in 1756 but did not become dominant until the oath requirements when Test Laws of the American Revolution made persecution official and harsh (see chapter 19). When one faction of Quakers subsided into passivity with the intention of testifying faith by endurance, an opposed faction abandoned absolute pacifism to become activists for other tenets of their creed. Resulting strains became impossible to maintain, the activists turned to other religions, and the Society of Friends in Pennsylvania settled into patterns observable today.

(But not everywhere. It is a minor shock to find that Herbert Hoover and Richard M. Nixon were Friends in western offshoots. Philadelphians were so shocked by Nixon that they set up a vigil around his White House.)

Only the beginning of transformation loomed in 1756. Neither Franklin nor the Friends had been transformed overnight. To deduce from this moment of emotional identification that their separate interests and aspirations became one thereafter would be a grave mistake. The old Quaker party of pre-Braddock days fragmented, and its non-Quaker following began to look elsewhere for leadership. A political revolution got under way in which Franklin and his friends were the most dynamic element. "Defense" Quakers like Isaac Norris hailed Franklin, but only for the duration of the war. "Strict" Quakers—Franklin's "stiffrumps"—were at odds with him almost immediately after the Braddock crisis. If they voted for his measures, they did so with reservations, and only because the available alternatives were even less attractive.

Other novelties appeared. The Germans he had coaxed and bulldozed into leasing their wagons were delighted at the bargains they had made. Braddock sang his praises to the crown and the governors.[12] The "electrical genius" had suddenly become the political prestidigitator and the martial magician. He had become a force.

The astonishing fact is that he held no position of power, and his financial means, though respectable, were limited. His secret was that he reciprocated the interest of other men. With omnivorous curiosity, he caught ideas everywhere, compared them, shaped them systematically, and gave them again to his world. Not a ruler, he was a superb leader, skeptical about and a little ahead of, but nearly always with his own people.

Franklin differed fundamentally from Smith. Smith was more preacher than teacher, more priest than minister, more critic than artist, more patron than scientist. He wanted to be a bishop rather than a priest, and a governor rather than a politician. He was not merely conceited as Franklin was; he was immodest—a condition different in kind as well as degree. His college's best historian has remarked, "His gifts for leadership were mediocre; he had no capacity for cooperation or ability to understand the views of other men."[13]

Smith and Franklin continued to work together on joint projects. Franklin had become obsessed with Governor Morris, and he did not believe his friend Smith was the writer of the *Brief State*. When Smith wrote a pamphlet to allay German suspicions of the charity schools, Franklin's press printed it; moreover, when Smith proposed to start a new German newspaper to counteract Christopher Saur's, Franklin helped freely. Though the Lutheran minister, Heinrich Mühlenberg, had originally suggested the newspaper, and the Reformed minister, Michael Schlatter, was superintendent of the charitable society's schools, Smith was emphatic that "Schlatter must not be seen in it, nor yet the society." Even after Franklin attacked the governor, Smith and the other trustees were "resolved that the press shall still keep Mr. Franklin's name, who is very popular among the Dutch, by his Waggon-project." Franklin amiably went along with the deception.[14]

Franklin, as president of the College's board of trustees, thought Smith would be "very serviceable" as provost, though the College began to take a direction away from Franklin's first conception of it.[15] Franklin and Smith were brother Masons, and no record suggests that Franklin had any objection to Smith as preacher of the commemorative sermon to the Masons on St. John's Day, 24 June 1755. Smith boasted to Thomas Penn that he gave the sermon "a Turn toward public Affairs," but its language, though typically strong, was cautious.[16]

All the while, however, Smith built his own political machine. When the Coetus (conference) of Reformed Ministers, through Schlatter, requested that the charitable society give them a lump sum to divide among themselves, Smith rejected the proposal at once. He would pay each one individually to keep them dependent. Otherwise, "they would give themselves no Trouble to forward the Schools, nay they might perhaps openly oppose them." He needed the leverage; the ministers were highly dubious about the schools.[17]

Smith attempted to gain control of Anglican Christ Church in Philadelphia, slurred its rector, and averred that he himself was better qualified than its ministers to conduct the church.[18] He curried favor with some of the Christ Church parishioners by extracting a very reluctantly given lot of ground from Thomas Penn for the building of a new, offshoot church.[19] Looking to the future, Smith began to exert what was to become a controlling influence over the SPG missionaries in the province. His protégé Thomas Barton, in a mission that included York and Carlisle, became especially valuable as a grateful partisan of the Penns.[20]

In short, Smith was no less busy than Franklin as Edward Braddock's long train of roadbuilders, wagoners, and soldiers hacked their way through virgin forest and dragged their cannon over the corrugated Appalachians toward French Fort Duquesne at the forks of the Allegheny and Monongahela rivers. In England, Smith's master was waited upon by a delegation of London Friends who found him "reserved, tenacious, & inflexible." Their hopes dashed, the Londoners saw no immediate hope of reconciliation and were frightened; for they had observed that any pretext in Pennsylvania would be seized upon by two strong groups of antagonists in England. London Quaker Dr. John Fothergill, who was a major correspondent for Pennsylvania's Friends, reported confidentially that "some very active and powerful people near the head" of the Board of Trade "would be very glad to crush every appearance of liberty abroad"; and the Presbyterians would "gain a most important point" if they could "so far irritate those in power here, as to induce them to exclude" Quakers from the Pennsylvania Assembly. London Friends mapped out a campaign of their own to bring pressure on Thomas Penn. Having among them some of the wealthiest merchants in London, they were not without resource.[21]

Then came the smashing defeat and rout of Edward Braddock and his British Regulars by a savage rabble inferior in numbers and equipment, but wiser in the ways of the woods. The news trickled down the mountain passes, gathering mass and momentum, washed over the back settlements to the coastal cities, and grew by the turmoil it stirred up until, when it finally struck England, it surged upon the island with the force of a tidal wave. No longer could the fighting in the colonies be just a backwoods affair. Now England and France were to be pitted together in a worldwide struggle for empire. The petty squabbles of provincials would now have to give way to imperial designs and interests. In the confusion even this stark fact took some time to be understood.

In Pennsylvania the defeat of Braddock changed only the pressure at first; issues and antagonists were, if anything, more stubbornly fixed than before. Governor Morris scented political opportunity. He had first news of the defeat in a letter that also urged the immediate creation of a militia to defend the frontiers.[22]

Morris waited for nearly a week while he perfected his strategy. Then, on 16 July, he sent out his writ to call the Assembly into session. The news was so staggering that many people refused to believe it. Confidence in Braddock's army had been so great that Franklin had been asked to start a subscription for victory fireworks. Morris complained that, after the newspapers published the defeat, Assembly partisans attacked his announcement as a trick and insulted him in the street.[23]

The Assembly met on the 23rd. On the 24th, Morris informed it officially of the defeat and pressed for defense measures in a message that was more assault than appeal. Accusation was implicit in his sarcastic hope that the Assembly "wou'd not by an ill-timed Parsimony, by reviving any Matters that have been in Dispute, or from any other Motive, suffer the People to remain any longer undefended, or the Blood of the Innocent to be shed by the cruel Hands of Savages."[24]

He played with the idea of circumventing the Assembly entirely as the Assembly had earlier bypassed him, by borrowing on his own authority from rich Proprietary supporters through a subscription device. The £20,000 or £30,000 so raised would be repaid "by a Tax laid equally upon the Province, or in any other way the Crown may direct." His proposal met with total

lack of enthusiasm from men whose vaunted patriotism was
restricted to sending other men to fight. When that became
clear, Morris substituted a plan to award trans-Appalachian
lands on special terms to all men who should enlist in an expeditionary force.[25]

Morris told Penn that he did not really expect the offer to
make much impression in Pennsylvania; he knew that Virginia
had made a better offer of equivalent lands, and a conversation
with Franklin had convinced him that his own inferior offer
would never be accepted by the Assembly. He hoped, however,
to put the Assembly "in the wrong at home"; i.e., in England.[26]
It is painfully apparent that the assemblymen were for Morris
greater enemies than the French.

Matters were made no better by the news that Colonel
Thomas Dunbar, the new commander of the survivors of Braddock's debacle (who still outnumbered the French at Fort Duquesne), had decided to retreat all the way back to Philadelphia,
"not thinking himself safe," as Franklin contemptuously observed, "till he arriv'd at Philadelphia, where the inhabitants
could protect him." Even most supporters of authority and prerogative were disgusted. "The whole transaction," Franklin recalled later, "gave us Americans the first suspicion that our
exalted ideas of the prowess of British regulars had not been
well founded."[27]

Morris concealed his private reservations. Informing the Assembly that Dunbar's retreat would expose the frontier settlements, he pressed again for defense measures.[28]

The nerves of assemblymen were steadier than those of
Braddock's surviving officers. Considering the news of Braddock's defeat, the assemblymen voted the largest supply bill in
the province's history, for £50,000, but Franklin's influence is
very plain in their device for raising the money, which was to tax
"all Estates, Real and Personal, within this Province."[29] Quite
suddenly, roles were reversed. The previously defensive assemblymen had taken the offensive, and Morris was in a dilemma.

He heard of the tax measure before it was formally presented
to him. The Proprietaries' principal supporters saw a "hard alternative" for Penn. Either his estate would be taxed by the
people's assessors or he would have to bear the blame for "refusing to contribute any thing towards the defence of the Prov-

ince." (In England, even the king's lands were taxed.) Morris
knew there was no possibility of permitting the tax except by
forfeiting his bond to Penn. His problem therefore became di-
version of blame for refusing to assent to the tax. To this end he
offered the trans-Appalachian lands noticed above.[30]

Morris proposed at the same time to amend the tax bill in
order to exempt the Proprietary estates from its provisions. This
effort had been expected. Speaker Norris impatiently asked
Morris to get immediately to the point and not waste time: did
he have instructions from Penn to veto such a tax? Norris
showed one, but he insisted that he had other reasons besides.
He knew that the Proprietaries' "Love and Affection" for their
province were so great that they would want to contribute to
defense if they had been on the scene. Because they were absent,
he had proposed in their behalf to offer the western lands.

The Assembly acidly rejected such love and affection. It
noted that the quality of land to be allotted had not been specified. "Good" land had not even been mentioned. The worst
feature of Morris's offer was that "it may be fully complied with,
and yet nothing in Reality be granted." The assemblymen knew
about Virginia's better offer. They told Morris that even the
best lands of his proposal "in those Parts on that Quitrent would
be neither more nor less than this, That for the Encouragement
of such as shall, with the Hazard of their Lives, recover the
Proprietaries Country from the Enemy, he will graciously sell
them a Part of the Lands so recovered at twice the Price demanded by his Neighbour."[31]

Morris took a little time to digest the long message. Meantime, to make trouble for the Quakers and to renew the initia-
tive, he demanded the establishment of a militia.[32]

Through July and August, petitions had been accumulating
in the hands both of the governor and the Assembly, pleading
for arms to be given to the inhabitants. So long as Dunbar's
troops remained in the west, the Assembly laid all such petitions
on the table. However, when Morris transmitted a message
on 11 August that Dunbar's troops had been ordered to leave
Pennsylvania entirely, the Assembly could no longer depend
on their former shield. It authorized a committee, "with the
Consent and Approbation of the Governor of this Province,"
to spend £1,000 for arms. Morris was later to charge that he had

been bypassed, but Franklin wrote his friend Collinson, within a week after the Assembly acted, that he had been buying quantities of arms "with the Governor's approbation, as to the Disposition; for as he is Captain General we think it our Duty not to arm the People without his Consent, tho' we are otherwise at Variance with him."[33]

In any case, this issue lay temporarily dormant. The Assembly adjourned for three weeks in the hope that "our Superiors" would have by then determined the relative powers of Governor and Assembly.[34]

Franklin had become a very angry man. Some of his former friends in the Proprietary camp were now defaming him "by every base Art" with abuse that grew so strong he thought briefly of running away to Connecticut, but the thought was ephemeral. He had evidence enough among his papers that his services were appreciated by the agents of royal authority, and he would defend himself.

Franklin at last decided that the Quakers could be depended on in a military emergency. He was satisfied that they were acting "as Representatives of the *Whole People,* and not of their own Sect only." They had shown that they could give money for defense "as freely as any People."[35] He felt more secure now on his political flank. When the Assembly reconvened, he hit out harder than before.

"The *Politicks* and the *Calumny*" of the governor's charges, he wrote, "we can easily trace to their Fountain Head, though he does not vouchsafe to quote it at all. The perfect *Sameness* of Sentiment, and even of Expression, are sufficient to show, that they are all drawn from a late famous Libel, intituled, *A Brief State of the Province of Pennsylvania.*" It was no secret, he maintained, "That there is a Design in the Proprietaries and Governor, to abridge the People here of their Privileges. . . . The Doctrine that it is necessary is publickly taught in their *Brief State.*"

To Morris's charges that the Assembly had been delinquent in supporting the war effort, Franklin not only gave a flat contradiction but in doing so identified the Assembly's aims with his own. His defense of himself became a defense of the Assembly including himself. He cited letters from General Braddock, from Braddock's secretary, from Colonel Dunbar, all acknowl-

edging the Assembly's support and generosity, and expressing
warm gratitude. He generalized the immediate situation into a
lesson in philosophy that has become famous (it is carved in
stone at Pennsylvania's Capitol building): *"Those who would give
up essential Liberty to purchase a little temporary Safety deserve
neither Liberty nor Safety."* He laid the Assembly's record on
the line for the electorate to judge. The assemblymen could be
removed by their constituents in a few days, he wrote; and
bitterly, would that "the Governor be as soon and as easily
changed."[36]

If ever an election was held in which two distinct and opposed sides could be clearly discerned, the Pennsylvania election
of 1755 was it. Whatever else might be said of the *Brief State*
and Morris's associated measures, this much was true: they had
polarized the province. The voters might misjudge the character
of the antagonists, but they knew the sides.[37]

The issues had been sharpening up all summer—ever since
the *Brief State*'s arrival. Strict Quakers had responded to it by
founding a Meeting for Sufferings; long historical experience in
England had taught them what such attacks portended. Franklin and his followers, with the support of the defense Quakers,
dug in at the Assembly. William Smith began to explore the
possibilities of other methods of forcing the Assembly's capitu-
lation; after Braddock's defeat, he scented an opportunity in the
western counties. Smith wrote a circular letter to SPG missionaries, attacking the Quakers and exhorting the missionaries to
stir up their flocks for self-defense. It was a priest's duty, he told
them, to show every man his proper station and duties in life,
not only in religious affairs, but in civil matters also. The office
of the priest, he stressed, was to *"instruct"* his flock in "what
GOD requires of them."[38] As usual in such cases, what GOD
required was fairly similar to what Penn desired.

Smith's protégé Thomas Barton responded energetically to
Smith's prodding. He preached strong sermons to spirit up the
people. He called them together at his house to organize for
defense. Indeed, in providing courageous leadership on the
frontier during the whole war period, Barton seems to have
been wholly admirable. He seems to have been just as active,
but with less success, in trying to lead his people to the polls.[39]

The evidence for Smith's second electoral gambit is circum-

stantial but strong. Following the anti-Catholic theme of his
Brief State, he seems to have attempted to work up a hysteria
against Catholics which would develop, if everything worked
out well, into a political movement against the tolerators of
Catholics. The oath that Smith wrote into the new charter of
the College of Philadelphia was, on the face of it, more anti-
Catholic than anti-Quaker, for it provided that Quakers might
affirm rather than swear; but some of the doctrines abjured
by the oath were essential to Catholic faith. Catholicism was
brought under strong attack by Proprietary partisans in Berks
County, when five justices—all Proprietary appointees under
the leadership of Penn's and Smith's henchman Conrad
Weiser—wrote an urgent letter to the governor containing most
alarming intelligence of papist strength, rumored priestly con-
tacts with the French, and the arming of the papist inhabitants
to massacre Protestants at an opportune moment. (I have
learned informally that a small Catholic community existed at
Bally, Pennsylvania.) Governor Morris promptly informed the
Assembly, but the assemblymen looked at the message with
a fishy eye. Whatever strange things might be happening out
yonder, they seemed stranger yet when relayed by Morris. Having read the *Brief State* with great care, assemblymen were ex-
traordinarily sensitive to every issue raised by it. They called in
for formal questioning one of the magistrates who had signed
the appeal to Morris, and some of them privately questioned
another of the Berks magistrates. They concluded that there was
"very little Foundation" for the scare, and they cautioned the
governor not only to care for the safety of the people but to
keep his actions "consistent with the Charters and Laws of this
Province."[40]

  When one considers what political temptation lay within
the anti-Catholic scare—the equivalent of anti-communism in
our recent Cold War—the Assembly's response appears in an
aspect of quiet magnificence. The witch-hunt was killed in embryo, and Smith later complained bitterly to his archbishop that
the Quakers "abused" all clergy who "distinguished" between
Catholics and Protestants.[41]

  But Smith's main reliance lay in intercession by Parliament
in Pennsylvania's government. He urged it on his friend James
Oswald, a Member of Parliament and one of the lords of trade

responsible to the crown for administration of the colonies. Smith sent a copy to Thomas Penn. Smith's political activities for Penn in the province continued to be under cover as much as possible.

At this distance in time it seems remarkable that Smith and Franklin continued to be friendly with each other, and even to work together in the German schools scheme. In spite of Smith's utter devotion to Penn's interest, he was reluctant to think ill of his friend. Smith excused Franklin to Penn, saying that Franklin had no desire to hurt Penn's estate, that he was but one member of the Assembly and must not be held responsible for the actions of the whole. Smith felt that he had as large a share of Franklin's confidence as anyone else had, and he remained convinced that Franklin had a secret scheme to overthrow the Quakers. (One wonders uneasily what grounds Smith had for this idea.) The two exchanged political views with each other; Franklin treated Smith as his "Bosom-friend." However, Smith's attitude did not amount to wide-eyed trust; it is clear from his reports to Penn that he was not telling Franklin what they contained.[42]

Among the many ironic coincidences of the Smith-Franklin relationship is the fact that Franklin was writing, probably by the same ship, that he thought Smith was not the author of the *Brief State;* but his mild remark does not stretch easily to the warmth of Smith's "Bosom-friendship."[43]

There was another letter from Franklin on that ship—one that has escaped historians' notice. On instructions from the Assembly he wrote to its agent in London to justify the land tax in a presentation to the lords of trade.[44]

The tax had been adopted under Franklin's urging, so he was naturally chosen to say why. Confidently—almost playfully—Franklin prepared the message in a tone adroitly mischievous if not malicious. In mock seriousness he related that Governor Morris had called for emergency defense funds after Braddock's defeat, with a caution to the Assembly that the time was wrong for reviving "former disputes." Here was the very advice that Franklin himself had given to the governor just before the latter took office; the temptation was irresistible. Franklin recited and described the whole list of disputes that had arisen since Morris's arrival in the province. Gravely, Franklin pointed out that "all former Disputes & every thing that might seem to interfere with Royal Instructions, Old or new, or Acts of Parliament, in Force, or not in Force here & the like were carefully avoided by the House in the formation of their Bill." Strictly speaking, he was right. Like the man who escapes a lot of little debts by making one backbreaking loan to pay them off, Franklin had escaped from the former disputes by starting a new one bigger than them all; to wit, a tax on landed estates, including the Penns'.[45]

After all the wild excitement of summer, while Franklin's message was still at sea, the election did come at last in the first week of October. Never did a popular party receive a more complete endorsement of its policies. Never was an active, vociferous challenger more absolutely repudiated. Every member of the old Assembly who permitted his name to be offered was re-elected. The western county of Lancaster chose an entirely Quaker delegation although, as Isaac Norris observed, there were "scarcely One Hundred of that Profession in The whole County." (It was, and still is, a "Pennsylvania Dutch" region.) The people were "very Unanimous" and it was "Absurd to call ye Opposition a Party."[46]

Modern observers have been puzzled by this popular support, even in a zone of imminent danger, for the Quaker minority, but there is no need to resort to theories of Quaker dictatorship or sorcery. The Proprietaries were unloved. In spite of their glow of aristocracy that radiates so glamorously at two centuries' distance, their hard dealings in land and their well-publicized foreclosures and evictions made few friends. Their rapacity was known and detested. And if someone objects today that the common people tried to cheat the Proprietaries also, the statement might or might not be true; but, either way, it would be quite irrelevant to the voting in a mid-eighteenth-century election. Quakers had stood up to the Penns for more than half a century and were trusted not to give way.

Just as Thomas Penn feared the people, they feared him, with plenty of justification. If the Assembly had created a "regular" militia, as Penn and Morris demanded, it would have been under the governor's control. William Smith himself phrased the objection to it very neatly in his *Brief State*. The Quakers, he said—for which, in this instance, we may properly read the people—suspected a design to impose a military hierarchy upon them "by creating a vast Number of new Relations, Dependancies, and Subordinations in the Government."[47] They were not alone or paranoid in that fear: the Whigs of Britain held it also and fought against militias there. (Events were to prove that when the Whigs lost to the militarists, they lost to the Tories who took control of government under George III.)[48]

In 1755, the net result of a summer's strenuous political struggle in Pennsylvania was an election that showed the antagonists firmly committed to its continuation. But now a new and terrible force launched itself on the province. For the first time in their history, Pennsylvania's inhabitants were attacked in force by Indians.

12 SOLDIER

Of all the Virtues, *Justice* is the best,
Valour, without it, is a common Pest;
Pirates and Thieves, too oft with *Courage* grac'd,
Show us how ill that Virtue may be plac'd;
'Tis Constitution makes us *chaste* and *brave*,
Justice from Reason and from Heav'n we have;
Our other Virtues dwell but in the Blood,
That in the Soul, and gives the Name of Good.

Poor Richard Improved, January 1756

INDIAN COHORTS did not gleam with purple and gold, but they did strike like a wolf on the fold. With one difference: their depredations had "civilized" leadership. Every raiding band was accompanied by a French officer masquerading as an Indian whose purpose was to guarantee *beaucoup de ravages,* in the phrase used by Canada's Governor General Vaudreuil bragging to the most civilized city in the most civilized nation in Europe. Vaudreuil had perfected the art of backwoods devastation, and he wanted Paris to understand his skill.[1]

The French did not much care where they struck so long as inhabitants were terrorized and resources destroyed. Delaware Indians, however, had particular objectives in the lands from which they had been dispossessed. After devastating westernmost settlers, they struck at the Palatines who had pushed them out of Tulpehocken Valley (between Lebanon and Reading) and the hapless Moravians who had been placed in the lands of the Walking Purchase, yet to become infamous.

Information about the raids came to Philadelphia, as did many refugees. At the end of the year, Secretary Peters reported to the provincial council that on 18 October 1755 "was committed the first Inroad ever made by Indians upon this Province since its first Settlement," in consequence of which "not less than one hundred and fifty miles in length and between twenty and thirty in breadth . . . has been entirely deserted, the Houses and Improvements reduced to Ashes, the Cattle, Horses, Grain, Goods, and Effects of the Inhabitants either destroyed, burned, or carried off by the Indians." Peters understood the power of French promises of "re-instating" the Indian nations, "formerly in our Alliance," in the lands they formerly had possessed.[2]

From various sources, I have tentatively calculated 317 Pennsylvania victims killed, 2 scalped but survived, 103 prisoners, and 19 missing.[3]

In the background of intertribal politics was some information about the Iroquois Six Nations that Peters kept secret except from his master in London: A letter from Shippensburg in the midst of the fray. The anonymous writer blamed the Iroquois for encouraging Delaware and Shawnee warriors so as to preserve the Ohio country as Indian territory. "And if they [the Indians] are permitted to distroy us, they intend to strike Lines with us [i.e., establish a boundary] and afterwards to fall foul of the French and drive them out of that part of the Country."[4] Later events were to validate this appraisal. When written, however, it had no effect on a government that depended entirely and blindly on its alliance with the Iroquois.

Not only the Quakers, but also most of the exposed Germans and Scotch-Irish of the borders, "had no notion of the Indians coming upon them," as Richard Peters was to say privately. "They took no Warning nor furnished themselves with arms or ammunition or any manner of defence."[5]

They had full confidence in what they thought was Pennsylvania's policy toward Indians, unaware of the very different real policy that had been suppressed from public understanding by Proprietary control of the agents and records dealing with the tribes. Arms and ammunition were almost nonexistent when the Indians struck within a month after the elections. Some officials, notably Conrad Weiser, attempted to form impromptu militia bands, but confused and terrified refugees, many of them barefoot, soon choked the roads.[6]

Governor Morris's conduct immediately before the raids was so reckless as to shock even Peters. Before the Indians struck in Pennsylvania, Morris had warning that they had begun raids in Maryland and Virginia. On 16 October, when the Assembly convened for the fall session, Morris laid before his council the news of the raids; *but he withheld the information from the*

Assembly. Peters leaked something to Speaker Norris. Two days later, an Assembly delegation pointedly asked the governor whether he had anything to present to them, "particularly any matter relating to Indian affairs." No, said the governor; if so, "he would have done it before now . . . nor had he any objection to their Adjournment to the first of December." On the same day the worried Peters wrote secretly to Conrad Weiser for advice about the Indians that "threaten this Province."[7] All the while that Morris played this dangerous game, messengers were on their way from the west to tell the terrible story of the annihilation of Penn's Creek settlement that had been wiped out on the very day, 16 October, when Morris suppressed from the Assembly the warnings in his possession.[8]

When news of Penn's Creek arrived, Morris was at New Castle, presiding over his separate government of the "lower counties" of Delaware. His only response, besides begging pro forma for arms from the neighboring provinces (themselves under attack), was political. "If the Assembly had paid the least regard to my Recommendations," he wrote to Weiser, for circulation among the threatened people, "as everything that has happened was reasonably to be expected, the people would not at this time have remained without protection or such a quantity of innocent Blood have been spilt." What was "reasonably to be expected" was precisely the warning that Morris had suppressed.[9]

While Morris framed political campaigns, Franklin was at work more practically. The first news of the raids came to Philadelphia on 25 October. On the same day, Franklin wrote to Collinson that "the People on the Frontiers have been and will be furnished with Arms and Ammunition by the Care of the Committee of Assembly." To the province's agent Richard Partridge, Franklin was specific: "600 good Arms have been purchased and sent up . . . with suitable Ammunition; to supply such as are without and unable to buy for themselves." He added that a considerable sum had been subscribed to help outfit New England troops on the march against Crown Point at Lake George, "which will be speedily forwarded."[10]

Peters confirms him, but again privately. Peters told Penn, "on the Application of the Inhabitants after the first attack . . . a vast Quantity of Arms and Ammunition was sent into Berks,

Lancaster and Northampton Counties." Writing later, however, Peters was forced to admit that "the Publick was dis-
appointed, for tho the best Men in the Counties had the
Distribution of them, yet this, tho an heavy Expence, was of
little or no Service, a great Number of the Arms being Lost, and
the Ammunition expended in private Uses."[11] The sinister hint
in Peters's letter is that the "best Men" in his jargon were always
the Proprietary's men. "Lost" firearms, in the circumstances, are
too much to swallow; "private Uses" for the ammunition betrays the direction in which the losing occurred. As fast as
Franklin sent the arms forward, the Proprietary's good men to
whom they were consigned sold those good arms at a good
price.

When Morris returned from New Castle, he was anything
but grateful for Franklin's efforts. He immediately ordered an
investigation into "this infringement on the rights of government." It was "a very extraordinary measure," thought Morris,
because it would teach the people "to depend upon an Assembly
for what they should only receive from the Government," i.e.,
himself. If it was not in fact a crime, Morris was sure "it ought
to be so."[12] Morris's own notion of how to protect the frontier
was to order a search of Philadelphia for Frenchmen rumored
to have been seen there. His single useful act of the whole day's
work was to commission Conrad Weiser as colonel of the volun-
teer forces being raised in Berks County.[13]

William Smith, when the news of the raid arrived, had a
project of his own afoot. Remembering Thomas Penn's earlier
advice that an appeal to the English public would not be so
effective as an appeal from the Pennsylvania public, Smith had
written a "Representation" appealing to the king for action
against the Assembly. Penn made sure that it was eventually
carried to the Privy Council, where the subject was seriously
debated whether Quakers should be disqualified by an oath
from holding office anywhere in Britain's American colonies.

For the moment, let us be content with a look at the means
of circulating this Representation. We have an account from
Richard Hockley, Penn's dimwitted kinsman and Receiver
General. Hockley reported indignantly to Penn that he had been
"call'd in by a Magistrate and ask'd to Sign a Petition that is to
be presented to the King (which I refused) setting forth the

defenceless state of the Province . . . and the reason given is, because a sett of People whose religious principles disavow self defence . . . thrust themselves into the Legislative Power." The petition had been signed by twenty persons when Hockley saw it, with William Allen and Mayor William Plumsted leading the list. This was a scandalous thing, thought Hockley, for everyone knew that Plumsted, "though he bears a Commission under You is deeply concern'd in the French trade."[14]

Shock and terror prevailed in the "back country." The governor was preparing his messages to the crown more carefully than the defense of the province. Smith was laying groundwork for royal intervention and the abrogation of William Penn's charter. In the midst of it all, the Assembly convened again on 3 November. Morris demanded money and a militia. "I have neither Money, Arms, or Ammunition at my disposal," he cried. "All I have . . . been able to do has been to issue Commissions." But he flatly refused in advance to pass any bill like those he had previously vetoed. In effect, he threatened to let slaughter and devastation continue unless the Assembly would capitulate and give him what he had contended for from the beginning.[15]

From the beginning of the crisis, the Assembly's responses had been different in nature and effect from the governor's. Equally stubborn in adherence to its positions, the Assembly had managed to find means to meet every demand and request made upon it to support Britain's war effort. Now, under Quaker inspiration, it began to evince interest in an additional policy of its own that happened to be what everyone had assumed was Pennsylvania's policy ever since William Penn. The Assembly inquired of Morris why the Indians had attacked, and offered to redress any wrong they might have suffered.[16]

For some reason—not a good one—this wholly rational proposal has drawn the scorn and wrath of countless writers who uncritically have adopted Morris and Smith's sedulously propagated notion that the Assembly was composed of a lot of Quaker bleeding hearts—vicious oafs who cared nothing for suffering white people but groveled in sentimental stupidity before the murderous savage. More, the libelous lie spread by Smith that Quakers had offered to cooperate with the French attackers as long as their own people were exempted from attack has been repeated in malice as recently as 1958.[17]

The fact that the Indians had indeed been badly wronged
has been glossed over and shouted down. The Quakers became
in image what crude bigots call "nigger lovers." The image is as
false to the reality as the epithet is false in its implications. (For
the record, I am not a Quaker or a pacifist, but I hate racism in
all its manifestations and will not tolerate its expression from
the most eminent of historians—*especially* from them.)

I regret that the continued repetition of the anti-Quaker
propaganda down to the present day bespeaks motives other
than objectivity. Morris's motive is clear as day. He needed
demagogic distractions as badly as any politician ever did. He
stood alone even in his own council, though a sociable, profes-
sionally pleasant man. Richard Peters sadly reported Morris's
total failure to influence public opinion in the province: "all
People lay the Blame on the Proprietaries."[18]

Responding to Morris's new demands for defense funds
within five days, the Assembly offered him a new bill to raise
£60,000. It was carefully drawn to eliminate every possible
source of objection but the one main issue which Franklin had
determined to push to a decision—the land tax. Morris was
equally determined. He immediately denounced the Assembly's
"ill temper" in "raising a dispute about the Proprietary Tax at
such a dangerous time as this," and set about framing a veto
message.

Despite the sameness of Morris's fulminations, the Assembly's bill—Franklin's—was *not* quite the same as its predecessor,
and the difference between them was carefully calculated to
expose what lay behind Morris's rhetoric. The new bill contained a clause that the right to tax the Proprietary estates would
be submitted to royal determination. If the crown declared
Penn's lands exempt at any time while the act was in force, all
taxes raised from them would be refunded, "and an additional
Tax laid on the People to supply the Deficiency." Opposition to
this bill could not be maintained on the grounds that it might
be inconsistent with the crown's desires; the crown would have
the entire life of the bill to make up its mind. The Assembly
called Morris's attention to this new and unique feature of the
bill, thereby discomposing him so much that he needed five
days to frame a new rejection message. It would have to be
good. Morris and the assemblymen knew how the crown was

likely to react considering that even the king's estates were taxed in Britain. But Morris had his instructions, cemented by his bond. When he rejected again, the assemblymen became so thoroughly angered that they threatened to petition the king for Morris's removal.[19]

Seeking desperately to gain some measure of popular acceptance, Morris kept stressing the miseries of the back country inhabitants, which were real enough, and their need for a militia for protection. He lost that battle too. The Assembly was convinced that even "in the Midst of their Distresses" the frontier people did not want the militia. Astonishingly—but very privately—Richard Peters agreed.[20] What the people did want was arms, not in the hands of a disciplined military body at some future date but in their own hands at once. The previous Assembly had responded to this desire with £1,000 worth, and the very unpacifist Franklin had bought those guns and sent them out; the governor's response was confined to manifestoes. Be it said in Morris's favor that he was intensely embarrassed by the contrast, and he made efforts to provide more tangible help, but necessarily within the limits of his orders. That he failed can be inferred from the nature of the efforts.

As we have seen, he asked for a subscription by Penn's wealthy supporters to a fund, and he promised to "subscribe largely for the Proprietaries." William Allen scotched this idea. Then Morris tried to borrow £1,000 from Penn's Receiver General out of the money received for rent and mortgages. This was to be a *loan*, not a tax, but Richard Hockley "excused himself by assuring the Governor that he had not £100 in the House," which he did not offer. He, too, had instructions. Morris importuned Richard Peters to make a draft on the Proprietaries for £500, and Peters refused. Yet Peters wrote Penn that it looked bad. "For the Proprietaries at such a time as this, not to contribute anything whilst Thousands are perishing has something so disagreeable in it, that all men's mouths are open."[21]

Probably guided by William Smith, the governor's supporters made a desperate effort to overpower the Assembly by pressures from many directions at once. Thirty-six persons from Chester County, led by Justice William Moore, sent a petition demanding that the Assembly set aside religious scruples, cease disputing with the governor, and stop neglecting the province's defense. The petition was rare in its mention of religion and not very impressive in its few signatures. Sponsor William Moore was president judge of the county court, a post signifying the special esteem and trust of the Proprietaries who appointed all magistrates; and Moore was soon to become William Smith's father-in-law. Moore's petition was something other than the voice of the people, no matter how inflated its pretensions. It merely irritated the Assembly where Franklin's committee rejected the petition as improper.

From a different direction the Assembly was embarrassed, shortly after receiving this petition against its presumed Quaker scruples, to get an address from twenty strict Quakers (also not the voice of the people) protesting that the Assembly's measures were already too military and asserting the willingness of many Friends to "suffer" rather than pay taxes like the land tax. Franklin's committee dismissed the Quakers' petition as "unadvised and indiscreet."

Then came Smith's "Representation" from Mayor Plumsted and 133 "Principal Inhabitants" of Philadelphia (which Hockley had earlier refused to sign).[22] This Representation branded the refusal to create a militia as "a Subversion of the very End of Government," and it hinted that "a sufficient number" of persons could be found to enforce its demands. Franklin's committee found it too "presuming, indecent, insolent" for presentation to the Assembly. Its hint "to force a Compliance by the Power of Numbers if its Commands are not obeyed" brought a reprimand to the mayor for being "a Promoter and Ringleader of such an Insult."[23] The threatened violence was known to be the menace of a minority. Everyone in Pennsylvania knew which side had popular support. Richard Peters told Thomas Penn that "the Body of the People are against You . . . there is no stemming a Torrent."[24]

The Representation's veiled reference to violence was repeated, 24 November, in a "Remonstrance" by the mayor, aldermen, and common council, once again written anonymously by William Smith. In a city where Peters was bewailing the "business as usual" attitude of the inhabitants, its officials suggested that they might not be able to preserve peace and quiet much longer.[25] Governor Morris laid the Remonstrance before his council on the same day that he showed them letters from Justice and Colonel William Moore in Chester County, and Justice and Colonel Conrad Weiser in Berks County, announcing that thousands of the country people would march on Philadelphia "to compel the Governor and Assembly to agree to pass Laws to defend the Country." For public consumption, Morris ordered measures to preserve the peace, but he gave the orders to the same officials who had signed the Representation and Remonstrance.

Privately, Morris knew ahead of time about the march, and it seems more than likely that he knew who had initiated it. He confessed doubt to Thomas Penn of its propriety. "This manner of applying is extremely dangerous," he wrote, "and I am satisfied will be productive of mischief of some sort or other, but time alone must shew where it will fall." Nevertheless, he cooperated. Both Weiser and Moore were his appointees, and he made no hint of disciplining either.[26]

The threatened crowds came, but their thunder rumbled more fiercely on the horizon than in the city. Moore's promise of two thousand men from Chester alone proved to be bombast. Morris estimated the total from all quarters, in a letter intended to inflate the size, at seven hundred. In a private letter, William Smith, who never minimized his own projects, boasted that the crowd was three hundred strong.[27]

They had no discernible effect. To be sure, a militia law was adopted, but *before* the mass action; indeed, Morris agreed to it in council on 22 November—which news he did not send to Weiser and Moore—and sent a copy to Penn the same day.[28] The marchers did not arrive until the 25th. Nonetheless, Smith crowed that "the Assembly have been *pelted* into a military Law, such as it is . . . they are broke to pieces." What actually happened is hard to see for all the sound and fury of its reporting. Morris said that Franklin harangued the mob, but no record exists of such an event; when some of the marchers were admitted to the Assembly, Clerk William Franklin recorded only Speaker Norris as speaking to them. Governor Morris wrote that the mob leaders declared "their dependance was greatly upon me." Only two men spoke to him. Speaker Norris wrote that "two or three" of the country people had called at his house, "and very gravely asked me whether the people had not a power to depose" the governor. The governor apologized to Penn for "letting Government down very low" by his "appeal to a Mob," but called his action "absolutely necessary even for the preservation of Peace." At bottom, Speaker Norris's talk in the Assembly room with the protest leaders reveals concisely how the people really felt. He asked them, "Whether they desired that the House should give up any Rights, which, in the Opinion of the House, the People were justly intitled to?" He was answered, "No, they were far from requiring any Thing of that Kind; all they wanted was that some Expedient might be fallen upon, if possible, to accommodate Matters in such a Manner as that the Province might be relieved from its present unhappy Situation."[29] Franklin, listening, could hardly have said it better himself.

After all the smoke had blown away, the new militia law was still there, but it had small resemblance to the law for which so much effort had been made by Penn's men. This law was Franklin's, not Smith's. It restricted the governor, in commissioning the militia officers, to a choice of persons nominated by election of the volunteers.[30] In this respect it was similar to militias in other colonies, and it was intentionally useless for making a patronage machine. Smith promptly set out to sabotage it, to force its replacement by one nearer his wishes and necessarily in direct conflict with Franklin's creation.

Even after the passage of the Militia Act, Smith reported to Penn, "I still continue in Terms with Mr. Franklin," though he no longer spoke of friendship between them. "The Good I can do," Smith said, "depends upon my doing it silently without being seen." Penn was content to have Smith "silently do what good you can, that method may render you of great Service."[31]

Two critical acts were passed in this tumultuous period: besides the Militia Act, the act for raising £60,000 also was maneuvered into law. We shall have to set aside militia developments for a while in order to give attention to the money law. In England, the news of the Assembly's help to Braddock had created favorable opinion despite Penn's connivings; and the Assembly's friends, according to Franklin, "rais'd a clamor against the proprietaries for their meanness and injustice," at which Thomas Penn was "intimidated." Penn himself indirectly confirms Franklin's judgment, in letters to his supporters. His soundings of influential men convinced him that the crown was not interested in militia bills. (Apparently these great statesmen were as uninterested as himself in the afflictions of the home-steaders.) Ministers of government said that the most important task before the province was the raising of supplies—i.e., the granting of money for the crown's use. Penn trimmed his sails. It would be best, he now suggested, to use "prudent methods" with the Assembly. He revoked his instruction requiring the governor's participation in spending all public money, and he offered a "free gift" of £5,000 to the province. Then he paid a call on Quaker John Fothergill (who was his own physician) to acquaint him with the new policies. Overjoyed, Fothergill at once advised the Philadelphia Friends to make peace with Penn and practice "a respectful condescension."[32]

As Pennsylvanians were to discover, Penn's "free gift" did not mean that he had capitulated. He had simply devised a new trick, and a successful one. He made his gift offer publicly, but simultaneously wrote in private to Peters to take exceptional measures to produce money from the estate.[33] In the circum-stances of the time, they included foreclosures and dispossession of refugees who were behind in their payments.

Governor Morris handled the free gift offer with finesse. Penn wrote three letters, two to Morris and one to the Assem-bly. Morris suppressed the letter to the Assembly, substituting a message of his own in which he gave Penn credit for being stirred to the gift by Braddock's defeat.[34] (Penn's own letter never mentioned Braddock; he was worried about political in-tervention against himself in England.) Morris knew better than to inform the Assembly of Penn's stated intention to make his "gift" out of *delinquent* quitrents that were virtually uncollect-ible. Instead, Morris gave the Assembly the impression that the "gift" was to be a spot cash benefaction; the Assembly rose to the bait and amended its tax bill to exempt the Proprietary estates "in consideration of" Penn's gift.[35]

Penn's solution for those delinquent quitrents was to blame them on the Assembly. "This is the time," he wrote, "and this is the most popular pretence that ever can happen for our forcing the Arrears." He insisted that no income from any other part of his estate should apply to the "free gift," and he urged his agents to seize properties from nonpaying owners. He also demanded that even a portion of the collections for the "free gift" should be forwarded secretly to him instead of the government, and this was done. When the truth of this sleazy device finally emerged, James Hamilton, former and future governor, was so disgusted that he advanced £1,000 out of his own pocket and shamed Penn into reimbursing him—but not before Penn protested that Hamilton's "goodness" was "not necessary, and will distress us beyond measure."[36]

Though deceived, the wary Assembly took precautions with its bill. Morris's share in the spending of the £60,000 was limited to naming two commissioners out of a total of seven. (The compromise was probably Franklin's.) As soon as the tax bill passed, Franklin published an appeal in his *Pennsylvania Gazette* for an end to party strife. But William Smith took advantage of the moment of relaxation to write another pamphlet renewing his denunciations of the Assembly and the Quakers. Like the *Brief State,* this *Brief View* was soon sent to England for anonymous publication.[37]

Smith wrote it with a particular object in mind: the ejection by Parliament of Quakers from the Assembly. William Allen joined in. He sent to England the petition that Smith had written for local signatures, and engaged counsel in England to push the petition all the way up to the Privy Council. Smith's role, as before, was to inflame public opinion.[38]

There is irony here again because the Quakers had ceased to be the strongest anti-Proprietary element in the province. "King of the Quakers" Israel Pemberton, Jr., was no longer happy with Benjamin Franklin and Franklin's friends. Pemberton disliked Franklin's land tax; he was dissatisfied with Franklin's "indecent and virulent Terms" in the Assembly messages; and he was afraid that things were tending to an "irreparable breach with the Proprietaries." Just as the moment seemed ripe, therefore, for Proprietary partisans to woo the strict Quakers away from their halfhearted support of Franklin, at just that moment Allen and Smith launched a new attack.[39] Irony or not, Allen was in deadly earnest. His petition probably traveled by the same vessel that carried Pemberton's letter.[40]

London politics shifted coincidentally, and lifted the pressures that had worried Penn. The devil was sick no longer, and no longer cared to be a monk. Penn seized on the Allen-Smith petition against the Quakers and pushed it with all his strength. He started, incredibly enough, by complaining to three key personages about the Assembly's *arming* the backwoods people in the turmoil after the first Indian raids![41]

The campaign moved quickly to the brink of action by Parliament to require an oath for members of colonial assemblies which would have disqualified all Quakers from membership. It was stopped in the nick of time by agreement of Lord Granville, president of the Privy Council, and the great Quaker merchant John Hanbury and his associates. (Granville was deeply interested in the colonies, being a lord Proprietary himself in North Carolina.) To avoid permanent disqualification by oath, the London Quakers pledged in behalf of Pennsylvanian brethren that "the greater part" of Friends in the Assembly would withdraw voluntarily from the Assembly in wartime. The London Meeting for Sufferings thereupon wrote a formal Epistle to the Meeting in Philadelphia, and sent two emissaries to personally exert all possible powers of persuasion on the provincials.[42]

The oath bill was stopped, but the atmosphere never really cleared up. A sad and weary Dr. Fothergill wrote to Pemberton that the anti-Quaker propaganda had been carried on "with so much steadiness, management and success, as to raise the most popular dislike to us as a people, that we have ever labour'd under from the restoration [of Charles II]."[43] Some ministers turned on Penn. (Quakers gave strong financial support to the Whigs in government.) Penn waffled. "It will be most prudent, and best approved here," he warned Smith, "for you to recommend it to every body to forbear any further controversy."[44]

It was a little too late to be giving such advice to Smith. The busy provost, by the time he received Penn's counsel, had already gotten deep into hot water by his attacks on Franklin's militia. Governor Morris had passed the law reluctantly; he regarded it as "impossible to carry . . . into execution, and . . . therefore no more than waste Paper." In opposition to it, Proprietary men started an independent voluntary company whose officers Morris commissioned while raising obstructions for the legal militia.[45] One is hardly surprised, therefore, to find Morris in difficulties with the legal militiamen. Let Richard Peters report the situation with his usual acute perspicacity:

The Inhabitants of the several Wards of the City whilst the Governor was at New York formed themselves into Companies and chose their Officers under the present Law, and presented them to the Governor for his Approbation, but without Lists of their Names or a Return of the Poll of Election, and the Governor with Advice of Council desiring them to do this, or he could not accept the Choice, the Officers put it to the Vote of the Electors standing before the Governors Door whether they should do this or no, and they unanimously voted they would not give in their Names, and then voted that what they had done should be as nothing, and all this unanimously, and in a rude indecent manner. The Reason given by the Officers for this Treatment of the Governor was that in Conversation he told some of them, as soon as he had the Names of the Companies, he would incorporate them with the Regulars which were coming from New York, and then they would be subject to military Discipline. This it seems the Governor denies he said with respect to the Militia, tho he did mention some such thing with respect to the Guards posted on the Frontiers and in the Pay of the Province; but such Umbrage was taken at the very Thought, that the whole City was in an Uproar, and the Governor treated most rudely in their Discourse, and by Papers thrown into his House.[46]

A moment must be taken to consider the British methods of military discipline for Regulars in the eighteenth century. They were nothing less than torture, inflicted by the lash: *one thousand* lashes for such offences as stealing a pound of butter or a shirt, laid on the bare back in front of the offender's own unit. The performance was intentionally horrific, designed to make the common soldier fear his officers more than the enemy.[47] Colonials knew about this; they were utterly outraged by Morris's scheme to trap their volunteers into such "discipline."

If there was to be a legal militia, it would not be on such terms. Morris was persuaded by other Proprietary supporters to have the militia officers' elections certified without an appended list of their men, and the companies were formally brought into being.[48]

At Morris's request, Franklin went off to the frontiers to build a chain of forts and organize defenses. (Penn's men did not hazard their own precious frames in such danger.) On Franklin's return he was elected colonel of the militia; and to the despair of the Proprietaries' men, Morris commissioned him.[49] But Morris held off the commission until the competitive independent company could hold a review. On 25 February 1765, the day after Franklin's commission was granted, William Smith's upper-class gang offered a Plan of Association to Morris "for promoting *Military Discipline* among the Freemen of Pennsylvania, who are not WILLING and DESIROUS to act under the present *Militia Law*." The name and idea were lifted bodily from Franklin's old Association of 1747; even his cannon were to be used for training; but the purpose was to block Franklin from accomplishing anything with his legal militia which, by now, loomed as a Frankenstein monster before Penn's men.[50]

Again there is irony, or perhaps only contradiction arising from lack of scruple. At the very moment that Penn's henchmen were obstructing the formation of a military force in Pennsylvania, he was trying to get their petition for an oath enacted to ban Quakers from office *because the Friends obstructed the formation of a military force in Pennsylvania*. Lord Granville and John Hanbury defeated Penn in London; Franklin defeated Penn's men in Philadelphia.

The denouement was colorful and comic. Notice was given that a public meeting would be held at the College of Philadelphia for the promotion of the anti-pacifist, anti-militia Association. We may be sure that Provost Smith had a rousing oration ready, but he never got the chance to deliver it. Franklin, on a few hours' notice, ordered the first review of the legal militia in State House Square on the same date as Smith's Association meeting. Then Franklin ordered his mustered troops, under arms, to parade the quarter mile through the city streets to the College. The Associators decamped in a great hurry.[51]

It makes a strange and fascinating picture. A bespectacled and bald, middle-aged, fat philosopher astride a probably rather stately horse and leading a wobbly column of untrained, ununiformed, enthusiastic, nonacademic youth to besiege the College he had founded and of which he was still president. Did ever town and gown confront each other in more dubious battle?

The routed enemy were further discomfited by the philosopher-colonel's pen. He published a set of "Queries" in his *Gazette* and wondered, among other things, "Whether inviting a Number of People to a Consultation, and shutting the Doors in their Faces, as soon as they appear, be a Compliment or an Affront."[52]

Replies condemned the militia and counterreplies condemned the Association. Both sides scored points, hot tempers
grew hotter. In the midst, Franklin—wearing his Postmaster
hat this time—started for Virginia. His admiring militia officers
gave him an armed escort out of the city, with drawn swords.
Governor Morris had never been so honored. Scandalized opponents fumed, and Franklin himself was somewhat embarrassed by the pomp.[53] He managed to switch from soldier to
philosopher again in time to accept another honorary degree in
Virginia from William and Mary College. That sort of honor
also had never been conferred on Morris.[54]

Meanwhile, William Smith at last had been exposed. Some
unfriendly person caught sight of the original manuscript of the
Brief State and recognized Smith's distinctive handwriting.[55]
Worse luck for Smith was on its way. He had written a polemic
letter to the London *Evening Advertiser* which was printed in
April with his signature. Indignant Dr. Fothergill sent it to
Pennsylvania with the information that the identity of the *Brief
State*'s writer was established by the handwriting of the
original.[56]

Franklin's rallying of his countrymen against enemies without and within was his finest hour. For once he made no calculation of personal gain; nothing in the gift of the Assembly or the
populace could compare with the patronage available to the
Proprietary whose service Franklin left to fight for justice as
tribune of the people. Thomas Penn had fantastically enormous
estates to dispense to persons who furthered his designs, and an
associate of Governor Morris once drew Franklin aside to say
that Penn would give him a "fat price" to cooperate.[57] When
Franklin refused, Morris tried to get him ousted from the post
office (but Franklin was making it pay a good income to its
sinecure holder in England).

Besides his tough political leadership in Philadelphia,
marked throughout by principle, Franklin's tour of the country-
side to fashion defenses was genuinely courageous in the face of
real danger. Indian enemies were everywhere, but no one knew
where. Hidden bowmen were quite as capable of bringing
down a colonel as a private. By his personal example, Franklin
stiffened the morale of his people.

Beyond cavil, and genuinely modest for once, he was heroic.

13 FRONTS AND FRIENDS

THE POLITICAL BATTLES between Franklin and Thomas Penn must be scored as a draw so far. Franklin won the militia issue (until the crown later disallowed) and Penn kept his estates free from taxation. Penn also gave a knockout blow to the third contesting party, the Quakers, by forcing all the orthodox pacifists out of the Assembly, but this was a Pyrrhic victory because their replacements were Franklin stalwarts to a man. Franklin hoped for "some fair weather which I have long sigh'd for."[1] Richard Peters had less optimism. The new assemblymen were "Old Churchmen" (Anglicans), as Peters called them, "meer Franklinists and will go which way he pleases to direct." Himself ordained in the Church of England, Peters thought "they may prove even worse enemys to the Proprietors than the Quakers."[2]

In a quiet moment Franklin meditated on recent events in a letter to his friend the English Quaker, Peter Collinson. He was "not much concern'd" about the Proprietaries' antagonism toward him, "because if I have offended them *by acting right,* I can, whenever I please, remove their Displeasure, *by acting wrong.* . . . I have some natural Dislike to Persons who so far *Love Money,* as to be *unjust* for its sake: I despise their *meanness* . . . I am persuaded that I do not oppose their Views from Pique, Disappointment, or personal Resentment, but, as I think, from a Regard to the Publick Good." He permitted himself "a little Vanity." He was "sometimes asham'd" for the Proprietaries "when I see them differing with their People for Trifles, and instead of being ador'd, as they might be, like Demi Gods, become the Objects of universal Hatred and Contempt. How must they have managed, when, with all the Power their Charter, the Laws and their Wealth give them, a private Person . . . can do more Good in their Country than they, because he has the Affections and Confidence of their People," and ever the businessman, Franklin added, "and of course some Command of the Peoples Purses." He apologized that this letter had too much in it "about my self." For that very reason, it is illuminating today.[3]

After all the fuss about it, the militia was really not very good. The raw and scared garrisons of Franklin's forts clung to shelter within them; instead of ranging the woods to find the enemy, they feared that the enemy would find them. Indians moved about at pleasure and struck where they wished, seemingly less often than in 1755, but perhaps because so many people had deserted the target farms. French supervisors of the Indian raiders bragged of having deprived the English of necessary resources, and refugees burned with hate for all Indians, allies as well as enemies.

For militarist Franklin, it was sufficient to set up defense. For Quakers, however, especially the orthodox kind, all their principles of religion were violated by the spectacle of Indians behaving like savages after they had been treated as human persons. Could that have been really so? James Pemberton (Israel Junior's brother) remarked that the Assembly had asked "for a strict enquiry into the cause of this change of Conduct in the Indians who had till now allways prov'd our steady Friends, being apprehensive it must arise from some cause unknown to us, and most likely from some failure of Land Contracts, to which we receiv'd an evasive answer." The dispute over taxes caused this desire for an enquiry to be forgotten, "which I think, could we have succeeded, might have prevented a great deal of bloodshed, to have found the Cause of the Indians dissatisfaction, and voted a sufficient sum to make them easy."[4] Thus the Quakers sniffed the stench of the Walking Purchase, still pungent after nearly twenty years; and thus early did they propose a remedy that Franklin would try to adopt later at Easton, in 1756.

Israel Pemberton, Jr., was one of the orthodox Quakers who resigned from the Assembly at the request of London Friends, but Israel did not intend to give up the struggle. He was every bit as determined as Franklin to work for justice, and he concluded that the way to pacify the Indians was to negotiate with them. That would require confirming the suspicion of secret ill-treatment and making restitution. And in the meantime, the victims of war must not be forgotten; refugees must be given

relief and shelter.[5] This three-pronged campaign of Pemberton's and his associates was wholly independent of all branches
of government. In that day, long before the welfare state, even
the representative Assembly felt no responsibility for the refugees' welfare, except to provide them with arms. The Quakers
took up the burden. (Perhaps other churches also helped; I
have researched only the Quakers.) Very certainly, however, the
absentee landlord in London contributed not one farthing. He
continued to demand his rents.

(Readers who think I am being too harsh with Thomas
Penn should ask Irishmen or Scotch-Irishmen about who made
their ancestors flee to America. About absentee landlords, the
Green and the Orange agree.)

A petty political war broke out in Philadelphia when Penn's
partisans demoted Franklin from the president's office of the
College, electing Richard Peters in his place.[6] Franklin kept his
place as a trustee because he had been named in the College's
charter in the days when he too was a sycophant, and he refused
now to resign. His wounded vanity was assuaged by news from
England that the Royal Society had elected him to membership
without a single blackball—the first time in its president's memory that election had been unanimous.[7] And in Philadelphia the
opposition to the Proprietary elected Franklin president of the
Hospital trustees.[8]

Money continued at issue. Provincial troops under arms
were expensive because they demanded pay and provisions under different terms than the militia. Englishmen tended to confuse the provincial troops with the militia, as Franklin carefully
distinguished them (and as historians still confuse them). The
provincial troops were hirelings, though volunteers, and under
different discipline than the militia. And more costly. In 1757, a
new money bill was passed, for £100,000 this time, and Speaker
Norris lamented that it was still not enough. Imperialist Franklin took credit for getting a tenth of it set aside to be at the
disposal of the new commander in chief from England, John
Campbell, Earl Loudoun, but Franklin soon came to regret
Loudoun's blustering ways; especially after the earl determined
to quarter troops on Philadelphia and Franklin had to contrive
shelter for them outside of the inhabitants' residences.[9]

A continuing bone of contention arose because of Catholic

deportees from French Acadia who had been dumped on Philadelphia late in 1755. William Smith scribbled much (anonymously) to assert that these exiles were plotting with other
Catholics in the interior to bring French invaders into the province. (German immigrants or French deportees, they were all
enemies to Smith.) The crown's action was a military measure
to secure Acadia, newly baptized Nova Scotia; royalty had no
intention of providing for the welfare of the deportees. Once
again, the old Quaker-dominated Assembly took on the task of
feeding and arranging shelter for the deportees, and the succes-
sor Assembly under Franklin's command continued to accept
responsibility, though without enthusiasm. As the Acadians
made demands instead of expressing gratitude, they became a
hair shirt, and its scratchiness was not lessened by the advantage
taken by William Smith to present them as treasonable
plotters.[10]

In the long run, however, the most crucial actions of 1756
and 1757 were Israel Pemberton's and his supporting orthodox
Quakers'. Since the Assembly had failed to follow through with
its enquiry about possible mistreatment for the Indians, Pemberton determined to do it by private means. Because Pemberton
has suffered a very bad press, it is first necessary to clarify his
motive; it was peace, indisputably central to the Quaker creed.
As peace could not be attained without Indian agreement, contact with the Indians had to be made, and Pemberton could not
accept Franklin's method of making it by combat.

In the most direct fashion, Pemberton first consulted a
Mingo refugee—Scarouady—in Philadelphia in flight from the
warriors of the Ohio country. All unknowing of past iniquities,
Pemberton asked Conrad Weiser for assistance. Weiser helped,
but recorded the doings with editorial adjustments. From this
consultation, Pemberton sent an urgent message to Superintendent of Indian Affairs Sir William Johnson in New York, but
Johnson would not tolerate intrusion on his political domain
from Quakers or anyone else. That approach became a dead end.

Pemberton and associates founded a new organization, the
Friendly Association for Regaining and Preserving Peace with
the Indians by Pacific Measures. I have dealt with it in some
detail in another book; for present purposes, it is important to
notice that, far from being the creature of the Assembly, the

Friendly Association was formed in opposition to measures taken by the Assembly under Franklin's domination. Pemberton deplored "the Darling Scheme of gaining some Advantage over the Governor and Proprietor, for the sake of which every other Consideration seem'd to be little regarded."[11] And when the governor declared war on the Indians and set prices on their scalps, Pemberton's Quakers were outraged.[12]

Regardless of their motives, William Smith, with Thomas Penn's secret guidance, continued to attack *all* Quakers. In point of fact, Penn and Smith conceived the war in terms very like Franklin's, but with different priorities. Pemberton's Friendly Association was an aberration, but a vigorous one. It collected large sums of money from members and from pietist Germans who shared its aims, and distributed help to refugees and notably to the besieged Moravians in the old Walking Purchase territory. Positively activist, Pemberton and the Friendly Association probed until they stirred up an eastern Delaware chief named Teedyuscung to accept overtures for peace with the minority of Delawares left behind when most of the tribe went west.[13]

A new governor, William Denny, treated with Teedyuscung at Easton in November 1756. and Denny was persuaded by Franklin to ask a fateful question: "Had the Indians received grievances from Pennsylvania's government or others?" Teedyuscung did not hesitate, or equivocate. "I have not far to go for an Instance," he responded, "this very ground that is under me (striking it with his Foot) was my Land and Inheritance, and is taken from me by fraud."[14] Thus returned the ghost of the Walking Purchase to confirm Quaker suspicions of mistreatment in Indian affairs.

Secretary Richard Peters pretended to such shock that he had to put down his pen and declare himself unable to record Teedyuscung's charge. This does not wash. Peters understood the Walking Purchase arrangements perfectly because he had been present at them and had been in charge of all the documents ever since. If a charge of fraud against Penn were to be sustained, Peters would be guilty as an accomplice. Perhaps his refusal to write at Easton should be considered as a tacit rejection of testifying against himself.

He was not the only person there with pen and ink. Among

the unofficial observers was Charles Thomson, the Presbyterian teacher in the Friends' school (who had resigned from the College rather than take orders from William Smith). Thomson recorded everything Teedyuscung said in a beautifully clear, tiny script. (He was later to become the Secretary of Congress in the American Revolution.) As Peters had stopped writing, Governor Denny ordered Thomson's minutes to be adopted officially "as the most Perfect." As indeed they were.[15]

Franklin was there also, as one of the Assembly's commissioners; and, as always, he proposed a practical remedy. If an uncompensated land grab was rankling the Delawares, why not settle the matter then and there regardless of who was culpable? He suggested that a payment of £500 could be arranged. The Assembly would have provided that in an instant to get peace.

This was one time when practicality was more complicated than Franklin realized. On the Indian side, Chief Teedyuscung *refused* the payment because he was not authorized to accept it. His phrase "my Land" was an Indian figure of speech meaning "land of my people." The particular aggrieved landowner had been old Nutimus, who would have to be consulted before Franklin's offer could be accepted.[16]

The other complication was Thomas Penn. He knew that when Virginia and Massachusetts had aroused Indian uprisings through oppression and misdealings, the crown had stepped in to change the governments. If the Walking Purchase fraud were proved against Penn, he could lose all his Proprietary power. He had been haunted by that ghost and had instructed Peters not to let Friends "throw any blame on us."[17]

Subsequent events have been described in my book *Empire of Fortune,* and are not immediately germane to Franklin's life. Indian affairs did not much concern Franklin; they were a Quaker issue. Franklin was not nearly so ready as Pemberton to give trust to Indians. He suspected treachery by the province's Iroquois allies. "I make no doubt but that the Six Nations have privily encourag'd those Indians to fall upon us; they have taken no Step to defend us, as their Allies, nor to prevent the Mischief done us. . . . In short I do not believe we shall ever have a firm Peace with the Indians till we have well drubb'd them."[18] Franklin had some grounds for suspecting the Iroquois. Whichever empire was to win the war, the Iroquois did not intend to

lose it; they worked both sides of that street until Britain's ultimate victory became clear. However that might be, Franklin
was impatient. He had built his system of frontier forts and
garrisoned them with provincial troops. He turned back to the
Assembly for what seemed like more important matters.

Taxes and appropriations were needed again, and the Assembly was as determined as ever to get around or through the
Proprietary instructions somehow while Governor Denny was
still bound by them. Complex new bills were passed by the
Assembly, and the familiar pattern of deadlock occurred again.
The Assembly gave ground on taxing the Penns' estates, but
other issues remained. Angry assemblymen presented an ultimatum: either Denny would agree with them or he could find
other sources to pay the troops, because he would get no more
money for that purpose from the Assembly. In the end, the bill
was passed because Lord Loudoun needed money for the
troops under his command, so he instructed Denny to sign the
Assembly's bill; and Denny did, thus infuriating Thomas
Penn.[19]

An interesting sidelight on this brawl is the report of Richard Peters to Penn with its denunciation of Franklin's "Billings-
gate Language" and its notice that Franklin's face "at Times
turns white as the driven Snow with the Extreams of Wrath."
This consorts badly with the *Autobiography*'s bland comments
that Franklin always kept his feelings under control. Perhaps
more important is Peters's judgment made even in the heat of
the battle: "I have a very high Opinion of B.F.'s virtue and
uncorrupted honesty."[20]

Even though Lord Loudoun's pressure had won passage of
the money bill, it could still be disallowed by the crown. Knowing that the Penns would fight against it tooth and nail, the
Assembly voted to send Franklin to London to persuade approval from the crown. While at it, they also commissioned him
to demand a royal inquiry into the Walking Purchase.[21]

A curious sort of arm's-length reunion took place in London
because William Smith had been smoked out of his anonymity
and had been summoned to the Assembly on charges that
amounted to libel and conspiracy against that body. (Franklin
was already abroad.) Smith was defiant, so the Assembly decided to cool him off with a jail sentence, and he ran off to

London, two jumps ahead of the police.[22] In England, he and Franklin took pains to traduce each other.

Still other parties joined in the reunion as the delegates of London Friends returned from Philadelphia to report their observations of the negotiations with the hostile Delawares and to suggest means for further progress.

Nor may it be forgotten for a moment that Britain's war with France and France's Indian allies continued as hotly as ever. In Pennsylvania, it required the utmost endeavors of the Friendly Association just to make contact diplomatically with the hostile Indians of the Ohio country who did not recognize the authority of eastern Chief Teedyuscung.

It is absolutely necessary to recognize that "the Delawares" had divided decades earlier into the Delawares who migrated to the Ohio country and the Delawares who remained in the east in villages in New Jersey and along the Susquehanna River's North Branch. Political relationships between east and west had sundered. The easterners scattered and lost morale until their young warriors chose Teedyuscung as a "pine tree" chief to unite them. The Ohio Delawares were much more numerous and included what a captive called the tribe's "royal family," headed by brothers Pisquetomen, Shingas, and Tamaqua (Beaver).[23] Accustomed to family leadership for generations, these chiefs were not about to knock under to an upstart like Teedyuscung.

Much of the difficulty of making peace arose from the jockeying for prestige and power between east and west. Adding to the confusion was Teedyuscung's acceptance of sponsorship by Quakers and eastern Iroquois, especially Onondagas, while the Ohioans clung to the French and the Seneca western Iroquois. Behind the strivings between eastern and western Delawares can be sensed, very murkily, much competition between Onondagas and Senecas, as well as their varied English and French allies.

For peace negotiations to be successful, they had to be conducted piecemeal and with infinite patience, all while outraged victims of Indian raids were screaming for the blood of all Indians and any persons who befriended them.

14 A WOBBLY OFFENSIVE

AFTER WHAT SEEMED LIKE interminable delays in sailing caused by Lord Loudoun's orders to the ship's captain, Franklin arrived in London, 26 July 1757.[1]

He wanted to be sure of his backing in London, so he first approached the Quakers there. He talked with Dr. John Fothergill, who had so devotedly sent valuable information to Pennsylvania Friends, and Fothergill received him courteously, with advice. It is to be feared, however, that the advice was founded on wrong assumptions. Good Quaker that he was, Fothergill could not conceive Thomas Penn as a conscienceless villain. Surely Penn must be open to reason if he were approached reasonably, so Franklin should appeal to Penn's better nature before approaching officials of the crown. Probably with some doubt, Franklin agreed to try.[2]

For several years he had held an opinion of Penn less charitable and more realistic than the Quakers'. And Franklin did not forget that Penn had felt no compunction to pay even his personal bills. He still owed for purchases made at Franklin's shop nearly twenty years earlier. Such matters were not trivial to Franklin. Though he had risen in the world, he retained the shopkeeper's respect for punctuality and accuracy in settling credit. Penn's lordly disdain and tightfistedness failed that test.[3]

Dr. Fothergill thought that it would be useful for Franklin to meet Lord Granville before talking to Penn. As president of the king's Privy Council, John Carteret, Earl Granville, could be very helpful to Franklin's appeal to the crown. Granville was deeply interested in Pennsylvania's problems. On one side, he was Thomas Penn's brother-in-law, but Granville was far from sharing Penn's hatred for Quakers. It was Granville who had contrived the device for Quakers to withdraw from the Pennsylvania Assembly voluntarily (and temporarily) in order to avoid being disqualified permanently by a loyalty oath. Granville was well connected to some of London's wealthiest Quakers.

But he had no sympathy with Franklin's mission though they met by intervention of one of the richest merchants in the City, John Hanbury, who had played a key role in frustrating the oath bill and who was "remarkable for his connection and intimacy with . . . most of the Lords spiritual and temporal of the Newcastle and Pelham administration"—i.e., the Whigs. Despite such a favorable introduction, Franklin met with no encouragement from Granville. "You Americans have wrong ideas," huffed the lord president; "you contend that the King's Instructions to his Governors are not Laws, and think yourselves at Liberty to disregard them," but they are, "so far as relates to you, the *Law of the Land,* for THE KING IS THE LEGISLATOR OF THE COLONIES." Of course, Franklin defended Assembly rights against such doctrine, and the two parted without a meeting of minds. The conversation "a little alarm'd" Franklin "as to what might be the Sentiments of the Court concerning us."[4]

Thomas Penn knew of Franklin's mission in advance. Before Franklin arrived, Penn had appealed to his patron the Duke of Cumberland (not a Whig) to put pressure on Franklin's superior in the post office. (Franklin was deputy to Sir Everard Fawkener, the Postmaster General.) Penn tried to arouse jealousy in the province's agent Richard Partridge about Franklin's supplanting him, and Penn summoned the respected former governor James Hamilton to cross the ocean to refute Franklin. Hamilton procrastinated. He had more personal status and independence than most of Penn's supporters, and he did not relish entanglement with Franklin.[5]

Neither Franklin nor Penn anticipated pleasure from their meeting, which took place on 20 August 1757. It consisted entirely of an exchange of statements of position, neither side showing inclination to budge an inch. They met again on comparatively minor issues, and they came to angry, final encounter about 12 or 13 January 1758. That meeting became legendary from Franklin's description. It deserves a long quotation.

Penn denied that the Assembly had any such privileges as were held by the House of Commons. He averred "That we were only a kind of Corporation acting by a Charter from the Crown and could have no Privileges or Rights but what was granted by that Charter in which no such Privilege as We now claim was any where mentioned." (In effect this was the same position as Lord Granville's.)

But says I [Franklin], Your Father's Charter expressly says that the Assembly of Pennsylvania shall have all the Power and Privileges of an Assembly according to the Rights of the Freeborn Subjects of England, and as is usual in any of the British Plantations in America. *Yes says he* but, if my Father granted Privileges he was not by the Royal Charter impowered to grant, Nothing can be claim'd by such Grant. *I said,* If then your Father had no Right to grant the Privileges He pretended to grant, and publish'd all over Europe as granted, those who came to settle in the Province upon the Faith of that Grant and in Expectation of enjoying the Privileges contained in it, were deceived, cheated, and betrayed. *He answered* they should have themselves looked to that. That the Royal Charter was no Secret; they who came into the Province on my Father's Offer of Privileges, if they were deceiv'd, it was their own Fault; and that he said with a Kind of triumphing laughing Insolence, such as a low Jockey might do when a Purchaser complained that He had cheated him in a Horse. I was astonished to see him thus meanly give up his Father's Character and conceived that Moment a more cordial and thorough Contempt for him than I ever before felt for any Man living—a Contempt that I cannot express in Words, but I believe my Countenance expressed it strongly. . . . I made no other Answer to this than that the poor People were no Lawyers themselves and confiding in his Father did not think it necessary to consult any.[6]

Apart from Penn's slur upon his father, he had expressed in embryo the basic proposition that was to explode the combustibles of the American Revolution. Compared to this, all other issues would be subordinate details. Penn denied the Pennsylvania Assembly's (or any assembly's) power and privileges "according to the Rights of the Freeborn Subjects of England." Thomas denied that his father was empowered to grant such rights. By implication, he propounded that those freeborn subjects had no rights whatever except what the crown chose to give them, under whatever limitations, and for however long the crown pleased. It was an assertion of royal prerogative that devolved not upon the colonists but rather, through royal favor, upon their lord the Proprietary. Oliver Cromwell had nullified that proposition at the center of the empire; it remained alive at the peripheries.

Franklin reacted so strongly from repugnance to Penn personally that the full implications of Penn's assertions seemingly

escaped him. He seems to have forgotten Lord Granville's assertion that the king's will was law for colonists without check. At
this stage in Franklin's development he was obsessed with the
need to end Penn's feudal powers. The will of the people could
be aroused to that purpose *within the province;* but at the center
of empire, as it seemed to Franklin, the feudalist could be over-
powered only by the greater power of the King-in-Parliament,
and Franklin believed in Parliament as the protector of the liberties of the subject. Long an imperialist, Franklin began simmering as a royalist.

He was liberated from demands to come to terms with Penn
because Penn furiously cut off all further interviews. Someone
had leaked Franklin's remark about that "low jockey," who responded in high dudgeon. Next to the tangibles of his estates,
Penn valued highest the pretensions of his status. After Franklin's personal attack, only war without quarter could exist between them.

Once more we must see the distinction between Franklin
and the Quakers, in England as well as in Pennsylvania. Quaker
John Hunt, who had been sent to the province to cool the
hotheads, was introduced there by Israel Pemberton to the
Friendly Association's negotiations with Teedyuscung's Delawares. Hunt was inspired by the treaties he attended; they gave
him "the most Satisfaction and best wages" of his visit. Returning to London late in January 1758—shortly after the showdown between Franklin and the Penns—Hunt took his
colleague Christopher Wilson to try to persuade Thomas and
Richard Penn that Friends desired an "amicable accommoda-
tion." Correspondence between Pemberton and Fothergill evi-
dences the sincerity of this desire.

The Proprietaries received these babes-in-the-woods cordially. They pumped information about exciting plans to organize a big Quaker company for trade with the Indians, thus to
win their friendship. After cordially dismissing them, Thomas
Penn—one can almost see him rubbing his hands in satisfaction—Thomas immediately ordered Richard Peters to block the
company as "it will be the means of acquiring power to the
party."[7] Hunt, Dr. Fothergill, and four other Quakers who
had put up capital for the company, eventually discovered how
Thomas had hoodwinked them. Ruefully reflecting on his gull-

ibility, Hunt confessed that the Penns' protestations to accommodate matters with Pennsylvanians "look to me like mere pretention and will end in nothing. I cannot discover that thing called sincerity in them."[8]

John Hunt had brought from Pennsylvania a manuscript to be printed as a book; and, like William Smith's *Brief State,* it caused a sensation, but in a reverse direction. Charles Thomson, whose minutes at the treaty with Teedyuscung had been made official, had become deeply interested in events involving Indians. He was a Presbyterian, not a Quaker, though he taught in the Friends' school; but, like Franklin, he had a passion for justice, and in politics he was closer to Franklin than to his Quaker employers. He wrote his damning findings in *An Enquiry into the Causes of the Alienation of the Delaware and Shawanese Indians from the British Interest.* (Thomas Penn's annotated copy is now in the John Carter Brown Library, Providence, Rhode Island.)

Thomson's employment by Friends clarifies why John Hunt should have the manuscript instead of an associate of Franklin. It is also rather startling to see that Franklin was not even permitted to read the manuscript until Hunt had delivered it to Lord Granville and received it back. When Franklin finally got hold of the Thomson manuscript, he arranged its publication.[9] There was even less camaraderie between Franklin and the London Quakers than had existed in Pennsylvania, where he and Friends had been yoked by necessity for teamwork in the Assembly.

Franklin's first priority at the Privy Council was forced on him by the appeal of William Smith against his conviction for libeling the Assembly. Despite Franklin's defense of the Assembly, Smith won on the technicality that the Assembly of 1758 could not punish a libel on the Assembly of 1757.[10]

Defeated on that issue, Franklin appealed against the Penns' Indian policies. Charles Thomson's book appeared and strengthened the case, but the Board of Trade feared to settle the matter in England. On their recommendation, the king in Council ordered Sir William Johnson, the Superintendent of Indian Affairs for the northern department, to hold an inquiry and make a report.[11]

Franklin's best efforts got him nowhere. He exploited all his warm connections with learned men, but they did not alarm Thomas Penn. "It is quite another sort of People, who are to determine the Dispute between us," wrote Penn to Richard Peters.[12] Quite naturally, printer Franklin turned to the press. As an agent on an official mission, he could not sign his propaganda, but he planted it, ā la William Smith, anonymously. (The tone of his squib is playful instead of dripping Smith's venom.) Two major publications aided the cause, the heaviest being Richard Jackson's ponderous *An Historical Review of the Constitution and Government of Pennsylvania, From its Origins; So far as regards the several Points of Controversy, which have, from Time to Time, arisen between the several Governors of that Province, and their Assemblies.*[13] Whatever effect Jackson's magnum opus may have had on officialdom compelled to read it, the general public of interested gentlemen was probably affected more favorably by an article signed by William Franklin, who had accompanied his father to London. In *The Gentleman's Magazine,* the most substantial of the monthly journals, William totted up the Assembly's grants "for the king's use," and described the Quaker pacifists' withdrawals from the Assembly. With understandable hyperbole, he asserted that "more is done for the relief and defence of the country without any assistance from the crown, than is done perhaps by any other colony in America." A foreshadowing of Benjamin's royalism appeared in the novel argument that "Neither the proprietaries nor any other power on earth ought to interfere between [the assemblymen] and their sovereign."[14]

The Penns, however, had their own methods for making propaganda and delivering it directly to the seats of power. The provincial council transmitted to Thomas Penn a formal report attacking persons who "from their unhappy religious Principles or from what other Motive they best knew, refused or declined to concur with the Governor in giving the Hatchet to and joining with those Indians against the Enemy." This was presented in the guise of an exhaustive inquiry into Teedyuscung's charges of fraud for which, council concluded, "there is not the least Shadow of Foundation."

Two Quaker grandees sat in the council, who could not by any means agree to the "report's" innuendo of treasonous motivation by Quakers; but the document was sneaked past them during their absence from sessions.[15] Penn pushed it at crown officers upon whom it made a serious impression regardless of what was appearing in the public press.

If Penn's followers were busy, so were Israel Pemberton and the Friendly Association. Pemberton had learned something from Franklin's former devices with General Braddock's army. When British Regulars under Colonel John Stanwix were stationed at Lancaster in the hope (a vain one) that they would protect the country people, Pemberton's Friendly Association shipped a hogshead of Madeira wine to Stanwix. Naturally, "common civility" obliged Stanwix to thank the Friends for this "testimony of their good will," and he added gratitude for Philadelphia's good winter quarters for his thousand-man battalion. In writing.[16]

Pemberton's greatest coup became possible after Brigadier John Forbes was assigned to create a new army and lead it against Fort Duquesne. Forbes was a soldier rather than a politician. He cared nothing for the interests of the Proprietaries or the Assembly or Superintendent Johnson. Forbes's single-minded objective was to take Fort Duquesne. He knew that Braddock had been defeated by Indian enemies for lack of Indian allies, and Forbes wanted those Indian allies for his own campaign. He quickly came to understand that the snake pit of Pennsylvania politics would produce no Indians, and he lost all confidence in Superintendent Sir William Johnson. A most astonishing deus ex machina burst in upon him in the person of Israel Pemberton with ideas for seducing Indians to abandon the French, and Forbes hesitated not a moment to seize his luck.[17]

A very strange political situation developed. Penn's Governor Denny and henchmen, and Superintendent Johnson, for reasons of their own blocked all efforts to establish direct contact with the hostile Indians of the Ohio. The Iroquois League and the Delawares' eastern chief Teedyuscung strove to preserve their own statuses as indispensable intermediaries, so they also created roadblocks. Against them all, His Majesty's Brigadier John Forbes linked forces with devout pacifist Quaker Israel Pemberton to get word through to the Ohioans. Wonder of wonders, in spite of manifold obstructions and sabotage, this almost impossible team at last aroused enough curiosity for two Ohio chiefs to come east to investigate; and machinery was set hazardously in motion for a great peace treaty at Easton in October 1758.[18]

When that treaty came to pass, it was to have far-reaching consequences. Indians and English both wanted peace, so they agreed to postpone argument about the Walking Purchase of 1737 in order to grapple with immediate problems of 1758. The Ohio Delawares held power of decision. With a French garrison in Fort Duquesne, they had experienced occupation by a foreign power which was precisely what they had emigrated westward to escape. They wanted the French out and a territorial boundary between their lands west of the Appalachians and English jurisdictions east of the mountains.

To win them over, English negotiators promised to drive the French away and to draw a boundary line, in return for which the hostile warriors must withdraw from the French and cease depredations against "back country" settlers. A deal was made, and the Ohio Delawares buried the French hatchet.[19]

Forbes's common sense and Pemberton's religious dedication triumphed over the multitude of striving factions and parties to create a united front against the French, at least for a while. Abandoned by their Indian allies, the French burned their fort and ran away.

When news of this great victory reached England, with its portent of a sharp turn in the war's tide, surely the feeling against Quakers would have to turn? To think so, however, betrays ignorance of the customs of military commanders. Forbes reported that *he* had taken Duquesne, and it was clearly visible that he was at the head of the troops marching in. Pemberton was the length of the province away at Easton, much less visibly winning the Indians to make Duquesne's capture possible. The teamwork of Forbes and Pemberton is evidenced only by some suppressed official minutes and Forbes's unique, never published, letter of thanks to Pemberton.[20] Perhaps if he had lived longer, Forbes might have set the record straight, but he was so incapacitated by illness that he had to be carried in a litter, and he died soon after his triumph. Pennsylvania's officialdom and Superintendent Johnson immediately reverted to their policies of ganging up on the Quakers, especially on pesky Pemberton.

The English had gotten what they wanted from the Easton Treaty, but the Delawares got mostly a lesson in the reliability of diplomatic promises. The English did drive the French away; but, violating Delaware expectations, they substituted a larger English garrison for the banished French one.

The promise of a territorial boundary was promptly forgotten until tribal wrath exploded in the liberation war called Pontiac's. To defuse it, royal statesmen reminded themselves of the Easton promise and issued the Royal Proclamation of 1763 with instructions to make an actual survey of the promised line, but with some fine print. The land east of the line was to be British, no problem. Indians thought that the land west of the line was to be theirs, but they were deluded. That land was also British and only *reserved* to the Indians as their *hunting* territories.[21]

Students must consider the precise language of the Proclamation. Historian Frederick Jackson Turner charged its line with tremendous false significance by identifying it as a line between *civilization* and *savagery,* and thus converted it into an excuse for seizing more, and yet more, tribal territory.

But we must not get too far ahead of Franklin.

Notably, neither Franklin nor anyone else in London understood what had happened to bring about the Easton Treaty or the fall of Fort Duquesne. Notably also, Franklin had nothing to do with the campaign or its victorious conclusion. While the struggle for Indian alliance went on in Pennsylvania, Franklin struggled over the Assembly's issues in London. His faith in British political institutions suffered great strain. To Joseph Galloway, his lieutenant in the Assembly, he wrote that England "knows and feels itself so universally corrupt and rotten from Head to Foot, that it has little Confidence in any publick Men or publick Measures."[22] Bitter enmity to the feudal Penns kept that thought submerged until it erupted in unforeseen circumstances sixteen years later.

Because Benjamin Franklin was of his own age, without sympathy for Indians, he could not perceive that the royal crown betraying promises to Indians could just as easily betray colonial Englishmen. When the crown turned to overtly oppres- sive measures against *his* people, he reacted in much the same way as an Indian chief, but a mind caged in racial conceptions still prevented him from seeing the parallel.

15 ROYALIST

FRANKLIN WAS FAR FROM VICTORIOUS in London. He failed to win the Assembly's case against William Smith. He failed to get the Penns' Indian frauds brought to official light. His efforts regarding Assembly legislation were complicated by unanticipated Assembly victories which that rambunctious body pushed to extremes.

After Governor Denny had obeyed Lord Loudoun to pass a money bill against Thomas Penn's orders (and Denny's bond), Denny had to think about the consequences. He seems to have concluded that he had signed his death warrant as Penn's appointee, so hanged for a lamb, hanged for a sheep. In effect he switched sides for what he could get from the Assembly. Joseph Galloway discovered this new amenability and poured on thousands of pounds of bribes to assuage Denny's pain. New legislation resulted, which Denny signed without struggle.[1]

There was triumph in Pennsylvania, but we must imagine Franklin's feelings when he suddenly was called on to perform miracles in London.

One of the new bills concerned the judiciary, canceling the appointment of judges during the lord Proprietary's pleasure and providing instead that they should serve during good behavior. The lords of trade and plantations found against this act the provisions of Pennsylvania's royal charter, which delegated "by the most express and positive Terms, a Right to the establishment of Courts of Judicature and to the nomination of Judges, under no limitation whatsoever."[2] Franklin's powers of persuasion were up against a wall when put up against the charter.

The Assembly had also attacked the very root of Proprietary power by an act innocently professing to be for recording warrants and surveys of land. The fact was that such documents were being very carefully recorded in the Penns' private Land Office, where a great many important transactions with political implications were kept secret. For the Assembly to record those documents in its own files, it had first to seize them from the Proprietary office, and did. The lords of trade saw merit in making records of real property public, but they objected to the Assembly's act because it also deprived the Proprietaries of the final right of conveying property by a patent. The Assembly had made the issuance of a warrant a legal right to the property. By no strange coincidence this would have brought the creation of property under the Assembly's own Land Office, with the effect of making the Penns' patent a rubber stamp. The crown disallowed.[3]

Though Franklin and the Assembly lost that battle, historians have much reason to be grateful for the fight over it because the Assembly had all the Penns' Land Office records copied before they were returned to secrecy, and most of the copies, dated until 1757, still survive with invaluable information. Some, with a card index, are now in Philadelphia City Archives; the rest are in the Commonwealth's Interior Department in Harrisburg.

Some lesser acts went by without much struggle. Franklin did win one when the lords of trade let him receive funds from the crown reimbursing the province for outlays "for the king's use." As Franklin was the Assembly's agent, this would be expendable at the Assembly's pleasure, and it was not negligible.[4]

Some lesser bills were disallowed or permitted to pass. They are not highly relevant to present concerns. The main battle was fought over the acts to raise and spend money. Thomas Penn's lawyers were the best that could be had; for such purposes he spent money freely. They were good at their trade, and they gave Franklin a very hard time, so much so that he salvaged only a small fragment of principle from the debacle. Franklin had argued that the economy of Pennsylvania would be gravely damaged if the crown disallowed the taxation of the Proprietaries contained in the act to print £100,000. Chief Justice William Murray, Earl of Mansfield, responded favorably to that point. He summoned Franklin and Penn's lawyers to his chambers where an agreement was made. The basic issue was equitability; the Penns were worried that hostile assemblies might tax them punitively. Suppose they were guaranteed fairness? Not wanting to appear obstructive before this highest tribunal, the Penns'

lawyers conceded the point, and it was agreed all around that
the £100,000 act could pass under certain conditions: if located
unimproved town lots were assessed at the lowest rate levied on
other lands; if waste lands were not taxed; if the Penns had a
right within the province to appeal assessments; if their governor had some right in disbursements of funds; and if quitrents
were not depreciated.[5] With these stipulations, the act was
passed by the crown though other money bills were disallowed.

The amount of money to be raised by such taxation was
small, as the Penns noted with satisfaction. Speaker Norris, who
had stressed to Franklin that disallowance of the £100,000 act
would be a "calamity" for the province, was sure that "we have
been contending for a matter of Right rather than Mony."[6] And
the stipulations Franklin had agreed to were capable, as passed
by the crown, of some latitude of interpretation that Franklin
and lawyer Galloway explored at the next opportunity.[7]

Apart from the mentioned slight gains by Franklin, Thomas
Penn had won, hands down, to Franklin's great discomfiture.
Despite his social acceptance by men of intellect and place, he
missed the popular adoration of Pennsylvanians, and he was not
sorry to return to it in August 1762.[8] "I grow weary of so
long a Banishment, and anxiously desire once more the happy
Society of my Friends and Family in Philadelphia," he wrote to
Galloway already early in 1760, but he was obliged to wait
until the Treasury should pay him the reimbursement owed
to Pennsylvania for its support of the king's forces,[9] and the
Treasury dawdled.

One might think that rejection by the crown would have
soured Franklin on royal government, but not so. He attributed
his and the province's setbacks to the malign power and influence of Thomas Penn. As early as April 1759, he confided to
Galloway, "I am tired of Proprietary Government, and heartily
wish for that of the crown."[10] His desire was strengthened by
the royal favor conferred upon his son William, who was his
boon companion during his travels in England and Scotland.
William saw his father honored with an honorary degree by the
University at St. Andrews, and William's studies at the Inns of
Court qualified him as a barrister. The young man's career rose
to climax with his appointment in 1762 as Governor of New

Jersey by George III. That William's birth had been illegitimate was known and disregarded. By his royal appointment his social status was guaranteed. As Sheila L. Skemp remarks, the Franklins, father and son, "in 1762 . . . believed that English prejudices were the result of ignorance, not ill will, and they had supreme confidence in their own abilities to educate good-hearted but misinformed leaders from across the sea. Benjamin, as a leader of the Pennsylvania assembly, and William, as the royal governor of New Jersey, would continue to work together in their efforts to secure and enhance the strength of the empire and the prosperity of America."[11]

Only a calculation of what might be politically feasible restrained Benjamin from immediately launching a campaign to make Pennsylvania a royal province. Then trouble with Indians arose again.

When Benjamin Franklin had petitioned in London for an official inquiry into Thomas Penn's Walking Purchase of Delaware Indian lands, the crown referred the matter to Sir William Johnson, the royal Superintendent of Indian Affairs. Thomas Penn immediately instructed Richard Peters to offer a bribe to Johnson, but the latter man made Penn nervous by avoiding commitment. Penn's mind might have been easier had he known of Johnson's personal agenda, which always centered on preserving his *exclusive* right to handle Indian negotiations. Johnson had become as anti-Quaker as Penn because of the Friendly Association's strong espousal of Chief Teedyuscung's cause. No bribe was needed to provoke Johnson to suppress the Quakers by depriving them of their cause.[12]

He held a hearing at Easton in 1762 at which he arbitrarily denied Teedyuscung a clerk (with consequences in the record) and forbade formal intercession by the Friends who were present. At a critical point, Johnson declared a recess and conferred with Teedyuscung "in the bushes" out of sight and earshot. When formalities reopened, Teedyuscung withdrew his charge of fraud, and Johnson promised him a generous "gift" from Thomas Penn. Thus old Nutimus and other Delaware landlords got masked compensation and Penn's "honor" was saved.[13] A rejoicing Penn wrote gratitude to Johnson and promised to be his friend at court. They became political partners.[14] In practical terms, the Indians got as much compensation as Franklin had been willing for the Assembly to pay in 1756, but Thomas Penn was obliged to disgorge in 1762.

However, what Johnson arranged was noticed by Indians who understood very well what had happened at the Walking Purchase, regardless of what information was transmitted to the crown. They knew also that that event had been only one of a series of cheats and seizures that had caused most of the Delawares to migrate to the Ohio country. Johnson could vindicate Penn to the crown, but he rubbed salt in the Delawares' old wounds.[15]

While Johnson whitewashed Penn in June 1762, Franklin at last wound up his affairs in London, returning to Philadelphia in September.[16] Weary though he was from manifold frustrations, a new crisis left him little time for rest as the Indian troubles arose once more.

During Franklin's absence abroad, Israel Pemberton and the Friendly Association had espoused reconciliation with hostile Indians while Franklin was insulated from the day-to-day struggles on that issue. But when Sir William Johnson absolved Thomas Penn, the Friendly Association lost its issue even as Franklin had run up against a wall in London. Lord Penn's power was unscathed.

Despite nasty slurs against Quakers in histories marked more by bigotry than research, the Friends had been right, and what Johnson did to squelch them added still another grievance to a new accumulation in Indian country.

Peace had been attained at Easton in 1758 by incessant efforts of the Friendly Association under the sponsorship of Brigadier Forbes, but a faultline lay between Forbes's motives and the Friends'. Great strains pressed upon it. At Fort Pitt, built upon the ruins of Fort Duquesne, Forbes's successors meant only to hang onto the territory commanded by it, whereas the Delawares thought they had been guaranteed a boundary line between Indians and Europeans and that the Indians' territory included the Ohio country dominated by Fort Pitt. Crown bureaucrats were well aware of the boundary line guarantee, but not overly inclined to bother themselves about promises to Indians. As disillusion set in upon the Delawares, they joined equally disillusioned Senecas to mobilize a widespread confederacy to

expel the British. (The Senecas had hoped to get back Fort
Niagara, commanding passage between Lake Ontario and Lake
Erie, but British conquest of Niagara, like conquest of Fort
Duquesne, only substituted a British garrison for the French.)
Senecas, Delawares, and many other tribes erupted in a liberation war that began at Detroit so that the war was named after
the local Ottawa chief, Pontiac (and was turned by Francis Parkman's morbidly irresponsible imagination into "Pontiac's Conspiracy").[17]

Just as during the Seven Years War, the new war could not
be contained. The Indians aimed to eject British soldiery and
roll settlers back east of the Appalachians. Fort Pitt (the former
Fort Duquesne) was the Delawares' main target. They besieged
it and cut off supplies. From headquarters in New-York, General Jeffrey Amherst raged against the savages, suggesting that
they be infected with smallpox. He was a little behindhand with
that advice; the idea had already occurred to the garrison. (One
must wonder how prevalent the practice was.)

Commander Simeon Ecuyer called in chiefs Shingas and
Turtle Heart for a parley and at parting presented them with
blankets and handkerchiefs. These were very special blankets
that had been used in the fort's smallpox hospital. "I hope it will
have the desired effect," wrote Captain William Trent, who
provided the blankets, and so it did. Shingas and his brother
Pisquetomen, who had been prominent in political affairs, never
appeared again, and an epidemic spread among the Delawares.
It is not known to have distinguished noncombatants from warriors. If Indian raiders who wiped out whole families deserved
to be called savages, what should Amherst, Ecuyer, and Trent
be called? In terms of pragmatism, their method "worked": the
siege was lifted.[18]

Warriors ranged far and wide to terrorize the settlers who
had intruded into Indian country, and their victims were generally of a type—Scotch-Irish Presbyterians who were penniless
and therefore had squatted on lands beyond the reach of
Thomas Penn's enforcers of law and property rights. Quite naturally, the more easterly Scotch-Irish brethren of the victims
became infuriated. They had been told by Provost Smith in his
Brief State and *Brief View* that they suffered because of Quaker
power and Quaker policies, and in an age when all political

organization formed around churches, Presbyterians nurtured murderous feelings toward both Indian harriers and the supposed Quaker sponsors and encouragers of those Indians.

The concept of tolerance was alien to the Scotch-Irish. They came from a corner of Ireland where they were constantly exposed to the violence of the "mere Irish," and they were ready to trade blow for blow. For them the "natives" of Pennsylvania fitted easily into their pre-formed attitudes toward the "natives" of Ireland.

Surreptitiously, Anglican Smith had planted the notion of lynch law in 1756 in his *Brief View*. Commenting on the need to oust Quakers from the Assembly, he suggested: "There was another way of getting rid of them, by cutting their Throats; which Expedient a great many sanguine People of the back Counties had resolved upon, and would certainly have executed, if Great Pains had not been taken to prevent it."[19] (A real sweetheart, that Smith.) With incitement like that, the antagonisms normal between different religions heated up almost to holy war.

Two communities of Indians had chosen to live among the colonials: the Delawares converted by Moravians, and the few remnants of Conestogas, etc., whose towns formerly had stood on the banks of the lower Susquehanna River. Angry menaces from Scotch-Irish colonials in the vicinity of Allentown caused the Moravian converts to be withdrawn to Philadelphia for protection. (They were quartered in the "pest houses" on Province Island in the Delaware River. Was it some grim humorist's idea of a joke? Many succumbed, and threats followed them even there.)[20]

A Scotch-Irish lynch mob of armed horsemen descended from Paxton on the Susquehanna to murder seven helpless Indians in the workhouse at Lancaster. When it was learned that survivors had been out in the town and thus escaped the mob, a second raid butchered them. One of them had a copy of the friendship treaty signed by William Penn in 1701.

A friend has taken me to task for identifying the lynchers as Presbyterians; but this was well understood at the time and confirmed by their leaders' admissions much later, though the most cited study of the affair smudges their identity under the general term "frontiersmen."[21] They were a particular group

of Presbyterian frontiersmen, as Brooke Hindle acknowledges
further on. They were, in short, an unrepresentative gang
performing acts of violence and plunder under sanction of
professed religion—a common historical phenomenon still
observable today. Franklin's denunciation of the Paxton Boys
distinguished them from others of their church as was demonstrated when Presbyterians generally welcomed him as their
leader against Britain in 1775. (See chapter 18 below.)

Given opportunity, these "heroic" Paxton Boys brutalized
neighbors other than Indians. They moved in a body to the
Wyoming Valley of the North (or East) Branch of the Susque-
hanna River where they joined forces with violent settlers from
Connecticut to drive away persons loyal to Pennsylvania and
thus seize their lands. The victims complained to Pennsylvania's
Assembly that the lynchers "had robbed them of their Horses,
Cattle, and other Effects, burnt their Houses, destroyed their
Grain, and abused their Persons." The Assembly, which in-
cluded other Presbyterians, granted £60 for relief.[22]

But Brooke Hindle made their lynching "democratic." He
remarked, "The next severe shock of revolution was able to use
lines already drawn and cracks already made. The march of the
Paxton Boys paved the way for internal revolution."[23]

One must distinguish between two purposes. Overtly, the
Paxton Boys proclaimed their desire to kill Indians, and denounced even the Moravian Delawares as covert enemies. (They
were pacifists and some of them had been killed for that reason
by other, pagan Indians.) When the Paxton Boys organized a
march upon Philadelphia to go through the city to massacre
the converted Delawares, Franklin and the Quakers (united for
once) sensed an ulterior motive to overthrow the government
on the claim that westerners were inadequately represented in
the Assembly. And when about 250 armed men actually rode
into Germantown on their way downstream into the city, there
was uproar. (Learning that the raiders were expected about
11:00 A.M. on Sunday morning, Presbyterian churches can-
celed services.)[24]

New Governor John Penn summoned the people and recruited a defense Association that included six companies of
foot, two of horse, and a battery of artillery from royal troops
in the city, nearly a thousand men in all. Very evidently, Penn

worried at this stage of proceedings that the Paxton Boys wanted to overthrow all government, not only the Assembly. At midnight, Penn rushed to Franklin's house to offer command of the defenders. Franklin rejected command in order to "carry a musket and strengthen his [Penn's] Authority by setting an Example of Obedience to his Orders."[25]

A delegation representing various constituencies, but no Presbyterians, went out to meet the marchers, who allowed themselves to be persuaded by words and cannon to withdraw. A couple were allowed to present grievances to the Assembly, including Matthew Smith, the leader of the lynchers (though not then identified as such). They were heard, sent home, and disregarded.[26]

The Assembly asked Governor Penn to summon Lancaster officials for questioning about the massacres, but Penn wailed that no one would give names of the lynchers, and he took pains to make sure that no one did. He protected his officials from cross questioning by assemblymen by merely requesting magistrates to send depositions.[27]

Grave justifiable suspicions arose that the riots had been incited secretly by men hating Indians, Quakers, and the Assembly—a description that fits William Smith like a glove. Suspicion was not lessened by Penn's total lack of further interest in the affair, and it was well understood that the magistrates whom he protected from rude questioning were Proprietary appointees holding office *during his pleasure*. We know now that they did indeed have information, but it pleased Penn to avoid pressing them for it.[28]

The instigators of the Paxton Boys, together with their political objectives, have never been thoroughly researched. Instead, a variety of attempts at vindication of the Paxtonites has multiplied over the years, starting with Thomas Barton in 1764[29] and continuing in modern times through Brooke Hindle to Melvin H. Buxbaum, in whose learnedly confused book Franklin was guilty of writing to make his readers "able to identify with them [the Indians] as human beings not essentially different from Englishmen."[30] How villainous!

I make no pretense of being loftily "objective" by indifference to these issues. I sicken when I have to wade through the outpourings of gentlemen who pride themselves on scholarship in which Indian lives and concerns are inherently inferior to those of Europe's descendants of any religion. Such stuff deserves contempt rather than respect. At the very least, it is bad history.

Apart from its political implications, the Conestoga event reached Franklin's conscience with a lesson about racism. "If an Indian injures me," he wrote, "does it follow that I may revenge that injury on all Indians?" The question echoes loudly still. Franklin's sympathy for Indians as such had strong limits, but the lynching broadened his awareness of the kinds of behavior sanctioned between different peoples. "The only Crime of these poor Wretches seems to have been, that they had a reddish brown Skin, and black Hair; and some People of that Sort, it seems, had murdered some of our Relations. If it be right to kill Men for such a Reason, then, should any Man with a freckled Face and red Hair, kill a Wife or Child of mine, it would be right for me to revenge it, by killing all the freckled red-haired Men, Women and Children, I could afterwards anywhere meet with."[31] Even in the heat of strong emotion, Franklin could generalize powerfully from a simple example.

Anglo-American law is very clear that crime is *personal,* not familial, clannish, or ethnic. Conestoga taught Franklin that racism is reversion to the barbarism that preceded law.

But Franklin also became certain that the Paxtonites were attacking *him* and his Assembly by way of diatribes against Indians and Quakers.[32] I think he was right, but the lack of research on this issue leaves a great hole in the behaviors of William Smith and his gang, not to speak of Governor John Penn.

Among other things, Brooke Hindle showed absolute ignorance by his offhand diktat that Franklin's *Narrative of the Late Massacres* pamphlet against the Paxtonites defeated him in the upcoming elections. Hindle did not even examine the defection of Germans from Franklin's party for reasons wholly distinct from the Paxton affair. (See chapter 16 below.)

And Hindle was merely bigoted asinine in his assertion that "the Quaker party" tried to get a royal government. As we shall see, what was left of Quaker political organization opposed and ultimately defeated Franklin's campaign to jettison the feudal propriety of Pennsylvania in favor of direct royal government.[33]

In the midst of the Paxtonite uproars, the Assembly was

once again locked in struggle with the governor over familiar
issues that Thomas Penn hung onto with bulldog tenacity. Taxation of the Penns' estates, creation of a new militia, and control
of its officers were as rigidly fought by John Penn as formerly
they had been by Robert Hunter Morris, and once more the
Proprietaries used Indian hostilities as pretext for their demands. The Paxton Boys had been so befuddled by whoever
aroused them that they could not comprehend how the Assembly—which was run by Franklin's Anglican machine and disowned "defense" Quakers rather than orthodox Quakers—
protected all Pennsylvanians from the Penns' power grab. Israel
Pemberton's following had become practically irrelevant to political action.

Franklin had had more than enough of Governor John
Penn: "all Regard for him in the Assembly is lost; all hopes of
Happiness under a Proprietary Government are at an End; it
has now scarce Authority enough left to keep the common
Peace. . . . In fine, every thing seems in this Country, once the
Land of Peace and Order, to be running fast into Anarchy and
Confusion. Our only Hopes are, that the Crown will see the
Necessity of taking the Government into its own Hands, with-
out which we shall soon have no Government at all."[34]

It must be realized that the man who wrote that was quite
sincere about wanting a government with authority (but as distinguished from one with power to dictate without restraints).
At this time, Franklin had absolutely no sympathy with radical
agitators such as he would later show for Tom Paine. When the
British House of Commons expelled John Wilkes for printing
"a false, scandalous and seditious libel," Franklin approved.[35]
(Connecticut men settling on the Susquehanna's North Branch
were to honor John Wilkes and Isaac Barré by naming their
town Wilkes-Barré, but royalist Franklin was a long way from
their outlook.)

Franklin did not believe in popular democracy because he
saw no virtue in people generally. The genial old fellow of his
Autobiography bears small resemblance to the sour apple of 1764.
To Dr. John Fothergill in London he wrote in a light tone that
had more sincerity than humor: "Do you please yourself with
the Fancy that you are doing Good? You are mistaken. Half the
Lives you save are not worth saving, as being useless; and almost

the other Half ought not to be sav'd as being mischievous. Does your Conscience never hint to you the Impiety of being in constant Warfare against the Plans of Providence? Disease was intended as the Punishment of Intemperance, Sloth, and other Vices; and the Example of that Punishment was intended to promote and strengthen the Opposite Virtues."[36]

But Franklin did believe that virtue abided among some people, as he expounded in his *Narrative of the Late Massacres.* . . . He stressed the sacred "Rites of Hospitality" with examples from the Old Testament and even from Black Africa. And he ended his passionate pamphlet with praise for military discipline. With a last condemnation of *Cowards* who "can strike where they are sure to meet with no Return, can wound, mangle and murder," he praised the alternative: "it belongs to *brave* Men to spare, and to protect."[37]

In his angry, no longer complacent frame of mind, he seems to have decided that such virtue as could be found among the people could not flourish without protection by strong government. Characteristically he began to campaign for the strongest available, the crown of Great Britain.

16 REBOUND

THE PAXTON BOYS had no sooner gone home than the same old struggles resumed between the Assembly and Governor John Penn. Assemblymen passed a money bill to raise £55,000; Penn vetoed because of its "inequitable" taxation of Proprietary lands, but assemblymen thought their formula was fair. They voted for a new militia; Penn vetoed because the bill withheld from him the appointing of all the officers. Franklin was convinced that less important vetoes arose from simple desire by Penn "to charge them with Disloyalty."

To make matters worse, as he complained to agent Richard Jackson in London, "a bitter Enmity has arisen between the Presbyterians and Quakers" (small wonder after the Paxton Presbyterians had threatened to kill all Quakers). "Abusive Pamphlets are every Day coming out on both sides, and I think there is some Danger of Mischief between them."[1]

Franklin was curiously willing to be evenhanded about the religious contentions, but it was intolerable for him and Galloway to let Governor Penn asperse the Assembly as he was doing with "Proprietary Misrepresentations and Calumnies."[2] They brought up a set of twenty-six resolutions that were passed by the Assembly unanimously, culminating in a decision to adjourn temporarily "in order to consult their Constituents, whether an humble Address should be drawn up, and transmitted to His Majesty, praying that he would be graciously pleased to take the People of this Province under His immediate Protection and Government."[3]

To gain popular support for their radical new policy, Franklin and Galloway issued special pamphlets. Franklin's was *Cool Thoughts on the Present Situation of Public Affairs;* Galloway's, written to respond to an opposition attack, was *An Address to the Freeholders and Inhabitants of the Province of Pennsylvania.* The basic issue became crystal clear by the Assembly's circulating a petition for royal government.

For once in his career, Franklin had misjudged the political winds because the constituents of the unanimous assemblymen were much otherwise than unanimous. Presbyterian leader George Bryan cautioned that "all dissenting from the Church of England would do well to consider how far their privileges would be likely to be impaired," and the Presbyterian ministers and elders of Philadelphia circularized churches outside the city to support opposition to evil-minded persons encroaching on "our *essential* and *charter* privileges."[4] Strangely, Presbyterians and the hated Quakers united on the same grounds of devotion to William Penn's charter. Neither wanted to see a royal province in which the Church of England was established.

The Quakers split more sharply than on any previous issue. Speaker Isaac Norris, who had backed Franklin all through the defense issues, resigned his post, and Joseph Richardson joined him in opposition. (Franklin became Speaker.) The opposition's newly prominent leader, John Dickinson (questionably identified as a Quaker by H. W. Smith), went head-to-head against Galloway in speaking and physical scuffle. He even challenged Galloway to a duel (not fought).

Pietist Germans worried also. Schwenkfelder Christopher Schultze fretted to "Beloved Friend Israel Pemberton" with a plea "to use all possible means to prevent the Destruction and depriving of religious Liberty in any respect" because "we hear that such a misunderstanding breaks out in our Legislature as [to] threaten a Revolution in our Constitution that our Charter should be delivered up in the King's hands," in which case he feared being deprived "of the First Article of the Freedom of Conscience"; and if his people were to "be subjected to Episcopal Jurisdiction and Military Actions it would be very hard and striking to the Heart."[5]

In the very dirty election campaign, Proprietary supporters hurled epithet and invective without restraint while Franklin and Galloway mistakenly assumed that their known records of accomplishment permitted them to discuss issues as statesmen above the storm. Franklin had so long been the people's darling that he forgot how vulnerable he was on several counts. Opponents charged him with wanting to be an all-powerful royal governor, and they pointed to William Franklin's post as Governor of New Jersey. While on the subject of William the attackers

stressed his illegitimate birth and charged Franklin with womanizing still (which probably was true). They smeared his careful attention to acquiring riches, for which they had some
foundation in fact. True enough, Franklin could have gained
much more wealth by soliciting Thomas Penn's patronage (and
acting accordingly), but his service for the Assembly in England, 1757–63, had been well recompensed by £3,000 plus
expenses, and the expenses had been carefully recorded and
claimed.[6] In contrast, his Quaker opponent Israel Pemberton
got nothing from public funds and spent largely on public activities from his private wealth.

In short, Franklin, the master of public relations, was out-
generaled by the strategists of John Dickinson's New Ticket
campaigning against his Old Ticket.

For practical effect, however, the impact of the publicity
campaigns was far less powerful than a land mine sprung by
William Smith. Smith resurrected Franklin's sneer at the Germans in his manuscript sent to London in 1753. At that time
Franklin's correspondent Richard Jackson gave Smith a copy of
the manuscript, and when Smith and Franklin became enemies,
Smith published the paper in his *American Magazine* in July
1758.[7] It was easy for him to draw attention quietly to it in 1764,
with devastating effect. Franklin mourned that it cost him a
thousand German votes. From being the province's champion
vote getter, he plunged to defeat in thirteenth place on a list of
fourteen Old Ticket candidates, dragging Galloway down to
defeat as well.[8]

Students have overlooked Smith's role in this, usually commenting that some unidentified Proprietary partisan had discovered the damaging manuscript.[9] For once, Smith laid no claim
to the victory. His former public association with Franklin in
the German charity schools project would have splashed the
new mud back upon himself. His satisfaction came from engi-
neering the greatest Proprietary coup in the Assembly to date
(or ever).

German motivations and roles were simple and rational.
They revenged themselves against Franklin's insults, but even
in their anger they made careful distinctions and sent one Old
Ticket member back from the German constituency in Lancas-

ter County. All the Proprietary party's gains were not enough to make a majority of Assembly seats.[10]

Quakers topped the vote in Philadelphia County. Proprietary men had hoped to split the Quakers permanently by putting Isaac Norris and Joseph Richardson on their New Ticket, and Franklin's Old Ticket retained them, so that they ran unopposed and piled up more votes than any other candidates; and in the new, revised Assembly, Norris became Speaker again. John Dickinson came in third. Nevertheless, the Old Ticket still commanded a majority because of its victories in outlying counties, so Franklin and Galloway could still determine basic policy. They conceived the election as an aberration unrepresentative of Pennsylvanians' true attitudes when voters should come to understand the Proprietaries' wicked history. Determined to punish Thomas Penn and make the province royal, Franklin contrived after the election to have the Assembly send him to England once more. When he took ship this time, the situation was very different from his journey in 1757. Then he had been the idol of his people; now, despite the festive sendoff arranged by his party, his support was far from universal. Nevertheless, he was still acclaimed as the province's most celebrated citizen, and he had many good friends to return to in England, where he arrived in December 1764. He was more strongly royalist than ever.[11]

While provincials struggled over provincial issues, crown bureaucrats attended to imperial issues. It is hugely ironic that they adopted Israel Pemberton's policy (with adjustments) to pacify the belligerent Indians by promising them a boundary between advancing colonial settlers and tribal territories. The result was the Royal Proclamation of 1763 which established many new colonial boundaries, being motivated in part by the royal desire to keep settlers east of the Appalachians where they could be controlled. The Proclamation was an act of high prerogative that curtailed a number of colonial chartered territories and aroused much hostility at just the historical moment when Franklin had become most strenuously partisan for the crown.[12] Precisely as the Proclamation mollified Indians trying to keep their land, it antagonized colonists trying to seize that land.

Because of its charter's definite provisions, Pennsylvania escaped the Proclamation's boundary revisions, but colonies with territories vaguely granted from the Atlantic to the Pacific— most notably Virginia—were up in arms. Among others, George Washington could no longer dispose of lands acquired near Pittsburgh during the Seven Years War. He consoled himself with the thought that a proclamation was not an act of Parliament; with sufficient pressure it could be nullified by another royal edict. When Sir William Johnson extended the royal promise of a boundary to the Indians, they did make peace without recognizing the "catch" in the promise; to wit, that the lands they understood to be recognized as *tribal* territories were identified on maps as *crown* lands reserved to Indians as hunting territories, and tacitly subject to being taken off reserve whenever the crown should decide. Johnson's treaties got Indian signatures accepting a surveyed boundary, though the signers had misgivings about how far west he pushed that line.

So far, the crown's bureaucrats had succeeded by political means in what the military had failed to accomplish by armed force. But this political victory had a heavy price in the violent reactions from colonial expansionists who were thereby frustrated in their schemes for speculation in western lands. The thrusting, encroaching squatters paid little attention to royal policy, and royal force was inadequate to discipline them.

In a sense, all these developments favored Franklin's mission after 1764. Crown ministers could feel only gratitude toward a prominent colonial glorifying royal government. Though Franklin had lost much support in his province, he was warmly welcomed at the empire's center.

Yet Franklin's mission was doomed from its first day because he regarded royal government as a means rather than an end, and there was an essential contradiction between his set purpose and the royalists' set convictions. Franklin's goal of eliminating Proprietary government in Pennsylvania conflicted directly with the crown's assumption of royal right to exercise patronage through a privileged class of nobles or gentry.

To use a modern term, Franklin was bent on ending "feudalism" in America, and there were many institutions of feudal privilege very much alive in Britain and its government. Franklin did not use feudal terminology. As Marc Bloch has revealed, such language was French in origin and only beginning to acquire acceptance in France in mid-eighteenth century.[13] Franklin identified his feudal target by calling it "proprietary government." He did not mean only Pennsylvania. The people of Maryland, he wrote, "agitated by the same Contentions between Proprietary Interest and Power, and Popular Liberty . . . are rendered equally unhappy with our selves." Indeed, disputes like Pennsylvania's had arisen "in ALL Proprietary Governments, and subsisted till their Dissolution."[14]

Even founder William Penn had contended with his original settlers, continuing "with some Intermissions, during his whole Life," and had been succeeded in similar disputes by his widow and sons.[15]

Seeking to get at fundamental causes, Franklin saw "no Reason to suppose that all Proprietary Rulers are worse Men than other Rulers, nor that all People in Proprietary Governments are worse People than those in other Governments. I suspect, therefore, that the Cause is radical, interwoven in the Constitution, and so become of the very Nature, of Proprietary Governments; and will therefore produce its Effects as long as such Governments continue."[16]

All this was written in Franklin's major campaign document in the election of 1764, which he lost by the defection of German supporters. Few elections have ever been marked by so high a level of analysis; in this, as in so many other matters, Franklin's thinking was far ahead of his contemporaries'. Because it was deeply felt philosophy rather than mere "campaign oratory," the election loss did not swerve him from determination for fundamental change. He resolved to end the Penns' lordship as his primary political goal. "British Spirits can no longer bear the Treatment they have received, nor will they put on the Chains prepared for them by a Fellow Subject. And the Irish and Germans have felt too severely the Oppressions of *hard-hearted Landlords* and *Arbitrary Princes,* to wish to see, in the Proprietaries of Pennsylvania, both the one and the other united."[17] When he took ship for England in November 1764, his goal was clear, and he still controlled the Assembly with his teammate Galloway.

Behind his desire to change the form of Pennsylvania's government lay Franklin's strong desire to do away with the *oppression* (his own term) of feudal rule. He was to find, however, that his faith in royalty had been naively idealistic. Relief from oppression was not high on the agendas of Britain's crown or of its ruling class.

17 SPOKESMAN

THIS BOOK HAS NOW essentially completed the task it undertook at the beginning, but there is still one serious question before it. We have seen the young craftsman and shrewd entrepreneur, the opportunist who cultivated patronage from whoever could give it: some from Assembly Quakers, more from the placemen of his lord Proprietary. We have seen his hot indignation at pacifists who resisted arming the province for defense, and his subsequent utter outrage when he learned how lord Penn prevented those pacifists from financing "the king's use" unless they first would accept the lord's yoke. We have seen how a hot sense of injustice aroused Franklin to become his lord's bitterest enemy and to reach out to the crown to take his beloved province under direct royal protection. What has not yet been seen is how this loyal king's man turned into a Revolutionary hero. Something more needs to be seen and said.

The change was gradual and slow; ten years elapsed this time before the royalist arriving in London departed in disillusion and anger. Most of that period of Franklin's life has been well examined, and I have little to add to competent descriptions long in print. For the sake of winding up loose ends, however, we may briefly note some episodes of major importance to mark transitions in Franklin's conceptions and attitudes.

The stamp tax made the first strain on his devotion. Enacted shortly after his arrival, it was passed despite the opposition expressed by all the colonies' agents, including Franklin, who suggested an alternative way to raise money by issuing interest-bearing paper money as the Pennsylvania Assembly had done. The ministers did not believe that his device would produce enough income for an empire struggling with the load of debt from the Seven Years War. The Stamp Act was passed, and the anticipated demonstrations of opposition occurred.[1]

At this stage of his life, Franklin's political instincts seem to have been blurred by idolatry of royalty. He had lost the Assembly election badly, and now he assumed that the stamp tax resistance would blow over after a little sound and fury. It was the same assumption as the ministry's. Franklin even accepted patronage to ease the pain of being overridden. He was granted the privilege of naming the stamp tax collectors in Pennsylvania, which would be a juicy plum for them and a substantial addition to Franklin's patronage system. He accepted this new offer and named John Hughes, his close follower in the Assembly, to be chief of the twenty-five collectors. Hughes delightedly grasped at this means to make himself rich on the commissions for stamp distribution.[2]

Proprietary partisans were equally delighted for different reasons. They sensed better than Franklin the grass-roots hostility to the tax. Colonists added to it with pamphlets and demonstrations. They would have rioted too if not for Joseph Galloway's firm suppression of agitation for that sort of violence. Indeed, Galloway saved Franklin from the consequences of his immersion in the rosy haze of majesty. During Franklin's absence abroad, Galloway matured as a tough political boss. Against threats to tear down houses, Galloway mounted guards from the "White Oaks" burly artisan supporters of his party. It seems likely that they had been recruited from Franklin's militia. They were quite sturdy enough to withstand attack from the agitated young gentlemen of Proprietary supporters, as the latter were well aware. Violence ceased.[3]

On the campaign front, Galloway corrected the mistakes of 1764. Instead of relying on reasoned argument, he organized an election machine that delivered to the polls every possible supporter, and he swamped the Proprietary candidates. Even their leader John Dickinson lost the election of 1765 and the next one in 1766. Proprietary defeat was so complete that Penn's men lost all political credibility, and their party dwindled into insignificance. Thenceforth, Galloway had undisputed control of the Assembly, and Franklin's back was protected. After the disintegration of the old Quaker and Proprietary parties, Franklin's reigned supreme.[4]

(Excuses are regularly offered that the Assembly was run by easterners because of disproportionate representation that doomed the westerners to lose every protest. This assumes that members from Lancaster, Cumberland, and Carlisle counties resented leadership from Philadelphians. One must read more than one set of statistics and one side's propaganda. Even in the 1764 election, members chosen from the western counties saved the majority of Franklin and Galloway's Old Ticket, despite the opposition New Ticket's gains in Philadelphia. Militarist Franklin of the 1747 Association and subsequent militias was at least as popular among the backwoodsmen as among urbanites.)[5]

In 1765, Galloway campaigned on a law and order program that appealed to sober citizens frightened by the uproars of the Proprietary men. It did no harm to Franklin in London that Pennsylvania confined its stamp tax opposition to dignified and orderly means of expression. Nor did it hurt Benjamin that his son William, as Governor of New Jersey, squelched opposition there. Royal ministers took note. When opposition elsewhere did not die down, and resistance to the stamp tax became so widespread and intense that effective administration seemed unfeasible, the ministers decided to repeal it. Whereupon they gave Benjamin a forum to declaim against the tax so that the colonial public would infer he had effected the repeal by his eloquence.[6] In 1765 Benjamin Franklin was as popular in London as he had been in Philadelphia.

But not so powerful. That Franklin's influence was mostly cosmetic shows very clearly in Parliament's Declaratory Act that accompanied repeal of the stamp tax. *What* was declared contradicted Franklin's most fundamental political belief, without reservation or equivocation. Here it is, as presented in Henry Steele Commager's *Documents of American History:*

WHEREAS *several of the houses of representatives in his Majesty's colonies and plantations in America, have of late, against law, claimed to themselves, or to the general assemblies of the same, the sole and exclusive right of imposing duties and taxes upon his Majesty's subjects in the said colonies and plantations; and have, in pursuance of such claim, passed certain votes, resolutions, and orders, derogatory to the legislative authority of parliament, and inconsistent with the dependency of the said colonies and plantations upon the crown of* Great Britain: . . . be it declared . . . that the said colonies and plantations in *America* have been, are, and of right ought to be, subordinate unto, and dependent upon the imperial crown and parliament of *Great Britain;* and that the King's majesty, by and with the advice and consent of the lords spiritual and temporal, and commons of *Great Britain,* in parliament assembled, had, hath, and of right ought to have, full power and authority to make laws and statutes of sufficient force and validity to bind the colonies and people of *America,* subjects of the crown of *Great Britain,* in all cases whatsoever.[7]

The words were plain, but the rosy haze of majesty still hung over Franklin. He simply could not believe that Parliament meant what it said. To Joseph Fox, the new Speaker of the Pennsylvania Assembly, Franklin advised keeping cool. "This is merely to save Appearances," he wrote, "and to guard against the Effects of the Clamour made by the late Ministry as if the Rights of this Nation were sacrificed to America. And I think we may rest secure notwithstanding such Act, that no future Ministry will ever attempt to tax us."[8] He could not have been more wrong.

Meantime the business for which he was in England suffered from official inattention. Franklin wanted to shuck off the Penns' lordship by having the crown buy their powers of government, a proposal for which precedent had been established by a never-consummated offer from William Penn early in the century. In the 1760s, circumstances were very different from those of William's time. If purchase were to be seriously contemplated, the price could only have become immense, and this while ministers were trying to raise money rather than spend it. Englishmen were already taxed to the screaming point to pay for the Seven Years War, and ministers were groping for ways to make Americans pay for the royal armies maintained among them. (Ostensibly those armies were to protect against Indians; in reality they were soon to occupy eastern cities to overawe riotous colonists.) Franklin had to wait.

Meantime, orthodox Quakers, worried about losing their chartered liberties, were still undercutting Franklin by trying to dicker with Thomas Penn for softening of his instructions to his governors. They got nowhere, but Franklin did not forgive.

Parliament wasted little time in proving Franklin wrong about its intentions to tax. Having passed the Declaratory Act in March 1766, Parliament passed the Townshend Revenue Act in June 1767. As this taxed goods imported by the colonies from Great Britain, it was rationalized as regulation of intra-imperial

commerce rather than direct taxation of the colonists. Franklin
considered that argument carefully, but he was beginning to
distrust Parliament, "it being difficult to draw lines between
duties for regulation and those for revenue." He thought that
"if the Parliament is to be the judge, it seems to me that establishing such principles of distinction will amount to little."

With that he tried to foresee the implications. "The more I
have thought and read on the subject the more I find myself
confirmed in opinion, that no middle doctrine can be well maintained, I mean not clearly with intelligible arguments. . . . Parliament has a power to make *all laws* for us, or . . . it has a power
to make *no laws* for us; and I think the arguments for the latter
more numerous and weighty than those for the former." He
played with the notion of a confederation of states governing
themselves under a common king (something like the domin-
ions of a later era). Rejection of Parliament's rule did not necessarily imply rejection of the crown's sovereignty. Franklin was
still under the spell of majesty though his faith was badly shaken
by Parliament's and the ministry's misbehavior.[9] His personal
goal is best described as colonial autonomy within the empire.

Parliament had quite different objectives. Townshend's law
provided not only for an income but also significantly for part
of its use. The ministers had finally realized that payment was
needed to guarantee their employees' obedience. Previously
they had dumped responsibility onto the colonists to pay for
their own government by agents of the crown. The consequences could have been predicted. Colonial assemblies required to pay governors used the power of the purse to make
governors cooperate more for the assemblies' desires than for
the crown's. Townshend proposed to remedy that fault by as-
suming to the ministry the payment of salaries for governors
and judges. The change baffled Joseph Galloway, who hardly
knew what to think. Perhaps the new law would aid the Assembly's desire to get rid of the Penns. "If Part [of Townshend Law
income] should be applied towards the Support of our Civil
Authority will not the Crown Name the Governor"—or, could
it be hoped?—"will it pay Men who are Named by its Subjects?"
Galloway knew how to get officials named by Pennsylvania's
subjects.

Cool thought worried this veteran politician: "I shoud

imagine . . . this Measure has been adopted to create a System of Influence in America dependant on the Crown . . . I confess I do not like the Scheme, and wish it had never been thought of" but "I see no probability of undoing it." Yet, "if the Governor and Judges are to be independant of the People, as they now really are, I think it will be infinitely better that they shoud also be independant of the Proprietors."[10]

Pennsylvania royalists Franklin and Galloway had an ax of their own to grind, so they had to keep on good terms with the ministers who would accept or reject their petition for change of government. Massachusetts was on a different footing. Townshend's law very deliberately struck at the common, almost institutional, practice of smuggling engaged in by Massachusetts merchants. It empowered customs agents to get writs of assistance from those newly crown-dependent judges "to search for and seize prohibited and uncustomed goods." It became legal for any customs officer in pursuit of his duty "to enter and go into any house, shop cellar, warehouse, or room or other place and, in case of resistance, to break open doors, chests, trunks, and other pakage there."[11] (Resentful memory of these writs of assistance would be preserved in Amendment IV of the Bill of Rights of the Constitution of the United States: "The right of the people to be secure in their persons, houses, papers, and effects, against unreasonable searches and seizures, shall not be violated. . . .")

Naturally, John Adams and the rebels in Massachusetts took the high ground of the rights of Englishmen rather than a more mundane protest against enforcement of laws against smuggling, but when the colonists finally decided to fight for independence the first name on their Declaration was that of John Hancock, the biggest smuggler of them all. Unlike the dedication of Pennsylvania's merchants to law and order, the mixed motives of Massachusetts's elite drove them to riot and rebellion.[12]

However his private thoughts might tend, Franklin had important material reasons to preserve amenities in his dealings with officials. As Deputy Postmaster General he drew a salary of £300 annually that depended on the crown's goodwill. When his long partnership with David Hall ended in 1766, Hall's annual payments of more than £600 expired with it and Franklin felt the pinch, the more so because calculations of accounts showed him owing Hall nearly £1,000. Shocked Franklin protested at that, and withheld settlement of the account. There is no record that he ever did pay Hall or Hall's heirs during his entire life.[13]

He was not desperately in need. The provincial Assembly paid £500 per year which, when added to his post office income, permitted living as a gentleman, but he clearly had been living high, Poor Richard notwithstanding. He could not afford to lose his royal post.

In 1769, an opportunity came his way to make a lot of money, to become really rich, but it also depended on royal favor. A Philadelphia Quaker named Samuel Wharton showed up in London with a scheme for a grant of millions of acres of western lands to a company of partners, and Franklin was included because of his supposed ability to wield influence. Wharton was a big dealer and a big spender. He entertained powerful men lavishly, and dressed as one of them. His Quaker background quickly vanished. As a wag commented, Wharton wore his sword as though he had been doing it all his life.[14]

The land grant scheme expanded until it included a number of noblemen and became a project for 20 million acres with a colony to be called Vandalia. Franklin helped as he could, but ministers were cooling to him as he resisted their policies to impose controls on the colonies. As Wharton realized that Vandalia moved along faster without Franklin than with him, the two Philadelphians saw less and less of each other, though Franklin maintained his share in the Grand Ohio Company organized by Wharton. They had to contend especially with obstructions from Lord Hillsborough, whose approval was necessary, and Hillsborough hated Franklin and colonists generally. (Vandalia died when news of the Boston Tea Party reached London.)[15]

The situation deteriorated as Franklin accepted invitations to act as agent for New Jersey (£100 per year), Georgia (£100 per year), and finally Massachusetts (£400 per year). The combined salaries neatly made up for the loss of his partnership with Hall, but the more he spoke up for one colony after another, the more he alienated ministers determined to reduce them all to proper subordination. For the ministry, Massachusetts was the last straw, and it was Franklin's undoing.

He could not have been unaware of the odor of brimstone wafting from Boston to London, and questions may be justified as to how fervently he believed in the "democratickal" nature of that colony. Certainly it did not follow the policies of law and order that he and Galloway pursued. But Franklin did believe firmly that a colony should have the right to govern itself, cooperating with the crown but not accepting royal dictation. That was not the ministers' belief. Besides, Franklin was not impervious to the lure of money, and Massachusetts's £400 salary carried weight. Perhaps he shared the general belief in his own ability to sway the ministers by reasoning with them. He was not modest about his powers of persuasion. I think more was involved than simply greed for money. Whatever his motives, he accepted the agency for Massachusetts.

Strictly speaking, he was appointed in October 1770 by only the House of Representatives—the lower house in Massachusetts's two-chamber legislature—and his acceptance was in itself an act of mild defiance against royal protocol that called for representation of the whole legislature. Lord Hillsborough quickly protested.[16] (The issue did not arise in Pennsylvania because its Assembly was unicameral.) Massachusetts was in a state of almost perpetual tumult as conservative pro-royalists complained of their mistreatment by radicals. Chief Justice Thomas Hutchinson wrote confidentially to Thomas Whately in England that "this is most certainly a crisis." Strong measures would be required to assure "the *dependance* which a colony ought to have upon the parent State." If nothing more were done "than some declaratory acts or resolves, *it is all over with us.*" Therefore, "There must be an abridgment of what are called English liberties."[17]

Provincial Secretary Andrew Oliver wrote to the same English correspondent, also in confidence. He was explicit that "the authority of government" could not be restored "while it's friends and the officers of the crown are left to an abject dependance on these very people who are *undermining it's authority.*"[18] Both men wrote in 1769 before Franklin became agent. Both were emphatic that the crown must itself pay its officers in order to make them independent of the popular branch of the legislature. Their letters slept in a London file as a sort of political time bomb that became all the more explosive when the Townshend Acts were only partially rescinded in March 1770. The acts' provisions for royal payment of royal officials remained in force, exactly as Hutchinson and Oliver had demanded, and there could be no doubt that the ministry intended this policy as just what Hutchinson had recommended—an abridgment of English liberties.[19]

Although Quakers complained of being snubbed by Franklin, he used his unique talents and status to gain influence in high places. In one direction, he improved his first official visit to England with scientific explorations and experiments that involved men with "philosophical" interests. One was Dr. John Pringle, erstwhile president of the Royal Society, who was physician to the queen during Franklin's first visit, and became King George's own physician later. Dr. Pringle happily accompanied Franklin on his travels exploring the country's "curiosities." Through Pringle, Benjamin pulled strings attached to first minister John Stuart, Earl Bute, and got an appointment for son William Franklin to the post of New Jersey's governor.

The *Franklin Papers* editors amused themselves by printing John Adams's prissy indignation over the "mortification of the pride, affront to the dignity and Insult to the Morals of America" constituted by this "Elevation to the Government of New Jersey of a base born Brat."[20]

On Benjamin's second visit to England, he cast a wider net, drawing in the friends of flamboyant Sir Francis Dashwood, Lord Ledespencer, a fantastically rich man, Chancellor of the Exchequer, and England's premier roué as well as premier baron. Bored with convention, Dashwood was also an intellectual and a connoisseur of art with the means to gratify grotesque whims. He delighted in Franklin's virtuosity and invited him for long visits to his country estate at West Wycombe. As early as July 1770, he discussed with Franklin a "Plan of Reconciliation" between crown and colonies. Franklin's astonished editors note wryly that Dashwood "was anything but a noted constitutional theorist."[21] Indeed, they seem to have had much difficulty preserving Franklin from the moral stench emanating from

Dashwood and his noble gang, who brought boatloads of prostitutes from London to his estate for orgies and black masses.[22] Despite Franklin's editors' embarrassment, it seems more than probable that he shared in this good, clean fun along with the noble rakes. Certainly he did not reprove the gentlemen for their wicked ways, and until official policy turned hostile to colonists, he was accepted as one of the boys. It must be said to Dashwood's credit that he defended Franklin to the very end when officialdom turned to persecution.[23]

Probably through one of Dashwood's chums, Franklin got his hands on the Hutchinson-Oliver letters. They had been passed around among some privileged gentlemen, and they were lent to Franklin on terms of honor requiring silence about the source, which may have been Dashwood himself. As chancellor he had access to such things, and he seems to have shared Franklin's belief that the letters would convince Massachusetts leaders that the ministry in England was more amenable to negotiation than those malicious letterwriters.

Carl Van Doren quotes Franklin to explain that this was another case of misjudgment. Franklin had hoped to turn Hutchinson and Oliver into scapegoats by making their wicked advice responsible for repressive measures that would have been avoided if the crown had been better informed. Thus, if his device had worked as he intended, the scapegoats could have been sacrificed while crown and colonists reconciled.[24] But the people of Massachusetts read crown policy more realistically than Franklin did. They saw that Parliament's Declaratory Act was not "merely to save Appearances" but fully intent on affirming Parliament's right to legislate for the colonies "in all cases whatsoever." And they held accountable both the American advisers for such policy and the principle it declared. In point of fact, the Declaratory Act had been passed *before* the letters were written by Hutchinson and Oliver. These officials were affirming settled policy. But their letters made plain that the officials were serving crown interests *against* the colonists rather than acting as honest brokers between the parties. If they were to be paid by the crown as the Townshend Acts prescribed, the colonists would lack the most potent means of pressuring them for the colonists' interest. Massachusetts erupted.

Because Franklin remained true to his promise of silence,

we still do not know how he got the letters. We do know that he forwarded them to Speaker Thomas Cushing of the Massachusetts House, hoping that they would be circulated privately, but Cushing printed them and the time bomb went off.

William Whately, the son of the letters' recipient (who had died), hurled charges and a challenge to John Temple, and Franklin confessed his role to prevent a duel. That ended his utility as a colonial agent.[25]

Why were the Massachusetts radicals so furious about these letters, and why could moderate, royalist Franklin sympathize with them? Neither they nor he were greatly wrought up about the amount of money that Parliament's proposed taxes would cost. They were outraged because the colonists were bypassed in the enactment of the taxes. "English liberties" had in fact been sharply "abridged," and more abridging was in prospect if royal officials could flout colonists' desires without fear of colonists' resentment. To point up the issue, Thomas Hutchinson had been made Governor of Massachusetts and Oliver had succeeded him as chief justice. Knowing their attitudes toward colonists' liberties, what could be expected from them in the highest offices of the province?

Franklin, for some time, had gradually become disillusioned, "first with one part" of the imperial structure, "then with another." In the sober judgment of the editors of his papers, "The ways in which Parliament used its authority over the colonies persuaded him . . . that that authority was illegitimate; and he reached the same conclusion about royal authority when he discovered that the King was deaf to American grievances."[26]

Franklin's mission had taken him to London to end the Penns' lordship because the Penns' governors were bound by rigid instructions that could be partly circumvented only because governors had to come to the Assembly for their pay. After 1773 Franklin faced the ghastly prospect that *all* colonial governors would be instructed without any possibility of circumvention. Franklin had failed more utterly in this mission than in his earlier one. Instead of circumstances improving, they were worse than at its beginning. This was the end of his political world, in fact and in conception.

He was left in no doubt about that.

18 PHOENIX

THE HUTCHINSON-OLIVER LETTERS entailed consequences intensely personal for Franklin and intensely political
for Massachusetts and the empire. William Whately sued Franklin in the Court of Chancery; if decision were adverse, Franklin
might have been sentenced to jail. Considering that he had
made a public confession and refused to name anyone who
might ameliorate his guilt, the verdict was fairly sure. Fortu-
nately, courts were as ponderously cumbersome as other agen-
cies of government, so Franklin's lawyers bought time for him
with stalling motions on technicalities.

He needed the time to fulfill his responsibilities and endure
what was in store. Samuel Wharton demanded his resignation
from the Vandalia project. The crown dismissed him from his
post office position. The province of Georgia ended his agency.
Few persons with status wanted to stay aboard his sinking ship.

Massachusetts added still more to his troubles by forward-
ing a petition to the crown demanding dismissal from office of
Hutchinson and Oliver. Fat chance. But agent Franklin duti-
fully laid the petition before the Privy Council and thus guaranteed himself the worst public humiliation of his life.

When the Privy Council ordered a hearing on the petition
in the Cockpit at the end of January 1774, it attracted an audience of London's most important people. They knew perfectly
well how the Council would have to act on the petition of
the Massachusetts House, but they were lured by the notoriety
Franklin had been getting in the press. (For once he could not
manage it his way.) "The question that intrigued the public was
how the government would handle the matter."[1]

Only a week earlier, news had reached London of the so-
called Boston Tea Party—the dumping of a ship's cargo of taxed
tea into Boston Harbor by a gang of men imperfectly disguised
as Indians. It could not have been more flagrant as a violation
of imperial authority, and it could not go unpunished. Royal

and popular wrath against Franklin's constituents struck at him as though he were one of his own lightning rods. More would come, of course, but he could be reached immediately.

Solicitor General Alexander Wedderburn gave very little attention to the legal question before the Privy Council—the petition from Massachusetts. Using that as a springboard, Wedderburn turned to a scurrilous attack on Franklin personally: "He has forfeited all the respect of societies and of men. . . . Amidst these tragical events, of one person nearly murdered, of another answerable for the issue, of a worthy governor hurt in his dearest interests, the fate of America in suspense; here is a man, who with the utmost insensibility of remorse, stands up and avows himself the author of all."[2] Wedderburn raged on for an hour. Franklin stood silent. The Privy Council, as expected, rejected the petition, omitting notice of Franklin, but Wedderburn's tongue-lashing scarred him for life.

Ironically his fame as a scientist, a *philosopher,* was rising precisely at this time when his repute as a politician plummeted. A French admirer translated his works into the language that was then the lingua franca of educated men in Europe, and traveling savants made a point of calling on him in London. Their admiration made no difference to the stupid arrogants in office, but it soothed Franklin's badly bruised self-esteem.

His most cherished desire was to somehow bring about a principled reconciliation between the crown and the colonies. In the bottommost depths of disgrace he still consulted with the few men capable of rational discourse, trying proposals for their reactions; but neither crown nor colonies would heed.

Carl Van Doren tells how Quaker merchant David Barclay and physician Dr. John Fothergill tried to lure Franklin to meet with Richard, Lord Howe, to discuss possible terms of reconciliation. One must smile at their device, which was to get Franklin to play chess with Howe's sister. She sounded him out, he replied amiably, her brother just happened to be available elsewhere in the house, and he responded quickly to summons. Whereupon Howe and Franklin discussed matters beyond chess.[3]

It is worth note that London's Quakers were not standing aloof from the contest. Rather, in their own fashion, they strove for solution by negotiation rather than war, much as Philadel-

phia Quakers had done with Indians during the Seven Years
War. (The new situation in London raises questions about
Franklin's hostility to the pacifists in Philadelphia after his re-
turn in 1775—see chapter 19.)

Even old William Pitt, Earl of Chatham, whose conquering
administration in the Seven Years War had produced the great
burden of debt—even he, after earnest talk with Franklin, tried
to get Parliament to consider measures of reconciliation, and
even his enormous prestige met only rebuff.[4]

The national debt was not the real issue. Expenses could
have been sharply reduced by withdrawing the regiments occupying the colonies and dismissing them from service; but to do
that would have weakened the base of Tory power in England
besides making a large concession to the colonists. Parliament
was not so much concerned with money, regardless of its revenue bills, as with power.

England's ministers were used to suppressing rebellions in
Ireland and Scotland and in England itself. Men still in office
had been part of the government that crushed the Scottish
Highlanders as recently as 1745. In their minds the king and
Parliament did not share power with overseas offshoots; they
ruled. Angry Members of Parliament, determined to show that
they had meant every word of their Declaratory Act: "to make
laws . . . to bind the colonies and people of America . . . in all
cases whatsoever." They passed a new series of laws to punish
Massachusetts—the Coercive Acts—and added the Quebec Act
as a gratuitous slap at the colonies with western ambitions.

The Boston Port Act closed the port to all commerce until
payment should be made for the tea dumped into the harbor.
(Distracted Franklin offered to pay for the tea himself, but was
ignored.)

The Massachusetts Government Act abolished all elections
by providing that all offices should be filled by direct or indirect
royal appointment.

The Administration of Justice Act struck especially hard at
Boston's great smugglers by providing that they should no
longer be tried in the province where their influence could sway
juries; in future their trials would be moved to other provinces
or to England.

The Quartering Act empowered army officers to override

civil regulations about where the occupying soldiers should be stationed and housed. Thus when riots broke out, the soldiers would be immediately at hand to quell them.

The Quebec Act redrew the boundaries of the new province of Quebec by extending the province southerly down the "backs" of the older provinces and making it impossible for westward-yearning land speculators to make their schemes effectual.[5]

All in all, Parliament achieved a monument of pigheadedness that seems especially designed to arouse opposition from moderate persons who had been willing to let Massachusetts fight its own battles. The Yankee radicals were much distrusted in Virginia, for example, but how could Virginia's Tidewater planters planning vast estates beyond the mountains permit their hopes to be smashed by the rotten representatives of Parliament's rotten boroughs? Suddenly Thomas Jefferson and George Washington rose to lead the opposition. (It is hard to think of men more unlike the Virginians than Sam Adams and John Hancock.) All the elected officials in all the colonies could see themselves as next in line whenever the crown should decide to abolish elections in their own provinces.

Virginians strode forward to propose "that the united wisdom of North America should be collected in a general congress of all the colonies," to be held in Philadelphia in September, and in August 1774 Virginia's burgesses chose their own delegates to that congress.[6] The response was general, and for the first time the colonists created a united front against royal dictation.

Franklin anticipated the event by a year. In July 1773 he wrote to Speaker Thomas Cushing in Massachusetts with advice that the *Franklin Papers* editors call "what the American radicals were looking for." When Governor Hutchinson obtained a copy of the letter by methods similar to those Franklin had used for Hutchinson's letters, the crown's minister believed Franklin's advice to be treasonous. The letter justifies a long quotation:

. . . as the Strength of an Empire depends not only on the *Union* of its Parts, but on their *Readiness* for United Exertion of their common Force: And as the Discussion of Rights may seem unseasonable in the Commencement of actual War; and the Delay it might occasion be prejudicial to the common Welfare. As likewise the Refusal of one or a few Colonies would not be so much regarded if the others granted liberally . . . this want of Concert would defeat the Expectation of general Redress that otherwise might be justly formed; perhaps it would be best and fairest, for the Colonies in a general Congress now in Peace to be assembled, or by means of the Correspondence lately proposed after a full and solemn Assertion and Declaration of their Rights, to engage firmly with each other that they will never grant aids to the Crown in any General War till those Rights are recogniz'd by the King and both Houses of Parliament; communicating at the same time to the Crown this their Resolution. Such a Step I imagine will bring the Dispute to a Crisis; and whether our Demands are immediately comply'd with, or compulsory Means are thought of to make us Rescind them, our Ends will finally be obtain'd, for even th[e odiu]m accomp[anyin]g such [compulsory] Attempts [will contribute to unite and strengthen us,] and in the mean time all the World will allow that our Proceeding has been honourable.[7]

No one could call this vacillating or equivocal. This Franklin of 1773 had turned his face against the Franklin of 1754 who had wanted to unite the colonies under a commander appointed by the crown.

Franklin was desperately trying to save the empire by forcing it to be just and fair to its colonists, a goal he had vainly pursued ever since beginning to campaign against the lords Penn. Finally he gave up. Perhaps partly in response to the news of his Debbie's death, perhaps stimulated by awareness that his trial for purloining the Hutchinson-Oliver letters could be stalled no longer, he took ship for Philadelphia in March 1775, just ahead of the constable.[8]

Carl Van Doren has remarked that Franklin "brought to the insurgents the prestige of the first American name," but this is an inadequate statement.[9] Franklin was not simply co-opted, he gave guidance and took leadership even to the fervid radicals in Massachusetts. (Cf. Speaker Cushing's fret before Franklin's letter about an intercolonial congress making matters "still more difficult." Note how Samuel Adams picked up and publicized Franklin's letter.)[10] Franklin's devotion to the empire assumed that the empire guaranteed English liberties, essential among which was the right of the colonists to govern themselves. This was more fantasy than fact. For freemen, colonial liberties were already greater than those much praised "English" liberties. As

The New Columbia Encyclopedia notes (article on "Reform Bills"), only about 435,000 Britons were qualified to vote in a population of 24,000,000 (including Ireland). These data seem to confirm a theory that revolutions are not made by people with everything to gain, but rather by those who have something they do not want to lose. Franklin approved the colonists' struggle to preserve what he conceived as the *natural constitution* of the empire which king and Parliament were violating.[11] He knew which side he was on.

By the time his ship docked at Philadelphia, he was a rebel, and soon George III proclaimed that "there is reason to apprehend that such rebellion hath been much promoted and encouraged by the traitorous correspondence, counsels and comfort of divers wicked and desperate persons within this realm."[12] When the king built a gallows for Franklin, he beatified the man for the revolutionaries. Now they, too, were sure about which side he was on.

Revolutions go to extremes. We must remember John Adams's much quoted remark that the American Revolution was a minority affair with support from one third of the populace, opposition from a third, and neutrality or indifference from the remaining third. George III was the most effective recruiter of moderates for the revolutionaries, and his first recruit was Benjamin Franklin.

Not everyone followed in Franklin's train. While he struggled and lost in London, his old ally Joseph Galloway struggled and lost in Pennsylvania, but they lost to different sides. Galloway suffered under pressure from the increasingly radical anti-imperialists led by John Dickinson (Franklin's old foe) and Charles Thomson (Franklin's old friend). They organized local committees and called a provincial convention to meet at the same time as Galloway's Assembly. Galloway maneuvered to exclude their delegates from the new Continental Congress, which he hoped to tame down to moderation. But Sam and John Adams met with Dickinson and Thomson outside the Congress sessions, and the Congress rejected Galloway's Plan of Union with Britain.[13]

Internally, Pennsylvanians elected Dickinson and Thomson to the Assembly, where they unseated Galloway from the

Speaker's post he had held for eight years.[14] (It should be noted that the radicals were elected by the city and county of Philadelphia. What does that do to the argument that democratic western counties were striving against repression from eastern oligarchs?)

Galloway's political career lay in ruins. He, too, had chosen a side, and his contrast with Franklin was so extreme that he ultimately fled as a Loyalist to Britain, where he proclaimed that it was to Franklin's intrigues, principally, that Britain and America "owe all their present misfortunes." (He gained a pension by that.)[15]

Franklin worked more and more closely with the revolutionaries as one of them. While Galloway tried to turn them back, Franklin was sent to the Second Continental Congress and chosen to Philadelphia's Committee of Safety, the radicals' means to suppress political dissidents. This was another switch for Franklin. Throughout his life in Philadelphia, he had been antipathetic to Presbyterians whom he regarded as enemies to liberty. Now he joined them, and that change meant that he, too, had become an enemy to some people's liberties. (More on this in the last chapter.)

By means wholly unanticipated or even conceivable, Franklin's great passion since 1755 was fulfilled: the revolutionaries overthrew the feudal lords of Pennsylvania and banished them forever. Within a year, the crown that had rebuffed his mission was itself overthrown, and Dr. Franklin, the philosopher, was credited on both sides of the Atlantic as the hero who had done most toward those revolutionary ends. We have seen that such judgments need modification, that the mastermind and great fixer often erred and that he has been made into a champion of ideas he did not share; but that he was a hero is beyond reasonable dispute. If he opposed democracy, he opposed tyranny more. In the jargon of today he may be called a hero of colonial liberation. Of all the colonists, he had become the best known on his side, venerated beyond all others. Even a critic may pay tribute to the long endeavors by which he earned that respect.

Franklin's long life, which spanned most of the eighteenth century, contradicts the efforts made by some writers to present the American Revolution as something of an aberration, an

unanticipated outcome of a series of arguments arising after the
Seven Years War: "if only the two sides had tried harder to
understand each other."

Nobody could have tried harder than Benjamin Franklin to
understand Britain; indeed, he came to understand it too well.
Colonial independence had been simmering for substantial reasons for a long time. Stephen Saunders Webb has dated it back
to seventeenth-century Virginia and Massachusetts when con-
vulsions in England made colonial secession seem feasible.[16]
Large numbers of immigrants to the colonies had small reason
to love the crown whose policies or sentences had driven them
abroad.

Crown bureaucrats were always on the alert for signs of
colonial independence, as they constantly watched Ireland and
Scotland for possible uprisings. Whig ministries tolerated much
colonial autonomy during the long period of "salutary neglect,"
and colonial politicians inched upward to more rights and privileges. The crown had cracked down with the appointment in
1757 of John Campbell, Earl Loudoun, as commander in chief
over all the colonies and authorized to rule by deputized royal
prerogative. His arrogance alienated all the colonial elites, and
his military incompetence against an inferior enemy brought his
dismissal. That was *during* the Seven Years War, not afterward,
and Loudoun's legacies are prominent in the Declaration of
Independence of 1776, which states that King George III "has
affected to render the Military independent of and superior to
the Civil Power" and itemizes "quartering large bodies of armed
troops among us."[17]

Franklin had adjusted to Loudoun, but when the crown
added more grievances later, he balked. Let it be stressed: he
was not converted by arguments, but by facts. The repressions
against which the colonists rose were real and hurtful, and
Franklin sat in the committee that supervised drafting of the
Declaration of Independence.[18]

When all has been said about Franklin's opportunism and
seeking after power, it is still necessary to add that this realist
had a character founded on human decency most of the time.
He fought lord Penn's rapacity when he could have benefited
more by collaborating with Penn. Learning the hard way of that
lord's imperviousness to provincial protest, Franklin reached

for the only power that could overthrow feudal privilege—the greater privilege of the crown's sovereignty. That he enjoyed to the hilt his residence in England and lived high is beyond dispute, but he threw it all away because moral outrage stirred him to bring royal rage down upon his head.

Morality includes conduct other than sexual. An irreducible judgment must acknowledge Benjamin Franklin as the irreconcilable foe of feudalism in America, who fought it in the political arena while Enlightenment *philosophes* still discussed it under the patronage of feudal lords. To recognize Franklin's shortcomings of personality cannot reduce his stature as hero. Despite defeat after defeat in his struggle against the entrenched power of the feudal Penns, he never turned back.

When Franklin returned to Pennsylvania in 1775, he had abandoned or rejected all his old power bases and sources of income, and he needed money. His Seven Years War teamwork with Quakers was a thing of the past, as also their cooperation in the building of Philadelphia's institutions. Not even the "defense" Quakers forgave his attempt to overthrow their cherished charter, which could not be separated from overthrow of the feudal lord whose father had granted it. Franklin's genial companionship with Penn's men had turned to hate. His Anglican supporters could not accept his new propaganda against the crown. Galloway, his lieutenant in the Assembly, was alienated. Son William Franklin preserved honorable loyalty to the crown he served as New Jersey's governor. It cannot be ignored that all these alienations had occurred because Benjamin had acted repeatedly on principle. Now there was no source of power for him to turn to except the Presbyterians whom he had fought throughout his career.

But not *all* Presbyterians. Franklin had distinguished, as we should also, Presbyterian Charles Thomson, loyal in the faith and also moved by principle. Thomson had stayed friendly with Franklin for many years. We need to know how many more were like Thomson, totally dissociated from the kind that threw up the lynching Paxton Boys; and outraged like Franklin by feudal and royal oppression.

In 1775, Franklin knew he had to join the Presbyterian radicals or subside into nonentity. In turn, they needed a leader with prestige, and no American colonial had more prestige than

Franklin despite all his setbacks. (They were famous setbacks.) *Realpolitik* drove the former enemies into each other's arms. Curiously, it was based on something more than cynicism. They united on the principle of opposition to feudal *and* royal prerogative, and at hazard to their lives they overthrew it.[19]

Thus we solve the mystery that has long baffled Franklin scholars—the process by which the strong royalist and imperialist became suddenly a leader of forces waging war against his formerly adored crown. Franklin had discovered, the hard way, that the feudalism he hated was ingrained in the crown's institutions, including Parliament, beyond his power to suppress it. He had striven to the point where it was no longer possible to stop; he had the lion by its tail, and if he let go he would be devoured. He had to kill the beast or at least to drive it out of his own homeland. Logical thinker that he was, he chose survival and its implied behavior.

This change did not require abandonment of one of his great goals, the vision of empire. Franklin maintained that dream as intact as ever, or even more so. He changed only one detail. He replaced the rule of Britain with rule by Americans who were soon to join with his help and guidance as the United States.

History and men's lives are capable of rational explication, but they are rarely simple.

19 CODA

LONG AGO, THAT GREAT SCHOLAR Charles M. An-
drews warned against teleological study of the colonial period
of the United States, as though everything happening then was
important only as leading to the Revolution.[1] He was right, and
he initiated a productive school of historians whose object of
study was the colonies of the British Empire rather than the
forerunners of secession from it.

With due tribute to that insight, one still must realize that
the Revolution was more than a matter of argument springing
up in 1765. We must see Franklin in a very real sense as more
than a genius, more than a man. He was a mirror of his times.
But a human mirror, which meant that his reflections could be
different from those of other humans of the same era.

Even son William was convinced that none but the most
infatuated colonists would ever voluntarily secede from England, and this he wrote while his father was intensely busy
preparing for just that eventuality. William's letter to Lord
Dartmouth was intercepted. After much political floundering
he was arrested and taken under guard to Connecticut at just
the time when his father served on the committee drafting the
Declaration of Independence.[2]

Historian Sheila Skemp writes that "Benjamin did not lift a
hand to secure his son's freedom or even to make his imprison-
ment more comfortable."[3] William's wife was poverty-stricken
while her husband spent three years in prison, and Benjamin
took out his spite even on her by providing the barest minimum
of necessary money for subsistence. At the height of glory, he
lacked grace.

There are different ways of seeing the dispute between father and son, and Benjamin expressed self-pity over being "deserted in my old Age by my only Son," but his spitefulness
toward his son's helpless wife does not evoke sympathy from
this reader.[4] It speaks volumes about the great man's great con-

ception of himself. The pitiful wail about being deserted "by my only Son" stands in contrast to Benjamin's idolatry by his countrymen, but daughter-in-law Elizabeth had no such compensation.

The massive ego is revealed more complexly in his callous conduct toward Quakers.

When Quakers had opposed Franklin's campaign to make Pennsylvania royal, they were concerned about the religious toleration guaranteed by William Penn's charter to his people. (It was not in the royal charter granted by Charles II to Penn.)[5] So long as William's charter was basic law, no church could be officially established, whereas if the province should become royal, it would be subject to establishment of the crown's Church of England.

Apart from this legal situation, Quakers were on excellent terms with King George III. In 1761, Provincial Counselor and Quaker grandee William Logan visited England and joined a deputation that presented an address by English Friends to the king, at which time Logan was overwhelmed by the king's interest and "condescension."

He recalled ecstatically another event when the king and the whole royal family came to the house of Quaker merchant David Barclay to view the grand procession of the Lord Mayor's Show. They stayed for five hours, chatting affably with Friends present, Logan among them.[6]

Already in that year of 1761, a rift was opening between Benjamin Franklin and the English Quakers. Logan found that "Doctor Fothergill, John Hunt, and other Friends here in London have no Extraordinary Opinion of [Franklin] nor Any Good he has done or Intends to do our Country."[7] It is clear from this and other sources that Franklin cultivated a very different type of society in London than Quakers.

When he plunged in 1764 for a royal takeover of Pennsylvania, the rift became an abyss that never was bridged. Not only orthodox Israel Pemberton, Jr., but even defense Quaker Isaac Norris, Jr., who had been Franklin's wheelhorse in the Assembly, turned against him.

Considering the king's benignity and Franklin's contempt, it was not surprising that Quakers refused to join his movement for secession from the crown. They, too, had formed a goal of autonomy within the empire; but, unlike Franklin, they were willing to accept Penn's lordship as part of the arrangement, and they were rigidly conservative. They held aloof from the American Revolution; and, doing so, they multiplied the vexations previously caused to Franklin. Not only did they reject his political leadership; they outraged his always sensitive ego. He took revenge.

It is highly instructive that this champion of liberty and freedom turned punishingly hostile against people who defined those great goals differently than himself. When the Quakers exasperated him by refusing to rebel against the oppression of king and Parliament, Franklin joined those other oppressors—the Presbyterians[8] who had fought ceaselessly to reject religious tolerance and to overpower the Quakers and their pietist German allies. These same Presbyterians were front-line soldiers in the Revolutionary battles for liberty as they conceived it, but their new Revolutionary Assembly enacted laws to preserve and extend its own powers against challenge by neutralists and loyalists. These laws required oaths of loyalty to the Revolutionary government—oaths impossible for any believing Quaker or pietist to swear.[9]

They included more than allegiance to the new government. They required also that the oath taker swear never to try to change the new constitution that empowered the revolutionaries. To sweeten these requirements, oath takers were exempted from taxes imposed on persons who refused.[10]

As O. S. Ireland has discovered, the "Republican" opponents of the Presbyterian "Constitutionalists" challenged this formally democratic document as "an instrument of tyranny."

Mr. Ireland counted the members of the provincial and state assemblies. Before the Revolution "about 80 percent" were Quaker and Anglican "most of the time." After Independence, proportions changed sharply to 58 percent Calvinist in 1776, and "in the fall 1777 election [when the test oaths took effect] this proportion increased to 82 percent."[11] The new government became what I have called the Dictatorship of the Presbyteriat.

Historians have frequently praised Pennsylvania's new constitution as the most democratic of the new states, but it seems a strange way to produce democracy.

Plausible justifications may be advanced on grounds of *real-politik*. The new "soviet-style" Assembly was locked in struggle against one of the world's great military powers, so measures to tolerate dissent had small appeal. This was war for survival, in which citizenship was reserved exclusively for the warriors and their supporters.

That justification becomes faint, however, after the war had been won and Great Britain accepted the new United States by formal treaty. The powers controlling Pennsylvania's recognized government hung onto their oath laws despite being no longer menaced from abroad. Historians call them the democratic party, but they required the oaths precisely because they knew that repeal would entail their downfall; and so it happened after the Anglican party (led by Anthony Wayne) ended the oaths in 1787.

(Curiously, though the newly adopted United States Constitution is often criticized as too authoritarian, in Pennsylvania it coincided with the restoration of citizenship to half the populace. Its Article VI stipulated that "no religious Test shall ever be required as a Qualification to any Office or public Trust under the United States.")

It seems proper to stress that these events occurred in the eighteenth century rather than now. Since then, all organized religions have evolved variously, sometimes to the extent that their old devotees would hardly recognize the modern forms; and Presbyterians have changed along with the others. Despite their anachronistic Westminster Confession, most of them no longer pride themselves as exclusive possessors of salvation in the midst of the multitude of foredoomed souls. Ubiquitous Presbyterian hospitals and retirement homes testify to their concern for helping other people.

Not all religions have changed in the same way. Recent events here and abroad demonstrate only too clearly how some faiths grasp after power and repression in programs barely short of holy war and sometimes degenerating into that sort of dreadful mass murder. In his classic history of Rome, Edward Gibbon "described the triumph of barbarism and religion." Surely it must not be fated to be ever thus.

Benjamin Franklin did not protest against Pennsylvania's oath laws. Worse, he stood aside as the Revolutionary executive

council, of which he was titular head, summoned and persecuted particular Quakers whom he knew well and with whom
he had teamed against Thomas Penn in the 1750s. These were
absolute pacifists as Franklin had often lamented, men who
would not dream of taking up weapons against the new rulers
but who insisted on speaking their own dissident truths to
the new powers. When they were denounced as dangers to
the security of the state, Franklin remembered how they had
foiled his earlier campaign to turn Pennsylvania into a royal
dependence of the same George III against whom he now rebelled; and Franklin took a mean revenge for their flouting of
his will.

He said nothing in their favor, either to notice the many
benefits they had conferred on the community (often in partnership with himself) or to ease the hardships of their banishment
to western Virginia, which was then a frontier outpost lacking
in comforts. Israel Pemberton, Jr., "King of the Quakers," was
one of those so punished, and his exile was transparently a political warning to all Quakers to shut up.

The victimized Quakers had been "framed" by a forged report of treasonable correspondence ostensibly from the Quaker
meeting of Spanktown, New Jersey, which had never existed.
New Hampshire's John Sullivan started the action to which
John Adams gave support. Enemies of Quakers in Pennsylvania
picked it up and broadened its scope.[12]

(This was in the Calvinist tradition of Massachusetts Bay
when that colony exiled Roger Williams and others in the seven-
teenth century under pain of death for returning. Four Quakers
then defied Massachusetts's ban and were duly executed.)[13]

Friend John Hunt died in his western exile, and aged Friend
Israel Pemberton survived only a few weeks after he was permitted to return to his family.

This episode is generally swept under the rug by writers
making Franklin an icon of virtue. That he had no intention of
including it in his unfinished *Autobiography* is attested by his
careful omission of any mention of Israel Pemberton, Jr., from
the whole work, including Pemberton's part in the institutions
they had built together. (The Pennsylvania Hospital comes to
mind, for which Pemberton worked harder and longer than
Franklin, but Franklin took the credit.)

More than the public relations is at stake. They obscure profound issues of the most serious pertinence for our own times. For instance . . .

The conflict of freedoms exemplified by Franklin and Pemberton. Is it beneficial to the human community when proponents of one kind of freedom resort to main force in order to suppress a competitive kind? This question especially concerns all kinds of revolutionaries. Is victory in such a struggle worth the cost in terms of human suffering? (I once would have given an offhand answer to that; I am older now, and not so sure.)

Another cost must be reckoned into the account, for the striving after power can be as corrupting as its attainment. Historians are ready enough to acknowledge the vices of the French and Russian revolutions, and of many struggles for liberation from colonial fetters. (Idi Amin is an educational example.) What of our own American Revolution, buried beneath an overburden of mythology? How many historians have seriously considered the implications of Nikolai Lenin's ecstatic praise for it? How true is it that ours was the *nice* revolution? Answers to these questions are not implied here.

This discussion must not run on, but one more nagging question needs to be raised: How much credit should be given to the memoirs of historical celebrities? Surely, it should be plain as day that the testimonies of such men as Richard M. Nixon and Henry Kissinger—men known as compulsive liars during their public lives—should be subject to most rigorous examination and cross-check. Can we really believe that the passage of time has somehow purified the writings and characters of other famous men such as Benjamin Franklin—men who presented themselves, like Nixon, draped in virtue? What is history worth when so based? My answer to that question is this book.

A NOTE ON SOURCES

THE STANDARD VERSIONS OF Franklin's life and his background in Philadelphia rely on the fabrications of Thomas Penn's lawyers in the Walking Purchase case. My doctoral dissertation research disclosed that the lawyers had destroyed the original records of dealings with Indians, substituting exculpatory documents falsely presented as valid.

Quakers discovered these falsehoods and tried to expose them. Penn's men thereupon traduced the Quakers, playing upon theological antipathies and smearing them as "Indian lovers." Franklin despised the Quakers for their pacifism, and turned against them when they worked against his campaign to make Pennsylvania royal. Much bigotry has colored statements of fact by subsequent historians about Quakers.

Quaker manuscripts have been ignored and left unread by historians. Anthropologist Anthony F. C. Wallace discovered the value of part of this evidence and aroused my curiosity to examine more.

Provost William Smith's intrigues and conspirings have been overlooked almost entirely. Worse, historian Francis Parkman adopted Smith's diatribes as authoritative sources. More temperate writers have celebrated Smith as one of the "most civilized" colonials. This must mean that the celebrants have not read Smith's polluted effluent. I have.

Filiopietist Pennsylvanians revere the memories of their aristocratic ancestors who were Thomas Penn's minions, and who naturally could not be suspected of collaborating in wrongdoing.

An air of glamour hangs over the Penn family because of the genuine nobility of William Penn. Englishmen understand how a Duke of York could commit atrocities to become King Richard III, but Americans simply cannot believe that a chartered Proprietary lord would stray from rectitude.

Benjamin Franklin's papers were inadequately collected and annotated until the recent great edition. I have read many of the manuscripts on which the editors based comment, have seen the correctness of those comments, and was able to cite them as a kind of shorthand. They also taught me about sources I had not seen heretofore.

Enlightenment on Pennsylvania's structure has come also from the Dunns' edition of *The Papers of William Penn* and the essays in their

conference proceedings of *The World of William Penn*. That such fundamental documents for Pennsylvania remained unpublished until late in
the twentieth century is testimony, I think, to the long, nearsighted
preoccupation of colonial historians with New England and Virginia,
which has channeled "the mainstream" into a mud puddle.

Something may be said additionally about an attitude prevalent
among historians today which colors their interpretations of the
sources. Writers have been overawed by Tory attacks on Whig interpretations that violate Tory notions of objectivity. Many writers protect
themselves by accepting the Tory outlook as valid. It is not.

A different sort of source was my experience of thirty years of life
in Philadelphia where Quakers are still a vital living presence. I learned
then that the Friends are human, ranging widely over personality types
and varied to some degree in personal creeds. With that background, I
could only reject and condemn modern writers who make colonial
Quakers demonic in a pattern highly reminiscent of modern anti-
Semitism, and as groundlessly malign.

My findings herein are strongly revisionist. I do not present them
as definitive—a claim I have never made for any of my books—but I do
provide evidence to justify revision, and I insist that critics have an
obligation to examine and respond to that evidence. To dismiss it with
an offhand sneer at the book's style (as has happened to a previous
book) would be merely to demonstrate the critic's ignorance and bias
(as also happened previously).

The evidence has given me great pleasure by its depiction of a giant
who was believably human rather than a manufactured icon. I have
tried to share that pleasure with readers.

NOTES

1 INTRODUCTION

1. Stephen Saunders Webb, *1676: The End of American Independence* (New York: Alfred A. Knopf, 1984).
2. Of the many editions of Franklin's *Autobiography*, I have used the beautiful volume edited by Leonard W. Labaree, Ralph L. Ketcham, Helen C. Boatfield, and Helene H. Fineman (New Haven, CT: Yale University Press, 1964). It is a pleasure to the hands and eyes.
3. The best authoritative and relatively brief introduction to early Pennsylvania is in the papers of *The World of William Penn*, Richard S. and Mary Maples Dunn, eds. (Philadelphia: University of Pennsylvania Press, 1986). Supplement it with Francis Jennings, *The Ambiguous Iroquois Empire* (New York: W. W. Norton & Co., 1984), Part 3.
4. *The Charters and Acts of Assembly of the Province of Pennsylvania*. 2 vols. (Philadelphia: Peter Miller & Co., 1762).
5. *The Papers of Benjamin Franklin*, Leonard W. Labaree, et al., eds. (New Haven, CT: Yale University Press, 1959–). Short title: *Franklin Papers*.
6. *Minutes of the Provincial Council of Pennsylvania* (spine title: *Colonial Records*), ed. Samuel Hazard. 16 vols. (Harrisburg and Philadelphia, 1838–53). Vols. 1–3 printed

in two editions with different pagination; *Pennsylvania Archives*, 9th series, 138 vols. (Harrisburg and Philadelphia, 1852–1949). *Votes and Proceedings of the House of Representatives of the Province of Pennsylvania, 1682–1776* (1752–76), 8 vols. continuously paged: 8th series, *Pennsylvania Archives* (Harrisburg, 1931–35). Recently a new volume should be extremely useful, though it appeared after I had done research on the present book: Craig W. Horle, *Lawmaking and Legislators in Pennsylvania: A Biographical Dictionary* (Philadelphia: University of Pennsylvania Press, 1991).
7. James H. Hutson, "Benjamin Franklin and Pennsylvania Politics, 1751–1755: A Reappraisal," *Pa. Magazine of History and Biography* 93:3 (July 1969), 303–371; James H. Hutson, *Pennsylvania Politics, 1746–1770: The Movement for Royal Government and Its Consequences* (Princeton, NJ: Princeton University Press, 1972).
8. Carl Van Doren, *Benjamin Franklin* (New York: Viking Press, 1938; reprinted Garden City, NY: Garden City Publishing Co., 1942). By general consensus this is still the best comprehensive biography, but it is an extended exercise in hero worship. Van Doren's Franklin is larger than life.

2 BOSTON

1. My outlook should not be confused with that of William S. Hanna, *Benjamin Franklin and Pennsylvania Politics* (Stanford, CA: Stanford

University Press, 1964), a long snarl that seems to me like slanted trash.

2. Franklin's lesson was the death of his young son who had not been inoculated. This was one instance when the genius admitted error.

Van Doren, 126, 296. Except where separately noted, I have relied for details of Franklin's personal life on Van Doren's biography.

3. *Autobiography,* 69.

3 PHILADELPHIA

1. For the royal grant to William Penn, see Stephen Saunders Webb, "'The Peaceable Kingdom': Quaker Pennsylvania in the Stuart Empire," in *The World of William Penn,* Dunn and Dunn, eds., 173–194; and "Negotiating the Charter for Pennsylvania," in *The Papers of William Penn,* Richard S. Dunn, Mary Maples Dunn, et al., eds. 4 vols. (Philadelphia: University of Pennsylvania Press, 1981–), 2:19–78.

Note well that the royal charter to Penn must be distinguished

from Penn's charter of liberties or "frame of government" to his people—*Papers* 2:137–140.

2. See Francis Jennings, "Miquon's Passing: Indian-European Relations in Colonial Pennsylvania, 1674–1755," Ph.D. diss., University of Pennsylvania, 1965, 188–197.

3. Ibid., 197–205.

4. *Autobiography,* 92–95, quotation at p. 94.

5. Ibid., 106.

6. Ibid., 106–107. Van Doren, p. 70, adds the detail about indebtedness.

4 DOMESTIC

1. Franklin confessed that "that hard-to-be-govern'd Passion of Youth, had hurried me frequently into Intrigues with low Women that fell in my Way, which were attended with some Expence and great Inconvenience, besides a continual Risque to my Health by a Distemper which of all Things I dreaded, tho' by great good Luck I escaped it." *Autobiography,* 128. The passage can easily be read as applying to his life in Philadelphia as well as London.

2. *Autobiography,* 128–129; Van Doren, 93–94, notes how Franklin blandly omitted the fact and significance of his illegitimate son. Debbie grew jealous of William when he grew to manhood. Van Doren, 231.

3. Van Doren, 125, 127. Franklin's first inclination was toward the Presbyterian Church, from which he became alienated by a heresy

hunt. Melvin H. Buxbaum concedes Franklin's honest indignation, but suggests that Anglicans had more patronage to dispense. I note that Deborah Franklin had attended Christ Church before marrying him, and I incline to the belief that Benjamin began his attendance there, and his purchase of a pew, simply to go along with her. Later the church became a bastion of political power for him. Melvin H. Buxbaum, *Benjamin Franklin and the Zealous Presbyterians* (University Park, PA: Pennsylvania State University Press, 1975), ch. 3, especially p. 114; *Franklin Papers* 2:188 n4.

4. Van Doren, 94.

5. Francis Jennings, *Empire of Fortune* (New York: W. W. Norton & Co., 1988), 243–244.

6. See Buxbaum, ch. 3.

7. *Autobiography,* 126.

8. Ibid., 130.

9. Collinson: ed. note, ibid., 278; Logan: ibid., 289.

10. Logan: *Franklin Papers* 1:191 n6, 251 n7.

5 PROTÉGÉ

1. *Autobiography*, 257.
2. Ibid., 196.
3. Ibid., 172.
4. Ibid., 208.
5. Van Doren, 210.
6. Van Doren, 212.
7. *Autobiography*, 187–188, 190.
8. *Franklin Papers* 1:191 n6.
9. Van Doren, 105; *Franklin Papers* 1:251 n8.
10. *Franklin Papers* 1:320–321.
11. Franklin collected after twenty-five years. *Franklin Papers* 7:157–158.
12. See Francis Jennings, "The Indian Trade of the Susquehanna Valley," *Proceedings of the American Philosophical Society* 110:6 (December 1966), 406–424; embezzlement explained at p. 420.
13. Jennings, "Miquon's Passing," 296–306.
14. Logan's warnings of Indian rights: Logan to J. Penn, 6 Dec. 1727, Logan Papers, 1:89, mss., HSP; Logan to the Proprietaries, 8 Oct. 1734, *Pennsylvania Archives*, 2d series, 7:171–172. See also Logan to Thomas Watson, 20 Nov. 1727, Logan Letter Books, 3:114, mss., Historical Society of Pennsylvania (HSP).
15. Robert Charles was commissioned in Logan's place to be Secretary of the Province and Clerk of Council, 20 March 1733, Patent Book A-6, 167–168. John Georges was commissioned Secretary of the Land Office, 2 April 1733, Commission Book A-1, 1–2. Benjamin Eastburn was commissioned Surveyor General in place of Logan's confidant John Taylor, 29 Oct. 1733, ibid., 4. All mss. in Pennsylvania Dept. of Internal Affairs. Logan was separated from administration of property by being made chief justice, 9 April 1733, mss., Patent Book A-6, 169.
16. *A Modest Enquiry into the Nature and Necessity of a Paper-Currency* (1729), in *Franklin Papers* 1:139–157.
17. Ibid., ed. note, 141.
18. *Autobiography*, 171.
19. See Theodore Thayer, *Israel Pemberton, King of the Quakers* (Philadelphia: Historical Society of Pennsylvania, 1943), 3–4, a valuable monograph.
20. Ibid., 33.
21. Norris to Charles, 29 April 1756, Norris Letter Book, 1719–56, mss., 70–71, HSP.
22. Thayer, *Israel Pemberton*, 27.
23. Gordon arrived in Philadelphia by authority of both branches of the contending Penns and the crown. Council minutes, 22 June 1726, 3:265.
24. G. Thomas to J. Penn, 5 Oct. 1736, Penn Mss., Official Correspondence, mss., 3:27, HSP.
25. J. to T. Penn, 17 Feb. 1737, Penn Letter Books, mss., 1:182, HSP.

6 THE WALKING PURCHASE

1. See Jennings, *Ambiguous Iroquois Empire,* Appendix B. Additional details are in Francis Jennings, "The Scandalous Indian Policy of William Penn's Sons: Deeds and Documents of the Walking Purchase," *Pennsylvania History* 37 (January 1970), 19–39.
2. Richard S. Dunn summarizes. "He preached bourgeois thrift, but he practiced noblesse oblige." "Penny Wise and Pound Foolish:

Penn as a Businessman," in *The World of William Penn,* Dunn and Dunn, eds., 37–54, quotation at p. 51.

3. Jennings, *Ambiguous Iroquois Empire,* 325–29, 318 n25.

4. Ibid., 330–331. The ms. quoted on these pages was unearthed by Anthony F. C. Wallace, whose guidance led me to it. Moses Tatamy's Account, mss., Etting Collection, Misc. Mss., 1:94, HSP.

5. Jennings, *Ambiguous Iroquois Empire,* 391–392.

6. Dunn, "Penny Wise and Pound Foolish," 50–51; when the mortgage was lifted, the trustees made a legal release to the Penns, 24 June 1735, for the agreement that had sprung William Penn from debtors' prison, 15 July 1727. Pa. Patent Book F-7, 338, microfilm in Philadelphia City Hall.

7. John to Thomas Penn, 20 Feb. 1735/36, Penn Letter Books, mss., 1:143–144, HSP.

8. John and Richard Penn to Thomas Penn, 12 May 1734, Penn Letter Books, mss., 1:118–121.

9. Jennings, "Miquon's Passing," 320–327.

10. Logan to the Proprietaries, 8 Oct. 1734, *Pa. Archives,* 2d series, 7:171–172.

11. Jennings, *Ambiguous Iroquois Empire,* 392–394; Nutimus, et al., to Jeremiah Langhorne, 21 Nov. 1740, Penn Mss., Indian Affairs, mss., 4:30, HSP.

12. James Steel to John Chapman and Timothy Smith, 27 April 1735, James Steel's Letter Book, 1730–1741, mss., 96; Joseph Doan to Thomas Penn, 29 May 1735, Indian Walk Mss., 1735 April 26–1737 Sept. 19, mss. photostat; James Steel to Henry Van Wye, 25 May 1734, James Steel's Letter Book, 1730–41, mss., 272; An account of charges accrued in walking the day-and-a-half journey, 5 May 1735, Indian Walk Mss., mss. All in Friends Historical Library,

Swarthmore College. Thanks to Frederick Tolles for showing them to me.

13. Jennings, *Ambiguous Iroquois Empire,* 394; Jennings, "Miquon's Passing," 350 n59. Teedyuscung's remark is in *The Papers of Sir William Johnson,* James Sullivan, et al., eds., 14 vols. (Albany, NY: University of the State of New York, 1921–65), 3:767.

14. Jennings, *Ambiguous Iroquois Empire,* 318–319 with notes.

15. Multiple mss. in ibid., 334–335 notes 25, 26.

16. J. and R. Penn to T. Penn, 4 Feb. 1735/36; J. to T. Penn, 17 Feb. 1736/37, Penn Letter Books, mss., 1:130–136, 181–187, HSP.

17. Ibid.

18. Jennings, *Ambiguous Iroquois Empire,* 395.

19. Logan tried to get Nutimus's lands for £2 per thousand acres. The Penns paid nothing and sold those lands for £155 per thousand acres. *Pa. Archives,* 2d series, 7:171–172. An example will demonstrate the profit in land speculation: In 1730, the Penns sold to Caspar Wistar 2,000 acres at about £7 per hundred acres. Seven years later he resold at about £53, Pa. currency, per hundred acres. After allowing for the exchange rate, the profit is on the order of 500 percent. Pa. Patent Book A-1:162, mss.; Zewitz's deed, Northampton Co. Deed Book, B-1:177–178, mss., Easton Court House. This range of profit was typical. For the Penns, additional perpetual income was produced by annual quitrent.

20. Logan to T. Penn, 16 Aug. 1733, 7 July 1734, *Pa. Archives,* 2d series, 7:145, 168–169: *Pa. Council Minutes,* 20 Aug. 1736, 4:53–56.

21. Jennings, *Ambiguous Iroquois Empire,* 314–315, 321–323, and 395–396 (italics added). Paul A. W. Wallace found the key documents for this arrangement.

22. Ibid., 336–345. Anthony F. C. Wallace pioneered the analysis of the treaty preceding the Walk. His biography of Teedyuscung, though I have differed with it in other respects, was a tremendous advance over the fabrications of Thomas Penn's lawyers, printed without question and without consultation of manuscripts in Julian P. Boyd, ed., *Indian Treaties Printed by Benjamin Franklin, 1736–1762* (Philadelphia: Historical Society of Pennsylvania, 1938), Introduction. Wallace became interested as

an anthropologist because of the myth that the Iroquois had conquered the Delawares and "made women" of them, which falsely led ethnologists to think that women's status was inferior to men's in Iroquois society.

A curious, perhaps unique, insistence of local Quaker historians in Bucks County that their ancestors had helped to swindle the Indians was denied by national professionals. See William J. Buck, *History of the Indian Walk* (Philadelphia: E. S. Stuart, 1886).

7 CLIMBING

1. In recent years, the event has been reported by two widely disagreeing students: Norman S. Cohen, "The Philadelphia Election Riot of 1742," *Pa. Magazine of History and Biography* 92 (July 1968), 306–319, is rejected as "partisan and somewhat inaccurate" by William T. Parsons, "The Bloody Election of 1742," *Pa. History* 36:3 (July 1969), 290–306. Parsons's evidence is the more convincing.

2. Extract from *Pa. Gazette* in *Franklin Papers* 2:363–364.

3. Parsons, "Bloody Election," 297, 299; Theodore Thayer, *Pennsylvania Politics and the Growth of Democracy, 1740–1776* (Harrisburg, Pa. Hist. and Museum Commission, 1953), 18–19; "Selected Letters from the Letter-Book of Richard Hockley, 1739–1742," *Pa. Magazine of History and Biography* 26 (1904), 40.

4. *Franklin Papers* 2:363.

5. Jennings, *Ambiguous Iroquois Empire*, 343–345.

6. *Franklin Papers* 4:480.

7. Ibid., 2:378–383, 406–407.

8. Ibid., 6:187n.

9. *Autobiography,* 240–241.

10. *Franklin Papers* 3:370–372.

11. Ibid., 4:360–363, 392.

12. Ibid., 4:366–369.

13. Ibid., 5:126–134.

14. Ibid., 5:331.

15. *Franklin Papers* 3:195 notes 4, 5.

16. *Autobiography,* 189.

17. *Franklin Papers* 3:188–204.

18. Ibid., 3:201–202 (italics in original as always when I quote him directly).

19. *Autobiography,* 186–187.

20. *Franklin Papers* 3:214–218.

21. Ibid., 3:186 headnote and n8.

22. Van Doren, 120.

23. *Autobiography,* 181–182.

24. The Franklin-Hall agreement for a period of eighteen years is in *Franklin Papers* 3:263–267. It specifies that "the Business, and working part of Printing" were to be Hall's responsibility. Franklin's editing privilege was left tacit. Explicitly, apart from provisions for equal division of profit and loss, Franklin had "free Ingress and Egress in the Printing house." Hall was a good businessman. He provided Franklin with an income averaging £673 per year, a very substantial amount in that era.

25. *Franklin Papers* 3:395–421.

26. Ibid., 3:428–429.

27. Ibid., 3:422–423.

28. Ibid., 3:421, headnote. When William Allen became Chief Justice in 1750, Tench Francis was

promoted to Allen's former post of Recorder. Ibid., 3:428 n9.

29. Ibid., 4:435 and n5.

30. *Autobiography,* 181.

31. Theodore Thayer, *Israel Pemberton: King of the Quakers* (Philadelphia: Historical Society of Pennsylvania, 1943), 34.

32. Francis Jennings, *Empire of Fortune: Crowns, Colonies and Tribes in the Seven Years War in America* (New York: W. W. Norton and Co., 1988), 226–227. *Franklin Papers* 4: n7.

33. *Franklin Papers* 4:511 n6.

34. Ibid., 5:263.

35. *Franklin Papers* 4:511–512, 5:59; Samuel Johnson to Archbishop of Canterbury, 29 June 1753, *Documents Relative to the Colonial History of the State of New York,* E. B. O'Callaghan, et al., eds. 15 vols. (Albany, NY: Weed, Parsons & Co., 1856–87), 6:777 (hereafter cited as *N.Y. Col. Docs.*); Archbishop to Thomas Penn, 19 Sept. 1753, and Penn to Archbishop, Penn Mss., Private Correspondence, mss., 4:123, HSP.

36. *Franklin Papers* 5:190, 207, 212, 120; William Smith Papers, mss., 2:1, HSP. (When I used them, the Smith Papers were not catalogued

because of fear that the owning family might retrieve them. This happened, but copies had been made.)

37. *Franklin Papers* 5:207, 212 (italics in original).

38. *Franklin Papers* 5:7–11.

39. Albert Frank Gegenheimer, *William Smith: Educator and Churchman, 1727–1803* (Philadelphia: University of Pennsylvania Press, 1943), 38.

40. *Franklin Papers* 5:263 n7.

41. Gegenheimer, *William Smith,* 41.

42. *Franklin Papers* 6:28–37.

43. Smith's retainer from Penn for what we now call covert operations is confirmed by letter, T. Penn to R. Peters, 21 Feb. 1755, mss., Peters Mss. 4:4, HSP: £50 per year, Pa. currency, was "my own private benefaction and therefore no address is to be made to the Proprietors for it."

44. *Franklin Papers* 6:34, 70–72.

45. Gegenheimer, *William Smith,* 51.

46. Minutes of the Trustees, 17 March 1755, mss., University of Pennsylvania Archives.

47. William H. Williams, *America's First Hospital: The Pennsylvania Hospital, 1751–1841* (Wayne, PA: Haverford House, 1976), 2–21.

8 GERMANS

1. [William Smith, Provost], *A Brief State of the Province of Pennsylvania* (London: R. Griffiths, 1755), 4; Benjamin H. Newcomb, *Franklin and Galloway: A Political Partnership* (New London, CT: Yale University Press, 1972), 31 n47; Henry Harbaugh, *The Life of Rev. Michael Schlatter* (Philadelphia: Lindsay & Blakiston, 1857), 201.

    The massive bulk of Pennsylvania Germans is missing from the pages of Bernard Bailyn, *Voyagers to the West* (New York: Alfred A. Knopf, 1986). This is another example of New England's historians' lack of interest

in Pennsylvania, which contorts and biases their portrayals of the colonies.

2. *Franklin Papers* 1:230–231; 233 n7.

3. Dietmar Rothermund, "The German Problem of Colonial Pennsylvania," *Pa. Magazine of History and Biography* 84:1 (January 1960), 5–6; *Franklin Papers* 3:184 n9. Saur is another missing person in the *Autobiography.*

4. *Franklin Papers* 4:120–121.

5. Rothermund, "German Problem," 6.

6. Ibid., 6 n9. It is especially noteworthy that these hostilities were

between Protestant churches. Today it is difficult to comprehend
the ferocity of such religious con-
flicts between Protestant sects. I
once taught a seminar in which
two students researched the same
events, one from the Moravian archives, the other from the Lutheran. Normally modest and
ladylike, these two young women
almost came to blows because of
the rabidly contradictory sources
they had encountered. I had to
turn Quaker for the time being, to
restore order.

7. Harbaugh, *Life of Schlatter,* 213.
8. Ibid., 206, 144–145.
9. Dietmar Rothermund, *The Layman's Progress: Religious and Political Experience in Colonial
Pennsylvania, 1740–1770* (Philadelphia: University of Pennsylvania Press, 1961), 161–163.
10. *Franklin Papers* 4:477 n5, 479 n2.
11. Ibid., 4:234.
12. Ibid., 4:484–485.
13. Harbaugh, *Life of Schlatter,* 270.
14. Horace Wemyss Smith, *Life and
Correspondence of the Rev. William
Smith, D.D.,* 2 vols. (Philadelphia,
1879), 1:29–38, quotation at 34
(italics added).
15. Ibid., 1:39.
16. Ibid., 1:30–34, 38; *Franklin Papers* 5:239.
17. *Franklin Papers* 5:237–239; when

Richard Peters mistakenly mentioned a grant from Penn to pay
William Smith's salary in the charitable schools' organization, Penn
corrected him. Smith's payments
were "my own private benefaction," he said; i.e., Smith was being paid to do Penn's business,
not an organization's. Peters to
Penn, 23 Dec. 1754, mss., Penn
Mss., Official Correspondence,
6:251–253; Penn to Peters, 21
Feb. 1755, mss., Peters Mss., 4:4,
both HSP.
18. *Franklin Papers* 5:208.
19. Harbaugh's *Life of Schlatter* is er-
roneous in certain respects because Harbaugh was unaware of
(or preferred to omit) the trip to
Holland by Schlatter in 1753. See
minutes, 30 Oct. 1754, *Minutes
and Letters of the Coetus of the German Reformed Congregations in
Pennsylvania, 1747–1792* (Philadelphia, 1903), 115; Penn to Peters, 7 Nov. 1754, postscript,
mss., Gratz Collection, Papers of
the Governors, Thomas Penn,
HSP.
20. *Minutes and Letters of the Coetus,*
157, 161, *et passim.*
21. Harbaugh, *Life of Schlatter,* 274.
22. *Franklin Papers* 2:358 n4; 5:204–
205, headnote; 5:418–421.
23. Ibid., 5:421 n4; 203 n3.

9 INDIANS

1. *Autobiography,* 197 and n4.
2. Nicholas B. Wainwright, *George
Croghan: Wilderness Diplomat*
(Chapel Hill, NC: University of
North Carolina Press, 1959), 35.
3. *Franklin Papers* 4:182–183.
4. Ibid., 4:184–186. Cf. accounts of
William Johnson in New York.
Jennings, *Empire of Fortune,* 78–
79.
5. *Franklin Papers* 4:184–188.
6. Ibid., 4:189 (italics added).
7. Cadwallader Colden, *The History
of the Five Indian Nations De-

pending on the Province of New-
York in America* (1727–47). I have
used the Great Seal Books reprint
(Ithaca, NY: Cornell University
Press, 1958). *Franklin Papers*
3:169, 175, 178.
8. Rouille to Duquesne, 15 May
1752, *Collections of the Illinois State
Historical Library,* Theodore Calvin Pease, ed. (Springfield, IL,
1936), 29:631.
9. [Archibald Kennedy], *The Importance of Gaining and Preserving the
Friendship of the Indians to the Brit-

ish Interest, Considered (New York: James Parker, 1751).

10. *Franklin Papers,* 20 March 1751, 4:118–119.
11. Loc. cit.
12. Franklin's publication of the treaty minutes is in *Franklin Papers* 5:84–107. For behind-the-scenes operations, see Jennings, *Empire of Fortune,* 54–60. Julian P. Boyd's interpretation suffers from ignorance of Indian affairs.
13. *Franklin Papers* 5:65.
14. Jennings, *Empire of Fortune,* 59 n41.
15. Peters to T. Penn, 5 July 1753, mss., Penn Mss., Official Correspondence, 6:73, HSP. Commissioners Peters, Franklin, and Norris fared better than the Indians. They picked up expenses totaling £600, compared to the £800 intended for the Indians. *Pa. Council Minutes* 5:748–749.
16. *N.Y. Col. Docs.* 6:788.
17. Ibid., 28 Aug. 1753, 6:800–802.
18. Jennings, *Empire of Fortune,* 94–95.
19. Weiser to R. Peters, 15 March 1754, mss., Weiser Correspondence, 1:44, HSP.
20. Paul A. W. Wallace, *Conrad Weiser, 1796–1760, Friend of Colonist and Mohawk* (Philadelphia: University of Pennsylvania Press, 1945), 41; Philip S. Klein and Ari Hoogenboom, *A History of Pennsylvania* (New York: Mcgraw-Hill Book Co., 1973), 171–172.
21. William Brewster, *The Pennsylvania and New York Frontier, 1700–*

1763 (Philadelphia: George S. McManus Co., 1954), 36, 47n; Jennings, *Empire of Fortune,* 101–106.
22. Frederick Jackson Turner, "The Significance of the Frontier in American History" (1893), in Turner, *The Frontier in American History* (New York: Holt, Rinehart & Winston, 1920), 15.
23. *Franklin Papers* 5:276.
24. Ibid. 5:277.
25. *Pa. Council Minutes* 6:48–49.
26. *Franklin Papers* 5:335–338.
27. "Personal Accounts of the Albany Congress," ed. Beverly McAnear, *Mississippi Valley Historical Review* 39 (1953), 731.
28. Alison Gilbert Olson, "The British Government and Colonial Union, 1754," *William and Mary Quarterly,* 3d series, 17:1 (January 1960), 22–34. Franklin, *Autobiography,* 210.
29. Thomas Pownall's memo, "Notes on Indian Affairs" (1754), mss., Loudoun Papers (LO 460), Henry E. Huntington Library; idem., letter to "My Lord" (apparently Halifax) in "Personal Accounts of the Albany Congress of 1754," ed. McAnear, 740, 742–743. See also Charles A. W. Pownall, *Thomas Pownall* (London: Henry Stevens, Son & Stiles, 1908).
30. *Autobiography,* 211; *Franklin Papers* 5:441–447.
31. Brewster, *The Pennsylvania and New York Frontier,* 36, 47n.

10 ASSEMBLYMAN

1. *Autobiography,* 212–213.
2. Morris received two sets of instructions dated respectively 14 and 16 May 1754. Penn Mss., Assembly and Provincial Council of Pa., mss., 64; Pa. Misc. Papers, Penn and Baltimore, Penn Family, 1740–1756, mss., 162; Cadwa-

lader Collection, Thomas Cadwalader, mss., Box 6a, folder Documents (Penn), all HSP.
3. Alan Tully, *William Penn's Legacy: Politics and Social Structure in Provincial Pennsylvania, 1725–1755* (Baltimore: Johns Hopkins University Press, 1977), 40–41. Simi-

lar struggles in other colonies are detailed in Jack P. Greene, *The Quest for Power: The Lower Houses of Assembly in the Southern Royal Colonies 1689-1776* (Chapel Hill, NC: University of North Carolina Press, 1963).

4. Morris to Penn, indorsed "about 26 Dec 1754," Penn Mss., Official Correspondence, mss., 6:257, HSP.

5. Peters to Penn, 16 Dec. 1754, Penn Mss., Additional Misc. Letters, mss., 1:89, HSP.

6. *Votes and Proceedings of the House of Representatives of the Province of Pennsylvania* (reprinted from Franklin's rare first edition), *Pennsylvania Archives, 8th series,* 8 vols., paged continuously (Harrisburg, 1931–35), 5:3771–3772. Short title: *Votes of Assembly.*

7. *Votes of Assembly* 5:3789–3791.

8. Morris to Penn, ca. 26 Dec. 1754, Penn Mss., Official Correspondence, mss., 6:257; Penn to Morris, 17 Oct. 1754, Penn Letter Books, mss., 4:12, both HSP; *Votes of Assembly,* 3797.

9. Penn to Morris, 26 Feb. 1755, Penn Letter Books, mss., 4:58–63, HSP.

10. Penn to Smith, 28 Feb. 1755, Penn Letter Books, mss., 4:64–67; also in W. Smith Papers, mss., 2, both HSP.

11. Morris to Penn, cited n8; Peters to Penn, 23 Dec. 1754, mss., Penn Mss., Official Correspondence, 6:251–253.

12. [William Smith], *A Brief State of the Province of Pennsylvania . . . In a Letter from a Gentleman who has resided many Years in Pennsylvania to his Friend in London* (London: R. Griffiths, 1755). This vicious, fabricating diatribe had an influence hard to believe, both at the time and subsequently. I treated it in detail in Jennings, "Thomas Penn's Loyalty Oath," *American Journal of Legal History* 8 (1964), 303–313; and again in *Empire of Fortune,* 228–240. It has poisoned many histories because of its adoption by Francis Parkman, who shared Smith's racism and bigotry. Instead of reading what "authorities" have said about this book, reading the text of the book itself exposes the duplicity of both Smith and Parkman.

Compare the roles of Franklin and Smith in chapter 8, above.

13. Penn to Smith, 28 Feb. 1755, cited in note 10.

14. *Pa. Council Minutes* 6:202–203.

15. Peters to Penn, 21 Dec. 1754, mss., Penn Mss., Official Correspondence 6:247, HSP.

16. Penn to Peters, 7 Nov. 1754, Gratz Collection, Papers of the Governors, Thomas Penn, mss., HSP.

17. *Pa. Council Minutes* 6:298–299; *Pa. Archives,* 1st series, 2:252–253; *Franklin Papers* 6:63.

18. *Pa. Council Minutes* 6:307–308.

19. Ibid., 335–338.

20. *Pa. Archives,* 1st series, 2:286–288.

21. *Franklin Papers* 6:3–5 and long headnote; 53–54.

22. Quoted in Lawrence Henry Gipson, *The British Empire Before the American Revolution,* 15 vols. (New York: Alfred A. Knopf, 1958–70), 6:69–70. Gipson showed his pro-Proprietary bias by deploring the Assembly's (and Franklin's) "unconstitutional" action.

23. *Autobiography,* 216; *Franklin Papers* 6:12 n7.

24. *Pa. Council Minutes* 6:358.

25. *Military Affairs in North America, 1748–1765,* Stanley Pargellis, ed. (1936; reprinted Hamden, CT: Archon Books, 1969), 53–54. William Allen stated that Braddock had £25,000 in specie captured by the French. [William Allen], *The Burd Papers: Extracts from Chief Justice William Allen's Letter Book,* Lewis Burd Walker, ed. (Pottsville, PA, 1897), 22. I have been unable to find the original mss. letter book.

26. *Autobiography*, 217, 221–222.
27. Ibid., 217–221; *Franklin Papers* 6:13–27; Whitfield J. Bell, Jr., and Leonard W. Labaree, "Franklin and the 'Wagon Affair,'" *Proceedings of the American Philosophical Society* 101 (1957), 551–558.
28. *Military Affairs*, ed. Pargellis, 93–94.
29. Penn to Smith, 24 Oct. 1755, mss., W. Smith Papers 2, HSP.

11 CHANGING SIDES

1. Barton's arrival 24 April 1755 dated in *Pennsylvania Journal* no. 646. Discussion, Smith to Penn, 1 May 1755, Penn Mss., Official Correspondence, mss., 7:29–30; Penn to Smith, 28 Feb. 1755, mss., W. Smith Papers, 2:4; both HSP. Even Penn called it a "harsh" publication. See chapter 10, note 12, above. Cf. *Franklin Papers* 6:52 n5.
2. Penn called this "exceptionable . . . any one would imagine from what is said there was greater privileges granted them than to any other sort of People." Penn to Smith, 28 Feb. 1755, W. Smith Papers, mss., 2:4.
3. A study that has had too little attention notes that "the role of ethnicity and religion is . . . lost in the abstract theme of 'the growth of democracy' . . . the ethnic-religious conflict transcended section and class and was the most salient characteristic of the contending political forces in Pennsylvania." Wayne L. Bockelman and Owen S. Ireland, "The Internal Revolution in Pennsylvania: An Ethnic-Religious Interpretation," *Pennsylvania History* 41:2 (April 1974), 127.
4. Penn feared correctly that this harsh treatment of the Germans would "disoblige and sower them, and prevent their coming so cordially into the other Scheme." Cited in note 2. The "other Scheme" is depicted in chapter 8, above.
5. See Jennings, *Empire of Fortune*, 243–246.
6. Penn to Smith, 28 Feb. 1755, mss., W. Smith Papers, 2:4; Penn to Morris, 26 Feb. 1755, mss., Gratz Collection, Papers of the Governors, Thomas Penn; both HSP.
7. Norris Letter Book, 1719–56, 18 May 1755, mss., 72–73.
8. Minutes of the Meeting for Sufferings, mss., 1:11–19. When I consulted, they were in Friends Record Department; I understand they have been transferred to Friends Historical Library, Swarthmore College.

   This is a seminal document. It represents the beginning of a rift between "religious" Friends and the "political" kind.
9. Pemberton to Fothergill, 19 May 1755, mss., Etting Collection, Pemberton Papers, mss., 2:2.
10. *Franklin Papers* 6, 42, 49.
11. Ibid., 6:55; Norris Letter Book, 1719–56, mss., 72–73.
12. *Franklin Papers* 6:14.
13. Edward Potts Cheyney, *History of the University of Pennsylvania, 1740–1940* (Philadelphia: University of Pennsylvania Press, 1940), 170.
14. William Smith, *A Brief History of the Rise and Progress of the Charitable Society* (Philadelphia: Franklin & Hall, 1755); Smith to Penn, 3 July 1755, mss., Penn Mss., Official Correspondence, 6:81; *Franklin Papers* 5:418–421.
15. Cheyney, *History*, 172; *Franklin Papers* 6:88.
16. Smith to Penn, 2 July 1755, mss., Penn Mss., Official Correspondence, 8:81, HSP; William Smith,

Works, 2 vols. (Philadelphia: Hugh Maxwell & William Fry, 1803), 2:27ff.

17. Smith to Penn 2 July 1755, cited in note 6; *Minutes and Letters of the Coetus,* 138.

18. *Historical Collections Relating to the American Colonial Church,* William S. Perry, ed. (Hartford, CT: The Church Press, 1871), 2:268–269, 273–274.

19. Smith even managed to get the lot free of quitrent, which was a prodigious feat. Smith to Penn, 1 May 1755, mss., Penn Mss., Official Correspondence, 7:30; Penn to Smith, 24 Oct. 1755, mss., W. Smith Papers, 2:5; both HSP.

20. Barton's outlook and affiliations are clear in Marvin F. Russell, "Thomas Barton and Pennsylvania's Colonial Frontier," *Pennsylvania History* 46:4 (October 1979), 313–334.

21. Fothergill to Pemberton, 8 July 1755, mss., Etting Collection, Pemberton Papers, 2:3, HSP.

22. In a letter to Governor Dinwiddie of Virginia, Col. Innes cited the lack of militiamen from both Virginia and Maryland as a compelling reason for Pennsylvania to start its own force. *Pa. Council Minutes* 6:477–479.

23. *Autobiography,* 134–135; *Pa. Council Minutes* 6:479–480.

24. *Pa. Council Minutes* 487.

25. Ibid., 6:492, 497.

26. *Franklin Papers* 6:146 n6; *Pa. Council Minutes* 6:517–519, 504.

27. *Autobiography,* 133. Morris's dismay is in *Pa. Council Minutes* 6:513–514, 517. William Allen hurriedly ordered from London 1,000 muskets and a ton of balls. *The Burd Papers,* 22–23.

28. Pa. Council Minutes 6:502.

29. *Votes of Assembly* 5:3935; *Pa. Council Minutes* 6:510.

30. See note 26 above.

31. *Pa. Council Minutes* 6:525–526; *Votes of Assembly* 5:3936–3939.

32. *Pa. Council Minutes* 6:527–528, 534.

33. Ibid. 6:550; *Votes of Assembly* 5:4004; *Franklin Papers* 6:171.

34. *Votes of Assembly* 5:4006.

35. *Franklin Papers* 6:170–171.

36. Assembly's message, 29 Sept. 1755, *Franklin Papers* 6:193–210. The long message was signed by Isaac Norris as Speaker, but prepared by a committee including Franklin. The style is Franklin's.

37. Richard Peters despaired. "The greater the Danger, the more obstinate they grow." Peters to Penn, 12 Nov. 1755, mss., Gratz Collection, Peters Letter Book, 1755–57, 12, HSP.

38. Smith to Barton, 21 Aug. 1755, in Thomas Barton, *Unanimity and Public Spirit* (Philadelphia: Franklin & Hall, 1755), ix–x; Smith to Archbishop, 22 Oct. 1755, in H. W. Smith, *Life* 1:119.

39. Barton's political activity comes overtly into evidence in the 1756 elections, when he wrote about it to Smith, 23 Sept. 1756, in H. W. Smith, *Life,* 132.

40. *Pa. Council Minutes* 6:503; *Votes of Assembly* 5:3948.

41. 22 Oct. 1755, in H. W. Smith, *Life,* 1:119. This writer gives ample evidence that he shared his ancestor's anti-Catholic bias as well as others.

42. Smith to Penn, ca. first week in September 1755, mss., Penn Mss., Official Correspondence, 7:211–215, HSP. (Letter dated by date of Penn's acknowledgment of receipt, 24 Oct. 1755, allowing six weeks for delivery from Philadelphia to London and a week for incidental delays), W. Smith Papers, 2:5, HSP.

43. *Franklin Papers* 6:169.

44. I have reprinted this message in full in *American Journal of Legal History* 8 (1964), 264–266, and as an appendix to Jennings, *Empire of Fortune,* 485–486.

45. The new tax and Franklin's message split orthodox Quakers from him and from the political Quakers in the Assembly. Peters to Penn, 12 Nov. 1755, mss., Gratz Collection, Peters Letter Book, 1755–57; Pemberton to Fothergill, 27 Nov., 17 Dec. 1755, mss., Etting Collection, Pemberton Papers, 2:7, 8. All HSP.
46. Norris Letter Book, 1719–56, mss., 5 Oct. 1755, 83–85.
47. Smith, *Brief State,* 16.
48. See Jennings, *Empire of Fortune,* 257–258, 459–460.

12 SOLDIER

1. *Relation de la Prise du Fort Georges, ou Guillaume-Henry* . . . (Paris: Bureau d'Addresse aux Galleries du Louvre, 18 Oct. 1757), 1. Copy in John Carter Brown Library.
2. *Pa. Council Minutes,* 29 Dec. 1755, 6:767–768.
3. List, 16 Dec. 1757, mss., Conrad Weiser Correspondence, 1:115; "Lists . . . 1755–1756," *Pa. Magazine of History and Biography* 32 (1908), 309–319.
4. "Secret intelligence received from Shippensburgh," late 1755, mss., Penn Mss., Indian Affairs, 2:41.
5. Peters to Penn, 13 Nov. 1755, mss., Gratz Collection, Peters Letter Book, 1755–57.
6. W. Parsons to Peters, 31 Oct. 1755, *Pa. Archives* 2:443–445, et seq.
7. *Pa. Council Minutes* 6:639–644; *Franklin Papers* 6:230 n8; Weiser Correspondence, mss., 1:58, HSP.
8. *Pa. Council Minutes* 6:647.
9. Ibid., 6:652–653.
10. *Franklin Papers* 6:229, 231.
11. Peters to Penn, 28 Feb. 1756, mss., Gratz Collection, Peters Letter Book, 1755–57, 29–30.
12. *Franklin Papers* 6:229 n3.
13. Ibid., 6:234 n3.
14. Smith claimed authorship of the petition in his letter to the archbishop, 22 Oct. 1755, in H. W. Smith, *Life,* 1:119. He told Penn later that he had also written a Representation of prominent Philadelphians and a Remonstrance from the City Corporation. mss., Penn Mss., Official

Correspondence, 27 Nov. 1755, 7:173. Hockley's naive complaint about Plumsted should not be shrugged off as hostile propaganda; they were both Proprietary placemen and Hockley was kin to the Penns. Ibid., 25 Oct. 1755, 7:133, HSP.
15. *Pa. Council Minutes* 6:671–672.
16. Ibid., 6:678.
17. See Daniel Boorstin, *The Americans: The Colonial Experience* (New York: Random House, 1958), chs. 8, 9.
18. Peters to Penn, 8 and 12 Nov. 1755, mss., Gratz Collection, Peters Letter Book, 1755–57, HSP.
19. *Franklin Papers* 6:238–243.
20. Ibid., 6:242; Peters to Penn, 8 Nov. 1755, mss., Gratz Collection, Peters Letter Book, 1755–57, HSP.
21. *Pa. Council Minutes* 6:681; Peters to Penn, 12 Nov. 1755, Gratz Collection, Peters Letter Book, 1755–57, HSP.
22. *Franklin Papers* 6:245–246.
23. Ibid., 6:247–248 and notes.
24. Peters Letter Book, mss., 13 Nov. 1755.
25. Remonstrance at *Pa. Council Minutes* 6:734–735. Peters Letter Book, mss., 25 Nov. 1755.
26. *Pa. Council Minutes* 6:729, 741.
27. *Franklin Papers* 6:279–284; Smith to Penn, 27 Nov. 1755, mss., Penn Mss., Official Correspondence, 7:173, HSP.
28. *Pa. Council Minutes* 6:724.
29. The editors of the *Franklin Papers* 6:281 n7 describe this affair succinctly. William Smith boasted

that "Two of the Deputy Trustees of our free School at Providence were at the head of the Dutch who came down." Smith to Penn, 27 Nov. 1755, mss., Penn Mss., Official Correspondence, 7:173. Speaker Norris had a private interview with some of the marchers, who seem to have been confused as to why they were supposed to be there. Norris to Charles, 27 Nov. 1755, Norris Letter Book, 1719–56, mss., 91–92, HSP.

30. Text and informative comment on the new law are in *Franklin Papers* 6:266–273.

31. Smith to Penn, 27 Nov. 1755, mss., Penn Mss., Official Correspondence, 7:173; Penn to Smith, 14 Feb. 1756, mss., Penn Mss., Thomas Penn (Boxed), HSP.

32. *Autobiography,* 135; T. and R. Penn to Morris, 5 Oct. 1755, mss., Penn Mss., Official Correspondence, 7:121; Fothergill to Pemberton, 4 Oct. 1755, mss., Etting Collection, Pemberton Papers, 2:5, HSP.

33. Penn to Peters, 6 Oct. 1755, mss., Penn Letter Books, 4:166, HSP.

34. Penn to Morris, 4 Oct. 1755, *Pa. Council Minutes* 6:731; T. and R. Penn to Assembly, 5 Oct. 1755, mss., Penn Mss., Assembly and Provincial Council of Pa., 77; Morris's message, *Pa. Council Minutes* 6:733.

35. Ibid., 6:736.

36. Jennings, *Empire of Fortune,* 267 n33. Among other cute tricks, Penn ordered seizure of lands of refugees in arrears of quitrents.

37. [William Smith], *A Brief View of the conduct of Pennsylvania for the Year 1755* (London: R. Griffiths, 1756).

38. *Franklin Papers* 6:231 n3.

39. Pemberton to Fothergill, 27 Nov. 1755, mss., Etting Collection, Pemberton Papers, 2:7, HSP.

40. Penn's acknowledgment, 10 Jan. 1756, Penn to Peters, mss., Penn Letter Books, 4:206, HSP.

41. They were the king's second son, the Duke of Cumberland; the president of the Privy Council, Lord Granville; and Secretary Henry Fox. Penn to Morris, 10 Jan. 1756, mss., Penn Letter Books, 4:202, HSP.

42. See Jennings, "Thomas Penn's Loyalty Oath," *American Journal of Legal History* 8 (1964), 303–313.

43. Etting Collection, Pemberton Papers, mss., 16 March 1756, 2:10.

44. Penn to Smith, 14 Feb. 1756, postscript unique to duplicate dated 22 March 1756, mss., W. Smith Papers, HSP.

45. *Franklin Papers* 6:282, 415; *Pa. Council Minutes* 6:766.

46. Peters to Penn, 17 Feb. 1756, mss., Penn Mss., Official Correspondence, 8:29–32.

47. See Fred Anderson, *A People's Army: Massachusetts Soldiers and Society in the Seven Years' War* (Chapel Hill, NC: University of North Carolina Press, 1984), ch. 4.

48. *Franklin Papers* 6:383–389; *Pa. Council Minutes* 6:765–766, 769.

49. *Franklin Papers* 6:409. It was within Morris's legal right to refuse the commission and ask for an alternative nomination.

50. *Franklin Papers* 6:415–418.

51. Ibid., 6:416.

52. Ibid., 6:419.

53. *Autobiography,* 141.

54. *Franklin Papers* 6:430.

55. Norris to Charles, 28 April 1756, mss., Norris Letter Book, 1719–56, 65–70.

56. Fothergill to Pemberton, 8 May 1756, mss., Etting Collection, Pemberton Papers, 2:13, HSP. *Votes of Assembly* 5:4272–4274. Fothergill still did not suspect the extent of Penn's complicity in the anti-Quaker assault.

57. *Autobiography,* 213–214.

13 FRONTS AND FRIENDS

1. *Franklin Papers* 6:456–457.

2. Peters to Penn, 28 April and 1 June 1756, mss., Gratz Collection, Peters Letter Book, 1755–57, 47, 54, HSP.

3. *Franklin Papers* 7:14–15.

4. James Pemberton to Jonah Thompson, 25 4mo 1756, mss., Friends Historical Library, Swarthmore College.

5. A series of letters shows Moravian Bishop Augustus Spangenberg's gratitude for Quaker relief. Pemberton Papers, mss., 11:31, 35, HSP; Papers of the Friendly Association, mss., 1:133, 135, 139, 203; 2:75, Haverford College.

6. Franklin did not resign; he was dismissed. *Franklin Papers* 7:12 n4; 8:415–416.

7. Ibid., 6:375–376, 449.

8. *Pennsylvania Journal* 704 (3 June 1756).

9. Jennings, *Empire of Fortune,* 301–303. Lord Loudoun's attempt to rule the colonies by royal prerogative has received much too little attention. Resistance to his domination was a sort of rehearsal for later direct resistance to the King-in-Parliament.

10. Ibid., 246–247.

11. Ibid., 281; Pemberton's quotation, Pemberton to Fothergill, 17 Dec. 1755, mss., Etting Collection, Pemberton Papers, 2:8, HSP. Cf, Jennings, *Empire of Fortune,* chs. 12, 15, 17.

12. *Pa. Council Minutes* 7:78, 88–90.

13. See Anthony F. C. Wallace, *King of the Delawares: Teedyuscung, 1700–1763* (Philadelphia: University of Pennsylvania Press,

1949), a pathbreaking book. My interpretation differs in certain respects. See Jennings, *Empire of Fortune,* chs. 12, 15, *et passim.*

14. *Pa. Council Minutes* 7:324.

15. Minutes of the Friendly Association, mss., 20b, HSP. Presbyterian convert Moses Tatamy told Israel Pemberton the Indians' version of the Walking Purchase, which was resurrected in A. F. C. Wallace, *King of the Delawares,* 21, after centuries of neglect. Moses Tatamy's Account, mss., Etting Collection, Misc. Mss., 1:94, HSP.

16. Peters to Penn, 22 Nov. 1756, mss., Penn Papers, Official Correspondence, 8:203.

17. Penn to Peters, 14 Feb. 1756, mss., T. Penn Letter Books, 4:232–233, 237–238. In the background of all this was the historical fact of the crown's changing of colonial governments that could not keep "their" Indians under control.

18. *Franklin Papers* 6:487.

19. *Franklin Papers* 7:131–132; 152 n6.

20. Ibid., 7:132–133 n3.

21. Ibid., 7:109–114; 8:264–276.

22. Albert Frank Gegenheimer, *William Smith: Educator and Churchman, 1727–1803* (Philadelphia: University of Pennsylvania Press, 1943), 145–147.

23. Council at Easton, July 1756 (under 28 July 1756), mss., American Philosophical Society (unpaged); "Account of the Captivity of Hugh Gibson," in *Collections of the Massachusetts Historical Society,* 3d series, 6 (1837), 142–143, 148.

14 A WOBBLY OFFENSIVE

1. *Franklin Papers* 7:245.

2. *Autobiography,* 261, 262.

3. Ed. note, *Franklin Papers* 7:157–158.

4. Ibid., 7:249 n4; 250 n5.

5. Headnote, ibid., 7:248–249.

6. Ibid., 7:361–362.

7. John Hunt to [Israel Pemberton], 23 Feb. 1758, mss., Pemberton Papers, Box 3; Penn to Peters, 10

Feb. and 8 April 1758, mss., Peters Papers, 5:31, 32. All HSP.

8. Hunt to Pemberton, 23 Nov. 1758, mss., Pemberton Papers, Box 3, HSP.

9. *Franklin Papers* 7:376–377 n9; 266 n8.

10. Benjamin H. Newcomb, *Franklin and Galloway: A Political Partnership* (New Haven, CT: Yale University Press, 1972), 51–52.

11. Ibid., 55–57.

12. *Franklin Papers* 7:111 n9.

13. (London: R. Griffiths, 1759).

14. *Gentleman's Magazine* 27 (September 1757), 417–420.

15. The process is detailed in Jennings, *Empire of Fortune*, 347–348 and notes.

16. Ibid., 339–340.

17. Pemberton to Hunt, 18 June 1758, mss., Pemberton Papers, Box 3, HSP; Papers of the

Friendly Association, 31 May 1758, mss., 1:511, Haverford College.

18. Francis P. Jennings, "A Vanishing Indian: Francis Parkman versus His Sources," *Pa. Magazine of History and Biography* 87:3 (July 1963), 306–323.

19. See Jennings, *Empire of Fortune*, 384 n36, 387–388, and 402.

20. Forbes to Pemberton, 15 Jan. 1759, mss., Papers of the Friendly Association, 3:351, Haverford College.

21. Detailed analysis and text of the Proclamation's terms are in Jack Stagg, *Anglo-Indian Relations in North America to 1763* ... (Ottawa: Research Branch, Indian and Northern Affairs, 1981), 350–400.

22. *Franklin Papers* 7:375.

15 ROYALIST

1. Newcomb, *Franklin and Galloway*, 60–63.

2. *Franklin Papers* 9:161.

3. Ibid., 9:153–157, 210.

4. Ibid., 9:209.

5. Ibid., 9:207–208; Newcomb, *Franklin and Galloway*, 66–67.

6. *Franklin Papers* 9:181.

7. Newcomb, *Franklin and Galloway*, 77–78.

8. Ibid., 69.

9. *Franklin Papers* 9:17.

10. Ibid., 8:315.

11. Sheila L. Skemp, *Benjamin and William Franklin: Father and Son, Patriot and Loyalist* (Boston: Bedford Books, 1994), ch. 2, quotation at p. 37.

12. In 1757, Johnson was hostile to Penn, who worried that "We must not be too fond of leaving everything to Sir Wm. Johnson." *N.Y. Col. Docs.* 7:329–333; T. Penn's Letter Books, mss., 7:30–31, HSP.

13. See Jennings, *Empire of Fortune*, 435–436. Penn had been willing

as early as March 1757 to pay up to £500 as a "gift" to the Delawares if they would clear his name of "crime." Penn to Peters, 11 March 1757, mss., T. Penn's Letter Books, 5:82–89, HSP. Johnson's expert management gave Penn exactly what he had been striving for.

14. Penn to Johnson, 8 Jan 1763, mss., Penn Papers, Thomas Penn (Boxed), HSP.

15. See Jennings, "Brother Miquon: Good Lord!" in *The World of William Penn*, Dunn and Dunn, eds., 207–210.

16. *Franklin Papers* 10:150 n5.

17. See Michael N. McConnell, *A Country Between: The Upper Ohio Valley and Its Peoples, 1724–1774* (Lincoln, NE: University of Nebraska Press, 1992), ch. 8.

18. See Jennings, *Empire of Fortune*, 447 and refs. in n 26.

19. [Smith], *Brief View*, 7on.

20. Brooke Hindle, "The March of the Paxton Boys," *William and*

Mary Quarterly, 3d series, 3:4 (October 1946), 461–486. This brazen excuse for a lynching is full of verifiable misstatements of fact and has remained standard much too long for very bad reasons. For a better account, see [John Heckewelder], *The Travels of John Heckewelder in Frontier America,* Paul A. W. Wallace, ed. (Pittsburgh: University of Pittsburgh Press, 1958), ch. 6. Effect of "pest house" reduced Moravian convert Indians from 140 to 83. *Franklin Papers* 11:87 n3.

21. Hindle, "March," avers that the uprising was against "control by the Quaker Party" (p. 463), omitting to notice that the Assembly has passed from Quaker domination seven years earlier and was being effectively ruled by Franklin. Hindle also passes over Franklin's support from western county frontiersmen.

22. Anne M. Ousterhout, "Frontier Vengeance: Connecticut Yankees vs. Pennamites in the Wyoming Valley," *Pennsylvania History* 62:3 (Summer 1995), 343.

23. Hindle, "March," 486.

24. Ibid., 475, 478; John Penn to T. Penn, 17 March 1764, mss., Penn Mss., Official Correspondence, 9:216. HSP.

25. *Franklin Papers* 11:69–75, ed. note, provides a concise factual summary, though I have to differ with the editors in this instance because of their reliance on Hindle, "March of the Paxton Boys," for interpretation of events. See also Franklin to Richard Jackson, ibid., 77–78.

26. *A Declaration and Remonstrance of the distressed and bleeding Frontier Inhabitants of the Province of Pennsylvania, Presented by them to the Honourable the Governor and Assembly of the Province, Shewing the Causes Of their late Discontent and Uneasiness and the Grievances Un-der which they have laboured, and which they humbly pray to have redress'd* (no place: no publisher, 1764), in *Pa. Council Minutes* 9:138. This is vintage William Smith, including his repeated fabrication that Quakers had given the Indians "a Rod to scourge the white People."

27. *Franklin Papers* 11:104; James H. Hutson, *Pennsylvania Politics, 1746–1770: The Movement for Royal Government and Its Consequences* (Princeton, NJ: Princeton University Press, 1972), 110–111 and n174.

28. Moravian missionary John Heckewelder, who was not involved in Franklin's political machine, commented: "Although at first it was believed, that the only object of the rioters was the destruction of all the Indians . . . it soon became evident that they aimed at nothing short of overturning the whole form of government." *Travels of John Heckewelder,* Wallace, ed., 80. (Cf. Bacon's Rebellion in seventeenth-century Virginia.)

29. [Thomas Barton], *The Conduct of the Paxton-Men Impartially Represented: with some Remarks on the Narrative* (Philadelphia: Andrew Steuart, 1764). Authorship ascribed to Barton in 1873 in the copy at the Library Co. of Philadelphia, and definitely stated by Governor John Penn in a letter to T. Penn, 16 June 1764, mss., Penn Mss., Official Correspondence 9:238. John stated that Barton's authorship was kept secret for fear of the Assembly's "vengeance." Barton was one of William Smith's closest collaborators.

A slanted selection of contemporary pamphlets is in *The Paxton Papers,* J. R. Dunbar, ed. (The Hague: Martinus Nijhoff, 1957). Paul A. Wallace commented that the defenses of Moravian converts made by their missionaries "are available, but not among these pamphlets." *Pa. Magazine of History and Biography* 82:229.

30. Melvin H. Buxbaum, *Benjamin Franklin and the Zealous Presbyterians* (University Park, PA: Pennsylvania State University Press, 1975), 202. Buxbaum actually cites Franklin's hot comment: "my very Zeal in opposing the Murderers, and supporting the Authority of Government, and even my Humanity, with regard to the innocent Indians under our Protection, were mustered among my Offences, to stir up against me those religious Bigots, who are of all Savages the most brutish." *Franklin Papers* 11:434.

31. *A Narrative of the Late Massacres in Lancaster County, of a Number of*

Indians . . . (1764). In *Franklin Papers* 11:55.

32. Even Franklin was unaware of the intrigues in the western counties, but he quickly caught on to their effects. "Violent suspicions . . . now begin to prevail, that the armed Mob in the Country, tho' not at first promoted, has since been privately encourag'd by the Governor's Party, to awe the Assembly, and compell them to make such a Militia Law as the Governors have long aim'd at." Letter to Richard Jackson, 14 March 1764, *Franklin Papers* 11:107.

33. Hindle, "March," 485.

34. *Franklin Papers* 11:104–105.

35. Ibid., 11:76.

36. Ibid., 11:101.

37. Ibid., 11:69.

16 REBOUND

1. *Franklin Papers* 1:107.

2. Ibid., 11:130.

3. Ibid., 11:132.

4. Newcomb, *Franklin and Galloway,* 84–85.

5. 4 April 1764, mss. in Schwenkfelder Library, printed in Dietmar Rothermund, *The Layman's Progress: Religious and Political Experience in Colonial Pennsylvania, 1740–1770* (Philadelphia: University of Pennsylvania Press, 1961), 181–182.

6. Newcomb, *Franklin and Galloway,* 80–81.

7. *Franklin Papers* 4:479 n2; *The American Magazine* (July 1758), 470–475, Franklin identified at p. 470. One of Smith's less successful efforts, this magazine lasted only a year and would not have been read by Germans until attention was called to it.

   James H. Hutson came close to perceiving Smith's decisive role among the Germans. "Too much attention must not be given to the

Presbyterians . . . for the Germans were the decisive factor." Hutson, *Pennsylvania Politics,* 173. But for some strange reason, Hutson persisted in identifying Franklin's supporters as the "Quaker Party."

8. "Election Results in Philadelphia County, 1764," *Franklin Papers* 11:long headnote and document, 390–394.

9. Franklin told Richard Jackson that his opponents carried "above 1000 Dutch [i.e., German votes] from me, *by printing part of my Paper sent to you 12 Years since on Peopling new Countries where I speak of the Palatine Boors herding together*" (italics added), *Franklin Papers* 11:397.

   Newcomb noticed the effect of the anonymous broadside, "translated into German . . . with appropriate commentary and circulated among the German voters." Newcomb, *Franklin and Galloway,* 94–95.

10. *Franklin Papers* 11:393–394.

11. Newcomb, *Franklin and Gallo-way*, 100–104.
12. Louis De Vorsey, Jr., *The Indian Boundary in the Southern Colonies, 1763–1775* (Chapel Hill, NC: University of North Carolina Press, 1961); Jack M. Sosin, *Whitehall and the Wilderness* (Lincoln, NE: University of Nebraska Press, 1961).

13. Marc Bloch, *Feudal Society* (1940), trans. L. A. Manyon, 2 vols. (Chicago: University of Chicago Press, 1961), 1:16–17.
14. *Franklin Papers* 11:158.
15. *Cool Thoughts on the Present Situation of our Public Affairs* (1764). In *Franklin Papers* 11:158.
16. Ibid., 11:159.
17. Ibid., 11:173.

17 SPOKESMAN

1. Newcomb, *Franklin and Gallo-way*, ch. 4.
2. Ibid., 113.
3. Ibid., 118.
4. Ibid., 122–124, 145.
5. Ibid., 98–99; Franklin, *Cool Thoughts,* in *Franklin Papers* 11:161.
6. *Franklin Papers* 13:124–125, 128.
7. Henry Steele Commager, *Documents of American History,* 7th ed., 2 vols. (New York: Appleton-Century-Crofts, 1963), 1:60–61. As its many editions show, this is a standard work. Unfortunately it omits all the documents relative to Pennsylvania's politics during Franklin's battles with Penn.
8. *Franklin Papers* 13:186–187 and n2.
9. Ibid., 15:75–76.
10. Ibid., 14:277.
11. Commager, *Documents of American History,* 1:64.
12. See John W. Tyler, *Smugglers and Patriots: Boston Merchants and the Advent of the American Revolution* (Boston: Northeastern University Press, 1986).
13. *Franklin Papers* 13:100–101.
14. Ibid., 16:200 n1. Samuel Wharton had teamed up with George Croghan and William Trent to press the claims of the "suffering traders" chased out of the Ohio country by the French in 1752. See Thomas Perkins Abernethy, *Western Lands and the American Revolution* (1937; reprinted New

York: Russell & Russell, 1959), chs. 2, 3.
15. See Peter Marshall, "Lord Hillsborough, Samuel Wharton and the Ohio Grant, 1769–1775," *English Historical Review* 80 (1965), 717–739.
16. *Franklin Papers* 17:257–258.
17. Ibid., 20:550 (italics in original).
18. Ibid., 20:562 (italics in original). An apologia for Thomas Hutchinson is in Bernard Bailyn, *The Ordeal of Thomas Hutchinson* (Cambridge, MA: Harvard University Press, 1974). Bailyn insisted that Hutchinson had not "served any interest but that of the public" (p. 68). He seems to have conflated the crown with the public, as perhaps Hutchinson did also.
19. Revenue from the Townshend Acts was intended "for defraying the charge of the administration of justice, and the support of civil government, in such provinces as it shall be found necessary." Translated, this meant that the salaries of governors and judges were to be paid by the crown directly instead of being dependent upon assemblies. In some ways this provision seemed more important to the colonists than the taxes themselves. Charles Thomson reported, "The Colonies see plainly that the Ministry have adopted a settled plan to subjugate America to arbitrary power."

Commager, ed., *Documents of American History*, 63; *Franklin Papers* 16:237.

20. Newcomb, *Franklin and Galloway*, 71 n1; *Franklin Papers* 10:146 n7.

21. Ibid., 17:199 and n1.

22. For a sensational, wholly undocumented account that yet rings true for the time, see Daniel P. Man-

nix, *The Hell-Fire Club* (New York: Ballantine Books, 1959). A more decorous account is in Van Doren, 437–439.

23. *Franklin Papers* 21:long headnote, 38–39; Benjamin's letter to William, 7 Sept. 1744, ibid., 286.

24. Van Doren, 445.

25. *Franklin Papers* 21:430–431.

26. Ibid., 21:xlii.

18 PHOENIX

1. *Franklin Papers* 21:38; Van Doren, 461.

2. *Franklin Papers* 21:48, 49; Van Doren, 468–474.

3. Van Doren, 495–504.

4. E.g., *Franklin Papers* 21:506–510. To Galloway (p. 510), Franklin likened Parliament's proceedings to those of a highwayman "who with a Pistol in your Face says . . . give me all your Money or I'll shoot you thro' the Head."

It was in 1774 that Franklin recommended Tom Paine for employment in Pennsylvania. After Franklin returned to Philadelphia, he suggested that Paine write "a history of the present transactions," which became *Common Sense*. Paine sent him the first copy off the press. Ibid., 21:325–326; Van Doren, 548.

5. Commager, ed., *Documents of American History*, 71–76.

6. Ibid., 78–79.

7. *Franklin Papers* 20:276–278; 281–282.

8. Ibid., 21:xlvii.

9. Van Doren, 527.

10. *Franklin Papers* 20:173, 282 n7.

11. "On Claims to the Soil of America," *The Public Advertiser*, 16 March 1773. In *Franklin Papers* 20:115–122.

12. *Documents of American History*, ed. Commager, 95–96.

13. Newcomb, *Franklin and Galloway*, 246–257.

14. Ibid., 258.

15. Ibid., 288, 289.

16. Stephen Saunders Webb, *1676: The End of American Independence* (New York: Alfred A. Knopf, 1984).

17. See Jennings, *Empire of Fortune*, chs. 13, 14. Loudoun's role in events leading up to the Revolution has been inexcusably neglected in what is called "mainstream" history. He is not even mentioned in the Commager *Documents of American History*, which skip from 1754 to 1761.

18. Van Doren, 549–550.

19. Inexplicably, Melvin H. Buxbaum stops his book *Benjamin Franklin and the Zealous Presbyterians* short of this alliance.

19 CODA

1. Charles M. Andrews, *The Colonial Period of American History*, 4 vols. (1934–38; reprinted New Haven, CT: Yale University Press, 1964), 1:xvi.

2. Skemp, *Benjamin and William Franklin*, 136–137, 145.

3. Ibid., 148.

4. Ibid., 183.

5. Stephen Saunders Webb, in *The World of William Penn*, Dunn and Dunn, eds., 189.

6. W. Logan to J. Pemberton, 14 Nov. 1761, mss., Pemberton Papers, 15:72, HSP.

7. W. Logan to John Smith, 20 Feb

1761, mss., J. Smith Mss., 5:207, Library Co. of Philadelphia.

8. In 1764 he had called them "those religious Bigots, who are of all Savages the most brutish." *Franklin Papers* 11:434.

9. Philip S. Klein and Ari Hoogenboom, *A History of Pennsylvania* (New York: McGraw-Hill Book Co., 1973), 94, 97–98; Jackson Turner Main, *The Sovereign States, 1775–1783* (New York: New Viewpoints, 1973), 277, 292; Thompson Westcott, *Names of Persons Who Took the Oath of Allegiance to the State of Pennsylvania Between the Years 1777 and 1789, with a History of the Test Laws of Pennsylvania* (Philadelphia, 1865). I found a copy of Westcott's very rare book in the Stewart Collection of Glassboro State College, now Rowan College.

For other repressive measures, see Anne M. Ousterhout, "Controlling the Opposition in Pennsylvania During the American Revolution," *Pa. Magazine of History and Biography* 105:1 (January 1981), 3–34. Refusal of the oath was not a simple matter. Nonjurors were declared to be incapable of holding office, of serving on juries, of suing for debts, of electing or being elected, of buying, selling, or transferring real estate, and they were liable to be arrested as spies if they traveled out of the city or county of their residence (Westcott, *Names of Persons,* xix). By estimate, "nearly one-half of the inhabitants of Pennsylvania were deprived of the privileges of citizens" (ibid., xxxvi).

10. Klein and Hoogenboom, *History of Pennsylvania,* 105–107. Chapter 8 is an excellent discussion, solidly grounded and moderately worded.

11. O. S. Ireland, "The Crux of Politics: Religion and Party in Pennsylvania, 1778–1789," *William and Mary Quarterly* 3d series, 42:4 (October 1985), 453–475. Cited data on pp. 455, 471.

12. See Thayer, *Israel Pemberton,* pp. 217ff.

13. Jonathan M. Chu excuses this judicial murder by writing that the court "had no other alternative if it were to expel the evil that was Quakerism." Mr. Chu and his sponsor Henry W. Bowden seem unable to grasp that this sort of alibi for righteous possessors of power could be made equally by Hitler and Stalin. Can Bowden and Chu be so hidebound as actually to believe Quakerism is evil? Jonathan M. Chu, *Neighbors, Friends, or Madmen: The Puritan Adjustment to Quakerism in Seventeenth-Century Massachusetts Bay* (Westport, CT: Greenwood Press, 1985), 46.

BIBLIOGRAPHY

THIS LIST is confined to works cited in the Notes. For other materials consulted from time to time, see the bibliographies in the titles listed below under Studies, Jennings, Francis, at p. 229.

MANUSCRIPTS

Easton, Pennsylvania, Court House: Northampton County Deed Books.
Harrisburg, Pennsylvania, Dept. of Internal Affairs: Commission Books; Patent Books
Haverford College, Haverford, Pennsylvania: Papers of the Friendly Association
Philadelphia:
  American Philosophical Society: Anonymous (possibly William Logan), Council at Easton, July 1756
  City Hall Archives Dept.: Warrants and Surveys; microfilm of Pa. Commission Books and Patent Books
  Historical Society of Pennsylvania
    Cadwalader Collection, Thomas Cadwalader
    Correspondence of Conrad Weiser
    Etting Collection, Pemberton Papers
    Gratz Collection, Papers of the Governors, Thomas Penn
    Gratz Collection, Peters Letter Book, 1755–57
    Minutes of the Friendly Association
    Moses Tatamy's Account, Etting Collection, Misc. Mss.
    Norris Letter Book, 1719–56
    Penn Letter Books
    Penn Mss., Additional Miscellaneous Letters
    Penn Mss., Assembly and Provincial Council of Pa.
    Penn Mss., Indian Affairs
    Penn Mss., Official Correspondence
    Penn Mss., Private Correspondence
    Penn Mss., Thomas Penn (Boxed)
    Pennsylvania Miscellaneous Papers, Penn and Baltimore, Penn Family, 1740–56
    Richard Peters Mss.
    William Smith Papers
  Library Co. of Philadelphia: John Smith Mss.
  University of Pennsylvania Archives: Minutes of the Trustees
Swarthmore College, Swarthmore, Pennsylvania: Friends Historical Library
    Indian Walk Mss., 26 April 1735–19 September 1737
    James Steel's Letter Book, 1730–41
    Minutes of the Meeting for Sufferings
San Marino, California:
  Henry Huntington Library: Loudoun Papers

EIGHTEENTH-CENTURY PERIODICALS

Boston: *New England Courant*
London: *Gentleman's Magazine*
    Public Advertiser
Philadelphia: *American Magazine*
    American Weekly Mercury
    Pennsylvania Gazette
    Pennsylvania Journal
    Pensylvanische Berichte
    Philadelphische Zeitung

PRINTED SOURCE MATERIALS

[Allen, William]. *The Burd Papers: Extracts from Chief Justice William Allen's Letter Book,* Lewis Burd Walker, ed. Pottsville, PA, 1897.

[Barton, Thomas]. *The Conduct of the Paxton-Men Impartially Represented: with some Remarks on the Narrative.* Philadelphia: Andrew Steuart, 1764 (Library Co. of Phila.).

Barton, Thomas. *Unanimity and Public Spirit.* Philadelphia: Franklin & Hall, 1755.

The Charters and Acts of Assembly of the Province of Pennsylvania. Philadelphia: Peter Miller & Co., 1762.

Colden, Cadwallader. *The History of the Five Indian Nations Depending on the Province of New-York in America.* 1727–47; reprinted Ithaca, NY: Great Seal Books, 1958.

Collections of the Illinois State Historical Society, Theodore Calvin Pease, ed. Springfield, IL, 1936.

Documents Relative to the Colonial History of the State of New-York; short title: *N.Y. Col., Docs.* E. B. O'Callaghan, et al., eds. 15 vols. Albany, NY: Weed, Parsons & Co., 1856–87.

[Forbes, John]. *Writings of General John Forbes Relating to His Service in North America,* Alfred Procter James, ed. Menasha, WI: Collegiate Press, 1938.

[Fothergill, John]. *Chain of Friendship: Selected Letters of Dr. John Fothergill of London, 1735–1780,* Betsy C. Corner and Christopher C. Booth, eds. Cambridge, MA: Harvard University Press, 1971.

Franklin, Benjamin. *The Autobiography,* Leonard W. Labaree, et al., eds. New Haven, CT: Yale University Press, 1964.

———. [A select list of publications with citation to *Franklin Papers* reprints at (vol.: pp.)]

Cool Thoughts on the Present Situation in Our Public Affairs. (11:153–173)

*An Edict by the King of Prussia. (20:413–418)

Experiments and Observation on Electricity ed. P. Collinson. (4:125–130: sections reprinted at 3:156–214; 126–135; 352–365; 365–377; 4:9; 9–34; 65–70)

*[Germans in Pennsylvania: correction of first printing in the *Gentleman's Magazine*] (4:477–486)

A Modest Inquiry into the Nature and Necessity of a Paper Currency. (1:139–157)

A Narrative of the Late Massacres, in Lancaster County, of a Number of Indians. (11:42–69)

Observations and Suppositions towards forming a new Hypothesis for explaining the several Phaenomena of Thunder Gusts. (3:365–376)

Plain Truth: or, Serious Considerations On the Present State of the City of Philadelphia, and Province of Pennsylvania. (3:180–204)

A Proposal for Promoting Useful Knowledge among the British Plantations in America. (2:378–383)

Proposals Relating to the Education of Youth in Pensilvania. (3:395–421)

Rules by Which a Great Empire May Be Reduced to a Small One. (20:389–399)

[Gibson, Hugh]. "Account of the Captivity of Hugh Gibson," in *Collections of the Massachusetts Historical Society,* 3d series, 6 (1837).

Harbaugh, Henry. *The Life of Michael Schlatter; with a full account of his Travels and Labors among the Germans . . . 1716 to 1790.* Philadelphia: Lindsay & Blakiston, 1857.

[Heckewelder, John]. *The Travels of John Heckewelder in Frontier America,* Paul A. W. Wallace, ed. Pittsburgh: University of Pittsburgh Press, 1958.

Historical Collections Relating to the American Colonial Church, II, "Pennsylvania," William Stevens Perry, ed. Hartford, CT: The Church Press, 1871.

[Hockley, Richard]. "Selected Letters from the Letter-Book of Richard Hockley, 1739–1742," *Pennsylvania Magazine of History and Biography* 26 (1904).

Indian Treaties Printed by Benjamin Franklin, 1736–1762, Julian P. Boyd, ed. Philadelphia: Historical Society of Pennsylvania, 1938.

[Jackson, Richard]. *An Historical Review of the Constitution and Government of Pennsylvania . . .* London: R. Griffiths, 1759.

[Kennedy, Archibald]. *The Importance of Gaining and Preserving the Friendship of the Indians to the British Interest, Considered.* New York: James Parker, 1751.

Military Affairs in North America, 1748–1765; Selected Documents from the Cumberland Papers in Windsor Castle, Stanley Pargellis, ed. 1936; reprinted Hamden, CT: Archon Books, 1969.

Minutes and Letters of the Coetus of the German Reformed Congregations in Pennsylvania, 1747–1792. Philadelphia, 1903.

Minutes of the Provincial Council of Pennsylvania (spine title *Colonial Records*), Samuel Hazard, ed. 16 vols. Harrisburg and Philadelphia, 1838–53. (Note: Vols. 1–3 were printed in two editions with different pagination.)

The Papers of Benjamin Franklin; short title, *Franklin Papers.* Leonard W. Labaree, et al., eds. New Haven, CT: Yale University Press, 1959–.

The Papers of Sir William Johnson; short title, *Johnson Papers.* James Sullivan, et al., eds. 14 vols. Albany, NY: University of the State of New York, 1921–65.

The Paxton Papers, J. R. Dunbar, ed. The Hague: Martinus Nijhoff, 1957. See P. A. W. Wallace in *Pennsylvania Magazine of History and Biography* 82 (1960).

Pennsylvania Archives. 9th series, 138 vols., Harrisburg and Philadelphia, 1852–1949.

"Personal Accounts of the Albany Congress," Beverley McAnear, ed., *Mississippi Valley Historical Review* 39 (1953).

Relation de la Prise du Fort Georges ou Guillaume-Henry . . . Paris: Bureau d'Addresse aux Galleries du Louvre, 1757. Copy in John Carter Brown Library.

Smith, Horace Wemyss. *Life and Correspondence of the Rev. William Smith, D.D.* 2 vols. Philadelphia, 1879.

Smith, William. *A Brief History of the Rise and Progress of the Charitable Society.* Philadelphia: Franklin & Hall, 1755.

[Smith, William]. *A Brief State of the Province of Pennsylvania . . . In a Letter from a Gentleman who has resided many Years in Pennsylvania to his Friend in London.* London: R. Griffiths, 1755.

——. *A Brief View of the conduct of Pennsylvania for the Year 1755.* London: R. Griffiths, 1756.

———. "Intercepted Letters, 1756," in *American Historical Association Annual Report for the Year 1896.* 2 vols. Washington, DC: Government Printing Office, 1897, 1:662–685.

——. *A Letter from a Gentleman in London, To his Friend in Pennsylvania; with a Satire; containing Some Characteristical Strokes upon the Manners and Principles of the Quakers.* London: J. Scott, 1756.

Smith, William. *Works.* 2 vols. Philadelphia: Hugh Maxwell & William Fry, 1803.

Thomson, Charles. *An Enquiry into the Causes of the Alienation of the Delaware and Shawanese Indians from the British Interest.* London: J. Wilkie, 1759.

Votes and Proceedings of the House of Representatives of the Province of Pennsylvania, 1682–1776 (1752–76). 8 vols. *Pennsylvania Archives,* 8th series, Harrisburg, 1931–35. (Short title: *Votes of Assembly.*)

Westcott, Thompson. *Names of Persons Who Took the Oath of Allegiance to the State of Pennsylvania Between the Years 1777 and 1789, with a History of the Test Laws of Pennsylvania.* Philadelphia, 1865. Copy in Stewart Collection, Rowan College, NJ.

STUDIES

Abernethy, Thomas Perkins. *Western Lands and the American Revolution.* 1937; reprinted New York: Russell & Russell, 1959.

Anderson, Fred. *A People's Army: Massachusetts Soldiers and Society in the Seven Years' War.* Chapel Hill, NC: University of North Carolina Press, 1984.

Andrews, Charles M. *The Colonial Period of American History.* 4 vols. 1934–38; reprinted New Haven, CT: Yale University Press, 1964.

Bailyn, Bernard. *The Ordeal of Thomas Hutchinson.* Cambridge, MA: Harvard University Press, 1974.

Bell, Whitfield J., Jr., and Leonard W. Labaree. "Franklin and the 'Wagon Affair,'" *Proceedings of the American Philosophical Society* 101 (1957), 551–58.

Bockelman, Wayne L., and Owen S. Ireland. "The Internal Revolution in Pennsylvania: An Ethnic-Religious Interpretation," *Pennsylvania History* 41:2 (April 1974), 125–159.

Boorstin, Daniel. *The Americans: The Colonial Experience.* New York: Random House, 1958.

Brewster, William. *The Pennsylvania and New York Frontier, 1700–1763.* Philadelphia: George S. McManus Co., 1954.

Bridenbaugh, Carl. *Mitre and Sceptre: Transatlantic Faiths, Ideas, Personalities, and Politics, 1689–1775.* New York: Oxford University Press, 1962.

Buck, William J. *History of the Indian Walk.* Philadelphia: E. S. Stuart, 1886.

Buxbaum, Melvin H. *Benjamin Franklin and the Zealous Presbyterians.* University Park, PA: Pennsylvania State University Press, 1975.

Cheyney, Edward Potts. *History of the University of Pennsylvania, 1740–1940*. Philadelphia: University of Pennsylvania Press, 1940.

Cohen, Norman S. "The Philadelphia Election Riot of 1742," *Pennsylvania Magazine of History and Biography* 92 (July 1968), 306–319.

Dunn, Richard S. "Penny Wise and Pound Foolish: Penn as a Businessman," in *The World of William Penn,* Dunn and Dunn, eds., 37–54.

Gegenheimer, Albert Frank. *William Smith: Educator and Churchman, 1727–1803*. Philadelphia: University of Pennsylvania Press, 1943.

Gipson, Lawrence Henry. *The British Empire Before the American Revolution*. 15 vols. New York: Alfred A. Knopf, 1966–70.

Gleason, J. Philip. "A Scurrilous Colonial Election and Franklin's Reputation," *William and Mary Quarterly,* 3d series, 18 (January 1961), 68–84.

Greene, Jack P. *The Quest for Power: The Lower Houses of Assembly in the Southern Royal Colonies, 1689–1776*. 1963; reprinted New York: W. W. Norton & Co., 1972.

Hanna, William S. *Benjamin Franklin and Pennsylvania Politics*. Stanford, CA: Stanford University Press, 1964.

Hindle, Brooke. "The March of the Paxton Boys," *William and Mary Quarterly,* 3d series, 3 (October 1946), 461–486.

Horle, Craig W. *Lawmaking and Legislators in Pennsylvania: A Biographical Dictionary*. Philadelphia: University of Pennsylvania Press, 1991.

Hutson, James H. "Benjamin Franklin and the Parliamentary Grant for 1758," *William and Mary Quarterly,* 3d series, 23 (October 1966), 575–595.

———. "Benjamin Franklin and Pennsylvania Politics, 1751–1755: A Reappraisal," *Pennsylvania Magazine of History and Biography* 93:3 (July 1969), 303–371.

———. "Benjamin Franklin and William Smith: More Light on an Old Philadelphia Quarrel," *Pennsylvania Magazine of History and Biography* 93:1 (January 1969), 109–113.

———. *Pennsylvania Politics, 1746–1770: The Movement for Royal Government and Its Consequences*. Princeton, NJ: Princeton University Press, 1972.

Jennings, Francis. *The Ambiguous Iroquois Empire*. New York: W. W. Norton & Co., 1984.

———. *Empire of Fortune . . . The Seven Years War in America*. New York: W. W. Norton & Co., 1988.

———. "The Indian Trade of the Susquehanna Valley," *Proceedings of the American Philosophical Society* 110:6 (December 1966), 406–424.

———. "Miquon's Passing: Indian-European Relations in Colonial Pennsylvania, 1674 to 1755." Ph.D. dissertation, University of Pennsylvania, 1965.

———. "The Scandalous Indian Policy of William Penn's Sons," *Pennsylvania History* 37 (January 1970), 19–39.

———. "Thomas Penn's Loyalty Oath," *American Journal of Legal History* 8 (1964), 303–313.

———. "A Vanishing Indian: Francis Parkman versus His Sources," *Pennsylvania Magazine of History and Biography* 87:3 (July 1963), 306–323.

Ketcham, Ralph L. *Benjamin Franklin*. New York: Washington Square Press, 1966.

———. "Benjamin Franklin and William Smith: New Light on an Old Philadelphia Quarrel," *Pennsylvania Magazine of History and Biography* 88:2 (April 1964), 142–163.

————. "Conscience, War, and Politics in Pennsylvania, 1755–1757," *William and Mary Quarterly,* 3d series, 20 (July 1963), 416–439.

Klein, Philip S., and Ari Hoogenboom. *A History of Pennsylvania.* New York: McGraw-Hill Book Co., 1973.

Leonard, C. S. J., Sister Joan de Lourdes. "Elections in Colonial Pennsylvania," *William and Mary Quarterly,* 3d series, 11 (July 1954), 385–401.

Main, Jackson Turner. *The Sovereign States, 1775–1783.* New York: New Viewpoints, 1973.

Mannix, Daniel P. *The Hell-Fire Club.* New York: Ballantine Books, 1959.

Marshall, Peter. "Lord Hillsborough, Samuel Wharton and the Ohio Grant, 1769–1775," *English Historical Review* 80 (1965), 117–739.

McConnell, Michael N. *A Country Between: The Upper Ohio Valley and Its Peoples, 1724–1774.* Lincoln, NE: University of Nebraska Press, 1992.

Middlekauff, Robert. *Benjamin Franklin and His Enemies.* Berkeley: University of California Press, 1996.

Newcomb, Benjamin H. *Franklin and Galloway: A Political Partnership.* New Haven, CT: Yale University Press, 1972.

Olson, Alison Gilbert. "The British Government and Colonial Union, 1754," *William and Mary Quarterly,* 3d series, 17 (January 1960), 22–34.

Ousterhout, Anne M. "Controlling the Opposition in Pennsylvania During the American Revolution," *Pennsylvania Magazine of History and Biography* 105:1 (January 1981), 3–34.

————. "Frontier Vengeance: Connecticut Yankees vs. Pennamites in the Wyoming Valley," *Pennsylvania History* 62:3 (Summer 1995), 331–363.

The Papers of William Penn, Richard S. Dunn, Mary Maples Dunn, et al., eds. 4 vols. Philadelphia: University of Pennsylvania Press, 1981– .

Parsons, William T. "The Bloody Election of 1742," *Pennsylvania History* 36:3 (July 1969), 290–306.

Pownall, Charles A. W. *Thomas Pownall.* London: Henry Stevens, Son & Stiles, 1908.

Rothermund, Dietmar. "The German Problem of Colonial Pennsylvania," *Pennsylvania Magazine of History and Biography* 84:1 (January 1960), 3–21.

————. *The Layman's Progress: Religious and Political Experience in Colonial Pennsylvania, 1740–1770.*Philadelphia: University of Pennsylvania Press, 1961.

Russell, Marvin F. "Thomas Barton and Pennsylvania's Colonial Frontier," *Pennsylvania History* 46–4 (October 1979), 313–334.

Skemp, Sheila L. *Benjamin and William Franklin: Father and Son, Patriot and Loyalist.* New York: St. Martin's Press, 1994.

Stagg, Jack. *Anglo-American Relations in North America to 1763, and an Analysis of the Royal Proclamation of 7 October 1763.* Ottawa: Research Branch, Indian and Northern Affairs, 1981.

Thayer, Theodore. *Israel Pemberton, King of the Quakers.* Philadelphia: Historical Society of Pennsylvania, 1943.

————. *Pennsylvania Politics and the Growth of Democracy, 1740–1776.* Harrisburg, PA: Pennsylvania Historical and Museum Commission, 1953.

Tolles, Frederick B. "Benjamin Franklin's Business Mentors: The Philadelphia Quaker Merchants," *William and Mary Quarterly,* 3d series, 4 (January 1947), 60–69.

Tully, Alan. *William Penn's Legacy: Politics and Social Structure in Provincial*

Pennsylvania, 1725–1755. Baltimore: Johns Hopkins University Press, 1977.

Turner, Frederick Jackson. *The Frontier in American History*. New York: H. Holt & Co., 1920.

Tyler, John W. *Smugglers and Patriots: Boston Merchants and the Advent of the American Revolution*. Boston: Northeastern University Press, 1986.

Van Doren, Carl. *Benjamin Franklin*. New York: Viking Press, 1938.

Wainwright, Nicholas B. *George Croghan: Wilderness Diplomat*. Chapel Hill, NC: University of North Carolina Press, 1959.

Wallace, Anthony F. C. *King of the Delawares: Teedyuscung, 1700–1763*. Philadelphia: University of Pennsylvania Press, 1949.

Wallace, Paul A. W. *Conrad Weiser, 1696–1760, Friend of Colonist and Mohawk*. Philadelphia: University of Pennsylvania Press, 1945.

Webb, Stephen Saunders. *1676: The End of American Independence*. New York: Alfred A. Knopf, 1984.

———. " 'The Peaceable Kingdom': Quaker Pennsylvania in the Stuart Empire," in *The World of William Penn*, Dunn and Dunn, eds., 173–194.

Westcott, Thompson. *Names of Persons Who Took the Oath of Allegiance to the State of Pennsylvania Between the Years 1777 and 1789, with a History of the Test Laws of Pennsylvania*. Philadelphia, 1865. Copy in Stewart Collection, Rowan College, NJ.

Williams, William H. *America's First Hospital: The Pennsylvania Hospital, 1751–1841*. Wayne, PA: Haverford House, 1976.

The World of William Penn, Richard S. and Mary Maples Dunn, eds. Philadelphia: University of Pennsylvania Press, 1986.

INDEX

ambivalent with Thomas Penn, 49
appeals for end to party strife, 133
apprentice, 25
approves want and misery as character
 builders, 61
arranges publication of Thomson's *Enquiry,* 150
arrives Philadelphia, 27
Assembly printer, 36, 43
Assembly sends him to London, 144
Assembly's presents to junior officers,
 103–4
Autobiography's omissions, 17
becomes royalist, 158
birth, 24
boyhood activity, 26
colonel of militia, 135–36
condemns campaign against liberties,
 116
consults Fothergill, 146
contempt for Dunbar's retreat, 114
contrives new tax bill, 127
controls Assembly, 138
cooperates with persecutors, 199–200
cost of Indian presents, 83–84
defeated in election, 170
defends tax on Penns, 119
degree from St. Andrews, 158
degree from William and Mary, 137
demoted from College presidency, 140
denigrates "Palatine Boors," 75
denounced as traitor, 191
denounces Morris, 109
denounces Paxton Boys, 163, 165
described by Peters, 144
devotion to "English Liberties," 190–91
disillusioned by British corruption, 154
dissipation and debt, 31
distributes arms, 124
duns Thomas Penn, 146
elected to Assembly, 81
elected to Royal society and presidency
 of Pennsylvania Hospital, 140
endorses paper money, 42
fails in London, 156
family refuses subsidy, 30
famous quote on liberty, 117
fatuous about William Smith, 68–69
first voyage to London, 30
flees Boston, 26–27
fools Morris, 101–2
friendly with Dashwood, 184–85
friendly with Peter Collinson and James
 Logan, 37, 39
genius, 15
goal of empire, 195
Hall's payments end, 180–81
hostility to Quakers, 197–98
illegitimate son, 32, 206 n.2
imperialist and revolutionary, 18
initiates Academy of Philadelphia, 67
interest in electricity and lightning, 62
interest in Indians, 60–61

joins Presbyterian revolutionaries, 192,
 194
journeyman, 28
Junto, Mason, *Pa. Gazette,* 34
kite and key experiment, 63
Library Co., 36
lobbies in England for royal government, 171
marriage, 32
meets Lord Granville, 147
meets Thomas Penn, 147–49
Morris offers bribe, 137
nepotism, 39, 81
not democratic, 166–67
offers compensation to Teedyuscung,
 143
on colonial unity, 86
on Declatory Act, 178
on Germans, 22
on political struggles, 138
on racism, 165
on smallpox, 26, 206 n.2
on stamp tax, 175–76
opposes parliament, 179, 185
overturns feudalism, 192
post office salary, 180
prestige rises, 110
printing "franchises," 66
prints treaty minutes, 88
promotes military Association, 64–65
proposes ban on German immigrants,
 76
proposes Continental Congress, 189–90
proposes Indian affairs policy, 85–86
proposes institution for scholarship, 61
punished and humiliated, 186–87
quoted on Morris, 94
rejects Denny's bribe, 38
relations with Smith, 119
repulsed by Germans, 72–73
retains Assembly control, 171
retires from business, 66
returns to Pennsylvania, 160
returns to Philadelphia, 190
reviews militia against Smith, 136
rises in post office, 38–39
royalism confirmed, 166
schooling and *New England Courant,* 25
seeks patronage, 47, 59
Silence Dogood papers, 25
Speaker of Assembly, 169
spite against son's wife, 196–97
suspects Iroquois, 143
talks to Braddock, 103–4
talks with Lord Howe, 187
to treat with Ohio Indians, 86–87
trustee of German charity schools, 78
undercut by Quakers, 178
understanding of the Iroquois League,
 86
vanity, 21
womanizing charge, 169–70, 206 n.1
wrong about Germans, 79–80